Michael Gr

Context-Aware Data Management

Michael Grossniklaus

Context-Aware Data Management

An Object-Oriented Version Model

VDM Verlag Dr. Müller

Imprint

Bibliographic information by the German National Library: The German National Library lists this publication at the German National Bibliography; detailed bibliographic information is available on the Internet at http://dnb.d-nb.de.

Any brand names and product names mentioned in this book are subject to trademark, brand or patent protection and are trademarks or registered trademarks of their respective holders. The use of brand names, product names, common names, trade names, product descriptions etc. even without a particular marking in this works is in no way to be construed to mean that such names may be regarded as unrestricted in respect of trademark and brand protection legislation and could thus be used by anyone.

Cover image: www.purestockx.com

Publisher:
VDM Verlag Dr. Müller e. K., Dudweiler Landstr. 125 a, 66123 Saarbrücken, Germany,
Phone +49 681 9100-698, Fax +49 681 9100-988, Email: info@vdm-verlag.de

Copyright © 2007 VDM Verlag Dr. Müller e. K. and licensors
All rights reserved. Saarbrücken 2007

Produced in USA and UK by:
Lightning Source Inc., La Vergne, Tennessee, USA
Lightning Source UK Ltd., Milton Keynes, UK

ISBN: 978-3-8364-2938-2

You can fall but you must not lie down.

–Dougie MacLean: "Not Lie Down"

Don't waste your time or time will waste you.

–Muse: "Knights of Cydonia"

Die Welt liegt uns zu Füssen, denn wir stehen drauf.[1]

–Die Fantastischen Vier: "MfG"

---

[1] The world is at our feet because we stand on it.

Abstract

Context-aware computing has been recognised as a powerful solution to address the requirements of many modern application domains. For example, in mobile computing, context is used to augment the user's experience when interacting with a system by adapting responses to their current situation. In the domain of ubiquitous and pervasive computing, the role of context is often to compensate for the lack of traditional user interfaces. Finally, in web engineering, context is used to adapt content delivery to numerous factors. Building on context information, recent web systems support multi-channel and multi-modal interaction as well as personalisation and internationalisation. While several frameworks and models have been proposed to gather, represent and process context, very few of these solutions consider the management of context-aware data.

In the past, database systems have been used to manage data for applications from various domains. To address ever changing requirements, database systems have undergone a remarkable evolution from monolithic heavyweight databases to lightweight personal information stores. Continuing this evolution, it is our approach to extend database systems with concepts to cope with the challenge of context-aware data management. The proposed solution is based on a two-dimensional version model that allows context-dependent variants to be managed, while, at the same time, keeping track of the revisional history. Within the scope of this version model, query processing is realised based on a matching algorithm that uses the current context state of the system to select the best version of every object that is accessed during query evaluation.

Our version model has been specified based on the OM object-oriented data model and has been implemented as part of a database management system that is based on OM. As an application of this extended database management system, a web content management system has been designed and implemented. The intention of this Extensible Content Management System (XCM) is to provide a powerful implementation platform for web engineering applications. Most model-driven design methodologies in this application domain feature some notion of context-driven adaptation. However, suitable implementation platforms to support these methodologies are sparse or tied in with a specific design method. To implement web engineering systems, XCM separates the concepts of content, structure, view and presentation. Metadata about these concepts is managed within our extended database and therefore all four aspects of a web system can be made context-aware.

The EdFest mobile tourist information system serves as a proof-of-concept for XCM, that is used as a content management component in this system. EdFest is an application that provides information about the Edinburgh Festivals to tourists while they are visiting the city. The system offers multi-channel interaction by supporting standard web channels as well as a novel paper-based channel. In terms of context information, EdFest has established new requirements, as not only traditional factors such as location, device and user context are considered, but also the interaction context. Due to specific requirements of the interactive paper delivery channel, not only the content that is delivered to a tourist has to be adapted but also the interaction process that leads to the content delivery.

Even though our version model for context-aware data management has been defined within the framework of the OM data model, the concepts can be generalised to data that is represented in other models. In particular this is the case for relational database management systems, as our version model has its origins in solutions that have been proposed for temporal and engineering databases that were developed based on the relational model. Unfortunately, most of today's information is not managed by database systems but rather stored in plain files and it is therefore not possible to take advantage of the proposed version model. Concepts from web content management such as the explicit representation of the internal structure of a file or the reuse of different content components in different places could be used to improve today's file systems. Only in this setting, can the full potential of context-aware data management be finally unleashed in handling everyday information such as wordprocessing, spreadsheet or presentation documents.

Zusammenfassung

Der Einbezug von Kontextinformation ist eine anerkannte und mächtige Lösung für die Anforderungen vieler moderner Anwendungsbereiche. So wird Kontext beispielsweise in mobilen Applikationen verwendet, um die Interaktion mit dem Benutzer zu verbessern, indem sich die Anwendung an dessen Situation anpasst. Kontext wird auch dazu verwendet, um in allgegenwärtigen Systemen den Umstand zu kompensieren, dass diese oft keine traditionelle Benutzerschnittstelle haben. Aber auch in der Entwicklung von Webangeboten ist Kontext zur Anpassung an verschiedenste Faktoren essenziell. Neuere Websysteme nutzen dabei Kontextinformation, um Inhalte über mehrere Ausgabekanäle zu publizieren, sowie zur Personalisierung und Internationalisierung von Webseiten. Obwohl Systeme und Modelle zur Akquisition, Repräsentation und Bearbeitung von Kontext entwickelt wurden, blieb die Verwaltung kontext-sensitiver Daten bisher aussen vor.

Datenbanksysteme wurden in der Vergangenheit wiederholt dazu eingesetzt, Daten verschiedenster Anwendungen zu verwalten. Um mit den sich ständig verändernden Anforderungen Schritt zu halten, durchlebten Datenbanken die bemerkenswerte Entwicklung von monolithischen Datenbankservern hin zu flexiblen persönlichen Informationsspeichern. Das Ziel dieser Arbeit ist es daher, diese Entwicklung fortzuführen, indem Datenbanken mit Konzepten erweitert werden, die die Verwaltung kontext-sensitiver Information ermöglichen. Die vorgeschlagene Lösung basiert auf einem zweidimensionalen Versionierungsmodell, das sowohl die Verwaltung von kontext-abhängigen Varianten wie auch das Verfolgen der zeitlichen Evolution erlaubt. Die Auswertung von Anfragen erfolgt dabei durch einen Algorithmus, der anhand des gegenwärtigen Kontexts die bestmögliche Version jedes Objektes auswählt, auf das im Zuge der Anfragebearbeitung zugegriffen wird.

Unser Versionierungsmodell wurde unter der Verwendung des objektorientierten Datenmodells OM spezifiziert und innerhalb eines darauf basierenden Datenbanksystems implementiert. Als Anwendung dieser erweiterten Datenbank wurde ein Web Content Management System implementiert. Die Absicht dieses Extended Content Management System (XCM) ist es, eine mächtige Implementationsplattform für Webapplikationen anzubieten. Die meisten modellbasierten Ansätze zur Entwicklung solcher Systeme verfügen bereits über Methoden, kontextabhängige Anpassungen auszudrücken. Bisher wurden jedoch noch keine genügend allgemeinen oder geeigneten Plattformen geschaffen, um diese Modelle umzusetzen. XCM unterscheidet die vier Grundkonzepte Inhalt, Struktur, Sicht und Gestaltung. Metadaten zu diesen Konzepten werden in unserem erweiterten Datenbanksystem verwaltet und es ist daher möglich, jedes einzelne kontextsensitiv zu machen.

EdFest, ein mobiles Informationssystem für Touristen verwendet unser Content Management System als Komponente zur Informationsverwaltung und dient als Leistungsnachweis von XCM. Die Aufgabe von EdFest ist es, Touristen, die Edinburgh besuchen, mit Informationen über die dortigen Festspiele zu versorgen. Das System bietet neben dem gewöhnlichen, webbasierten Zugang auch papierbasierte Interaktion an. Im Hinblick auf die berücksichtigte Kontextinformation geht EdFest weiter als bisherige Systeme, da neben orts-, benutzer- und gerätespezifischen Faktoren auch der Interaktionskontext einbezogen wird. Als Folge der speziellen Anforderungen des Zuganges durch interaktives Papier reicht es nicht aus, nur die Inhalte anzupassen, sondern es ist auch notwendig, den Prozess zu adaptieren, über den auf Inhalte zugegriffen wird.

Obwohl unser Versionierungsmodell zur Verwaltung von kontext-sensitiven Daten im Rahmen des OM Datenmodells definiert wurde, lässt es sich auf Information ausweiten, die anhand anderer Modelle verwaltet wird. Dies trifft insbesondere auf das relationale Datenmodell zu, da unser Versionierungsmodell seinen Ursprung in temporalen und Ingenieurdatenbanken hat, die für das relationale Modell entwickelt wurden. Da der Anteil von Daten, die von Datenbanksystemen verwaltet werden verglichen mit denen, die in Dateien gespeichert sind, ziemlich bescheiden ist, ist es momentan nicht möglich vom vorgeschlagenen Modell zu profitieren. Wir glauben jedoch, dass Content Management Konzepte, wie die explizite Verwaltung der internen Struktur einer Datei oder die Wiederverwendung von Inhalten an mehreren Orten eine solide Basis darstellen, um heutige Dateisysteme zu verbessern. Nur so liesse sich das volle Potenzial kontext-orientierter Datenverwaltung im Umgang mit alltäglicher Information wie Textverarbeitungs-, Tabellenkalkulations- oder Präsentationsdokumenten verwirklichen.

Acknowledgements

First and foremost, I would like to thank Prof. Moira C. Norrie for the constant support she has given me over the last years. From the first time I met her as a student, Moira kept encouraging me to pursue my own ideas and I am grateful that she gave me the opportunity to do so in her research group. Whenever I needed to discuss something or sought guidance, Moira always had an open door and helpful advice for me. I am sure that the experience I have gained from working with her will be a valuable asset in my future life.

I would also like to express my gratitude to Prof. Stefano Ceri that was kind enough to agree to co-supervise my thesis. I have very much appreciated his invitation to give a seminar about my work at Politecnico di Milano. During the final stages of my thesis, Stefano's comments have always been helpful, constructive and encouraging.

Very special thanks go, of course, to my present and past coworkers at the Global Information Systems research group. Working together with every single group member was a joy and I am proud of the things we have achieved as a team. I will never forget the supportive and cooperative atmosphere that prevailed among us, both inside and outside the office. Some of my colleagues, however, deserve special a mention in the context of this thesis. I would like to thank Beat Signer and Corsin Decurtins for all the interesting discussions that we had when I shared an office with each of them. I am also very grateful to Beat for furnishing the template I used to layout this thesis and for the valuable feedback he provided. The meticulous proof-reading and critical comments of Ela Hunt have been very much appreciated and have helped me to improve the quality of this thesis substantially. Finally, I am also in Stefania Leone's debt for discovering many mistakes when she read through my thesis.

Apart from being my colleagues at the office, Alexios Palinginis and Alex de Spindler are both very good friends. Alexios and I walked the beginning of the path that led to the work presented in this thesis together and it saddens me that he decided to leave academia to pursue another road. I have met Alex when we were both students and it was his passion for carrying out his own projects that reassured me in my decision to pursue the academic trail. I am indebted to both of them for their support and the good memories I have when thinking back to the many happy moments we experienced together.

Finally, I would like to thank my good friends—Noëmi Lerch, Irena Ristic, Daniela Schaub, Lisa von Boehmer, Nicky Kern, Fabian Kristmann, Niggi Schäfer and Daniel Zweifel—for being there with me on various stages of the journey. Last, but by no means least, I am most grateful to my parents and my brothers that supported me throughout my whole life, regardless of whether times were good or bad. Thank you, this thesis would never have been possible without you!

Table of Contents

1
Introduction

Database systems have always played an important role in many applications across various domains. Originally conceived as a means for efficient storage of information in classic database applications such as library catalogues, financial accounting solutions, airline reservation systems or product inventories, database systems have evolved continually over time and have become widespread to a point where they form a part of nearly every type of application in existence. Nowadays, operating systems use them to maintain a directory of installed software and hardware, network management tools operate on top of a database cataloguing all users, hosts and the connections between them and computer-aided design tools employ database systems to keep track of the course of the product development process.

However, database systems are to be found not only in specialist applications and expert domains. More recently, these technologies have also progressed into the realm of consumer software. Multimedia tools such as image libraries or media players employ database systems to manage the vast amount of digital images, music files or videos. Personal organisers such as mail clients, calendar tools and contact managers also use databases to perform their tasks and to provide the user with advanced search and notification facilities. In modern web browsers, bookmarks are stored in lightweight data management systems that allow standardised querying and easy data exchange. Using techniques from the field of information retrieval, desktop search engines index documents on a personal computer's hard disk and thus constitute a powerful means to find files. When helping a driver to reach their destination, navigation systems as installed in most recent cars draw their knowledge from a geographical information system, a database system that is tailored and optimised to answer queries about route planning and features of the surrounding landscape. Lately, the trend towards omni-present database systems has even become visible in a manner that spawned discussions and plans to replace the hierarchical file systems used to manage data on disk today with file systems based on a database system. Such file systems could provide uniform database services to most of the applications discussed above and would eliminate the need for proprietary solutions.

To address the ever changing requirements that have arisen from their dispersion, database systems have undergone a remarkable evolution. Very early databases were built on a purely hierarchical data model and this was sufficient for many systems. When more complex applications required many-to-many relationships, the tree-based hierarchical model was abandoned and the graph-based network data model was introduced with CODASYL [71] as a standard. In parallel, data structure diagrams—later renamed as Bachman diagrams [9] after their inventor—were created as a way to graphically describe the data stored in a database system. Since the network model was designed for sequential data storage on magnetic tapes, a major drawback that resulted from this type of storage was the lack of a general search functionality.

With the advent of disk drives that were free of this limitation, random access to data became possible bringing forward database systems based on the relational model of data as first formalised by Codd [72]. Initially, the relational model was primarily adopted by the academic community which preferred its mathematical foundations over the technical specifications of commercial database systems based on the network model. As an approach to providing a "unified view of data", Chen proposed the Entity-Relationship (E/R) model [64]. Building on the idea of a graphical notation that describes a software system, E/R diagrams provided a clear separation of concepts by distinguishing between entities and relationships. At the time, these characteristics of the E/R model were major improvements. However, today the abstraction from the underlying implementation model and providing a conceptual view of data has also to be recognised as one of the model's major contributions. It is this property of the model that has propelled a continuing evolution manifesting itself in extensions to E/R or in other models developed to conceptualise specialist domains. Apart from performance, the E/R model was also one of the factors that led to the adoption of the relational model in commercial database systems as it also established a well-defined process for developing database applications.

Even though the relational model has nowadays been widely accepted as the standard technology to store and manipulate data in database systems, it was continually adapted, extended and optimised to suit the need of new applications. For example, when the requirement of representing the history of the stored data surfaced, attempts were made to represent this by simply adding additional attributes to existing relations to capture the time when a given tuple is valid. These approaches that merely used the relational model without altering the model itself, were soon found to be too simple in nature. Data cubes and three-dimensional relations were among the new concepts that were introduced to extend the foundation of the relational model to cope with temporal data. Other application domains such as computer-aided design, manufacturing and software engineering welcomed database systems supporting historic versions but also introduced additional demands such as the management of alternative versions, the definition of configurations and the possibility of merging data developed in parallel. To address these demands, a number of general version models have been proposed and integrated into database management systems.

As version models became more complex over time, the concepts of the relational model turned out to be a hindrance as they did not lend themselves to representing versioned objects. When object-oriented programming languages became the status quo in application engineering, the impedance mismatch between relational databases and object-oriented applications grew into a serious problem and object-oriented databases emerged also. As these systems provided the concept of an object, they were able to implement versioning at a natural level. At the same time, using the same data model in the database and for the programming language reduced the programming overheads to map data between the two models. As a reaction to this evolution, some relational databases were augmented by integrating object concepts into the relation model to form what is known as the object-relational model. While purely object-oriented databases were able to overcome the drawbacks of the relational model, they often lacked support for database management. For example, few systems implemented a standardised common query language such as Object Query Language (OQL) that was proposed by the Object Data Management Group (ODMG) and rather relied on the programming language to retrieve and manipulate data. These limitations and the fact that relational databases also provided some support for object-orientation, have restricted the success of object-oriented databases and today they only exist in certain niches such as embedded databases used in the automotive or aerospace industry.

Although the spread of database systems has already made these technologies an essential part of most of today's systems, their evolution is far from coming to an end. With the advent of powerful portable personal devices and global access to data, the whole domain of computer science launches into a new era which will bring new applications, new challenges and new demands. We believe that it is essential to continue addressing these demands by advancing the evolution of database systems one step ahead. An example of such a new demand that is currently perceived in most applications domains is the capability of systems to expose context-aware behaviour. Hence, it is necessary to develop core database system technologies to cope with these requirements. In this thesis, we propose a version model for object-oriented database systems targeted at context-aware data management. Continuing the evolution of version models, we have extended existing concepts to address today's requirements. The resulting model stores context-dependent versions of objects, while at the same providing more traditional, revisional versioning features that help to keep track of the evolution of a system. Further, through the use of a configurable matching algorithm that operates on top of this version model, our extended database system is able to deal with adaptation requirements of diverse applications.

1.1 Motivation

To corroborate the demand for context-aware database systems, we examine a set of fields within computer science that will provide evidence that there are applications being built that require such functionality. In these application domains, at least three major trends, that are already under way, can be witnessed at the moment. These developments have not yet been properly addressed in database systems research and will thus propel the future evolution of these technologies.

The globalisation of many modern applications is one such development that will have a strong impact on how database systems technologies will evolve in the near future. Global applications provide world-wide access to their functionality and the data they manage. Although they are built as a single application using a single source of information, they

are expected to behave everywhere as the local customs and culture demand. In its simplest form, globalisation means that such systems need
to be capable of dealing with multiple languages. More complex challenges arise from cultural differences such as whether text is read from
left-to-right or from right-to-left, how dates or numbers are formatted
and what information is considered offensive or even forbidden. Another
aspect of globalisation is collaboration across the globe. Clearly, every
region is most qualified to provide, edit and update the information that
is intended for local use. A modern database system should provide features to manage the same information spanning multiple nations and to
keep track of its evolution in a global collaborative environment.

Another important trend that information research must face is personalisation. In contrast to globalisation, personalisation demands that
an application adapts to the needs and desires of an individual user. Personalisation can either be effected based on user behaviour and history
or on explicit input by users specifying how the system should be configured. In the first case, a system can, for instance, adapt the way in
which it interacts with a user, thereby optimising the work processes a
user has to carry out to achieve their task. As an example of the second
case, users would like to be able to control the look and feel of an application, which parts of the stored data are presented to them and how
the application behaves in terms of when a specific piece of information
is displayed. Whereas, in the case of globalisation, information adapts
to well-specified rules of a whole set of users defined by their common
culture, personalisation leads to adaptivity at a much finer level of granularity, as the system alters based on arbitrary preferences of a single
person. A database system, therefore, does not only need to keep track
of the data managed by an individual user, it also needs to record the
configuration and preferences of these users.

The third development in computer science to affect database systems
is what we will call mobilisation throughout this thesis. With mobilisation we mean the influences that come from the fields of mobile, pervasive
and ubiquitous computing. Each of these fields essentially advocates a
shift from the traditional style of interacting with applications based on
a personal computer towards applications that are accessible through
small devices or are completely embedded in the environment. Database
systems technologies have already faced similar changes in computing
paradigms when they evolved from mainframe computers to workstations
and later to personal computers. This diversification led to a broaden-
ing of technologies that manifests itself in the range of database systems

available today. Corporate applications rely on highly configurable databases that manage large amounts of information, while consumer systems employ lightweight storage solutions that are optimised for much smaller data sets and are easier to administer. It is, therefore, only logical to assume that database systems will also take part in this latest transition of computing paradigms. In these novel environments, database systems need to address a whole set of additional challenges. While, for example, interaction with information in traditional systems was based on keyboard input and graphical output on screens, in these new applications, screens and keyboards are very limited in size or not available at all. Therefore, the so-called interaction bandwidth is drastically reduced and database systems need to provide support to use it as effectively as possible. Often applications will want to provide more than one interaction channel or combine arbitrary channels to offer complex interaction facilities. Especially in mobile scenarios, the physical environment of a user plays an important role. While personalisation requires adaptation to a user's preferences, mobilisation demands that an application and the information it delivers are also tailored to the conditions surrounding the user. As users are not assumed to be in constant interaction with an application as it is part of their entourage, a database system also needs to be proactive. When a new state in the user's environment is detected, that leads to the availability of updated or additional information, a proactive database system can notify the user about this new data without the user having to explicitly query for it. While this can be seen as extension of trigger mechanisms that are already prevalent in databases, it is also an example of how the limited bandwidth of such systems can be successfully used.

1.2   Challenges of Context-Awareness

To obtain a comprehensive list of requirements that need to be addressed in the field of database systems to cope with these three developments, globalisation, personalisation and mobilisation, we will have a look at a few existing application domains that have already begun to move in those directions. While examining those systems, the focus will, however, always be on investigating the challenges of data storage, management and delivery that are put forward by those applications.

The development of globalisation can be best observed in the domains of web engineering and web information systems. Starting out as a platform that would allow scientists to exchange their data and results, the World Wide Web evolved into the most important source of information on the planet. Nowadays, it used by private individuals to access up-to-date information, to communicate, to do e-commerce or to publish information about themselves. Corporate companies employ the web to present themselves to customers or partners and to do business-to-customer or business-to-business trade. More recently, the web has also become a platform to distribute and execute programs such as office or e-mail applications on-line. Along with this evolution of the web, the requirements to web engineering and web information systems have also changed. While, at first, web systems consisted of a collection of static web pages that were delivered by the web server to the client, more advanced applications demanded the presence of dynamic content and thus led to the integration of database systems in these applications. Originally, these databases served as a source for content, but it did not take long until they were also employed to store information about the structure and presentation of a web site. This development marked the birth of the first so-called content management systems that would create every requested page from the metainformation stored in a database system. These systems also led to the introduction of features targeted at globalisation as many of them were capable of handling multi-lingual sites. However, these features were always addressed at the application level and thus never made it into the core of the database system. When web sites still continued to grow in complexity and requirements, the need for CASE tools led to the development of model-driven approaches that allow a web application to be represented as a conceptual model. These models then serve as the basis for a generation process that implements the conceptual specification using off-the-shelf components. Lately, most of the model-driven approaches have begun to introduce some features to cope with globalisation such as the possibility to model adaptation of a web site under special conditions. Again, these features are implemented within the generation process and are thus not addressed within the database system. As most of the data and metadata of a web site are managed by a database system nevertheless, we believe that support for these globalisation requirements should be implemented at that level.

Not unlike globalisation, the requirements put forward by personalisation can also be witnessed in the fields of web engineering and web information systems. Portal sites providing personalised access to information while at the same time allowing content to be published by individuals, are a good source of such new challenges. As mentioned before, the functionality required to perform personalisation is not unlike the ones demanded by globalisation. The only difference is the granularity of adaptation that is now reduced to single individuals instead of cultural communities. Keeping this observation in mind, it is astounding to note that the systems that were developed to cope with personalisation differ greatly from the approaches that address globalisation. While numerous platforms exist to develop and implement portal sites, their capabilities are often orthogonal to the ones offered by content management systems or model-driven approaches, in the sense that neither side provides support to cope with the problems addressed by the other side. Once again, we believe that this perplexing situation exists because the requirements of personalisation have not been addressed at the proper level. Similar to content management systems and model-driven approaches, systems providing personalisation handle adaptation to an individual user within the application instead of empowering the database system to do so.

Finally, as briefly discussed in the previous section, the development of mobilisation is best noted in the fields of mobile, pervasive and ubiquitous computing. Unfortunately, not many applications in these fields currently rely on database systems to store, manage and deliver data. One reason for this is undoubtedly that most systems developed in these fields have very special hardware requirements that prevent traditional databases from being considered as components. As all of these systems are embedded in a user's surroundings, another reason for implementing proprietary solutions is the lack of support provided by current database systems to adapt to the context of a user and their environment or to become proactive if a certain state is detected. If database systems are to continue to play their important role in most applications, even as computing paradigms change, it is necessary to provide comprehensive support for mobile, pervasive and ubiquitous systems. It is our opinion that adaptation to complex context states as required in these applications, is not dissimilar to adaptation to individual users or groups of similar users. Therefore, it is possible to address all of these challenges with a single concept at the core of the database systems that will be used in the future.

1.3   Contribution of this Thesis

This thesis examines the field of context-aware computing from the perspective of database systems by determining the requirements of data management as put forward by applications from the domains of pervasive, ubiquitous and mobile computing as well as web engineering. A first contribution of this thesis is, therefore, a detailed analysis of context-aware applications that have been developed in these domains in recent years. To the best of our knowledge, relating these requirements to versioning concepts, that have already been developed for existing specialist databases, represents a novel approach to context-aware data management. Hence, the documentation of this connection between the two fields has to be seen as both a contribution and a validation of our work.

The in-depth presentation of the definition of our version model for context-aware data management stands at the heart of this thesis and, at the same time, represents its main contribution. Starting from existing solutions, our approach adapts and extends concepts proposed in earlier work to arrive at a version model that meets all demands of current context-aware applications and is flexible enough to cope with new requirements in the future. The formal definition of the version model is specified as an extension of the OM data model for object-oriented data management. OM provides a comprehensive graphical notation as well as an object algebra that can be used to specify complex constraints. Whereas the graphical notation is used to compare the structure of versioned objects to the one of traditional OM objects, we rely on algebraic expressions to specify certain rules and conditions unambiguously. Finally, the theoretical definition of our model is validated by a concrete implementation that takes the form of a database programming library providing context-aware data management to applications.

Apart from this database library, the presented version model has been thoroughly evaluated in two further projects leading to a rich body of experiences. The first of these projects is an implementation platform for web engineering applications that heavily uses context-dependent object variants to represent all of its core concepts. Based on this implementation platform an entire content management system consisting of a server component and client tools has been implemented. The architecture and functionality of this system is discussed in detail as it demonstrates the advantages of our approach. A mobile multi-channel information system for tourists visiting an international arts festival is the second project in which the version model for context-aware data management has been applied. In this system, our content management system has been used as the content management component that is responsible for delivering content across different channels to the visitors of the city. As the entire system has been demonstrated and used for several days at the festival itself, a substantial amount of information about how the version model performs in practice has been gathered. This comprehensive record of practical evaluation represents the final contribution of this thesis.

1.4   Thesis Overview

The remainder of this thesis is structured as follows. The next chapter is devoted to the analysis of application domains that have recently brought forward context-aware applications as well as models, frameworks and infrastructures supporting such applications. Typical sample systems from the fields of web engineering, ubiquitous, pervasive and mobile computing are presented. The analysis of these systems leads to the discussion of requirements for context-aware data management. The formulation of the hypothesis of our work that these requirements should be addressed with a version model within a database system, concludes the chapter. To motivate our approach of using a version model to manage context-aware data, the evolution of existing version models is examined in Chapter 3. However, before discussing concrete systems, we first establish a common terminology that serves as a basis for presenting these systems.

The object-oriented version model for context-aware data management is introduced in Chapter 4. This approach is an extension of concepts originally defined for version management in engineering databases. While it retains the notion of a version graph that supports both revisional and alternative versions, a contribution of our model is the generalisation of the way in which individual versions can be described. Version properties are used in our system to build dynamic configurations by adapting object graphs to the current context at query time. The model of context used in this work and the matching algorithm that uses the context information to select the best representation constitute further extensions to previously proposed versioning schemes.

To validate our version model by applying it in a concrete system, we have chosen the domain of web engineering as the demand for context-awareness and adaptation is well documented in this field. In web engineering, a number of model-based approaches allows context to be integrated into the conceptual specification of a web site. There are, however, still no general implementation platforms that provide satisfactory support for deploying such web sites and leverage the full potential of context-dependent adaptation. In Chapter 5 we propose our own content management system that has been built using our version model and is intended as a common basis for the implementation of model-based approaches.

The power of systems built on top of the version model for context-aware data management is demonstrated by examining the integration of the content management system presented in Chapter 5 within a mobile tourist information system. In Chapter 6, we discuss how this system is able to support tourists visiting an international arts festival by providing access to information about events and venues while on the move. All presented information services have been implemented using the technologies proposed in this thesis and were also tested in a complete system that was in use at the Edinburgh Fringe Festival in 2005.

We conclude this thesis with Chapter 7 where we review the contributions made in this work. Additionally, we summarise related work that is currently ongoing and issues that need to be addressed in the near future. An outlook on how this research could be continued argues that the concepts presented in this thesis could be opened up to other application domains than context-aware data management. Finally, we discuss systems that we believe would profit from these future developments of our technologies.

2

Context-Aware Computing

In this chapter, we start by giving a broad overview of context and the role it has played in various branches of science in the past. Then, shifting the focus to related research in the field of computer science, we summarise previous attempts to define and represent context as well as approaches to achieving context-awareness. Apart from establishing an understanding of the facets of context that are used in computer science today, the discussion of these works will also serve as a motivation for our work in the field of context-aware data management. Finally, a survey of concrete applications provides requirements to context-aware data management that arise from the use of context in these systems. At the end of the chapter, we revisit these requirements and formulate our hypothesis how the challenges of context-aware computing should be addressed in the field of information systems.

2.1 Forms of Context

Over the past years, context has been a subject intensely researched by a wide range of scientific disciplines outside computer science. Researchers from the fields of humanistic sciences such as linguistics, sociology and philosophy agree that context is a concept of utmost importance in the interpretation of speech, situations and actions. At any given point in time, the human senses constantly capture a vast amount of information from the environment and the individuals surrounding us. In addition to this sensory input, the human brain continuously draws on stored information, such as knowledge about past events, individual memories and a person's social background, to build a situational context. It is this context that enables and propels the processing and classification of new information in a subconscious but highly efficient manner. The power of the human brain lies in its ability to intuitively decide what is important and what is not or to assign meaning to phrases and events.

In linguistics, a typical application of context is its use to determine the meaning of polysemantic words [293] when reading a text or taking part in a conversation. For example, according to the lexical database WordNet [190], developed at Princeton University, the English word *row* has at least four significantly different interpretations—three as a noun and one as verb. Using the word *row* in an isolated sentence such as *"Fred had a row with a row of rowers."*, can, therefore, lead to considerable confusion. To understand what is being written or spoken, additional information contained in preceding or succeeding sentences, the position of the words within the sentence, or precedent knowledge about Fred is required. According to scientists working in linguistics, it is exactly this additional information that has to be considered as context and only through this context is the human brain capable of understanding language. The information, for instance, that Fred is a lout and has recently been to the harbour, would suggest that *"Fred had a quarrel with a line of oarsmen."* is a plausible interpretation of the above sentence. The importance of this notion of context is only amplified by the fact that most words have multiple meanings which can only be determined when the word is placed in a sentence. To provide this context, most modern dictionaries resort to examples that show the application and the meaning of a given word, rather than trying to explain the word by substituting it with synonyms.

Researches in social sciences observe how humans implicitly change and adapt their behaviour to the situation or environment they are in. Although the great importance of context was accepted in sociology long ago, the notion or understanding of context is somewhat different from the one presented before. While the discipline of linguistics focusses on the factors that empower the human mind to understand language, sociology endeavours to explore the mechanisms that are at work when people interact. In this setting, context is an unseen force that controls how our actions are perceived by other persons around us. For example, a joke that is well received among friends can have catastrophic consequences when told in a more formal environment. The study of context in social sciences aims at uncovering and understanding these processes with the promise to devise methods [93] that help to better exploit the power of context. Eliminating undesired contextual influences may help in the future to optimise the performance of individuals or the way in which people collaborate [135]. Also, the design of new products may be improved to make their handling more intuitive, by taking advantage of a profound knowledge of context and its impact on the user.

Finally, scholars of philosophy have probably the most theoretical notion of context [8]. One aim of the research related to context in philosophy is to describe its very nature in terms of what it really is. In contrast to the other presented disciplines, where context is perceived to be an influence or force that interacts with real and abstract objects, some philosophers look at context in isolation. It is their goal to reach a profound understanding that will allow them to provide a comprehensive definition of context. However, even philosophy itself is not immune against the influences of context and therefore another branch of researches examines how context affects philosophical reasoning [12, 154, 276]. In the course of their studies, philosophers have shown that context has an influence on the logic of an argument and that certain questions can only be contemplated legitimately if the context of the question is known and well-defined. Context in philosophy determines which aspects of a problem are taken into consideration and which are left out and therefore, it is reasonable to assume that context defines a question as much as the question defines itself.

While it could be very interesting to dwell more on these ideas and thoughts, it would be of little merit or relevance in the scope of the work presented here. Nevertheless, we think the broad perspective on context presented here serves as an important background to appreciate related research in computer science. For the remainder of this thesis, we have, however, decided to limit the focus to more technical approaches. Context has been a subject of research in many areas of computer science, with some of the first efforts dating back to the early 1960s. In the field of Artificial Intelligence (AI), for example, the impact of context on knowledge representation structures [124] and cognitive models [193] has been examined. Various endeavours to understand and formalise the uses of context have been made, and frameworks [27] to support applications have been developed. Another discipline within computer

science that has produced a lot of research in the area of context is the
field of Human-Computer Interaction (HCI). The main focus of most of
these works lies in exploiting context to build user interfaces that automatically and implicitly adapt to the user's needs, capabilities and
wishes [248, 247]. Multiple efforts have been made to create a shared
understanding of context [274] and a standardised set of context parameters that would facilitate the development and portability of adaptive
interfaces. Although these fields have made numerous and substantial
contributions to the exploration of context, we will limit ourselves to the
uses of context as found in the areas of ubiquitous, pervasive and mobile
computing as well as web engineering, as we believe that these application domains are most relevant to the work presented in this thesis.
In these fields, context has been widely accepted as a driving force for
augmenting the functionality of applications [75].

Most notably in the field of ubiquitous and pervasive computing,
many models, frameworks and infrastructures for context-awareness have
been developed to help the creation of applications that rely heavily on
context information. Due to the broad variety of existing approaches, we
will give a detailed presentation of some uses of context from the domain
of ubiquitous and pervasive computing in the following section. This will
serve both as the basis of our motivation of the importance of context and
as a source of requirements that need to be addressed in context-aware
data management. In addition to systems from ubiquitous and pervasive
computing, we will also survey a number of projects in mobile computing.
Clearly, location information is a very important dimension of context,
when working with a mobile system. However, there are also other, more
subtle forms of context that need to be considered when data is delivered
to such a client. Finally, we believe it is worthwhile to also examine a
set of important technologies that have been developed in the relatively
young field of web engineering. As a result of today's omnipresence of
the web, the systems that sustain it have to cope with a vast amount of
requirements. Web sites that adapt themselves to the different people,
languages or geographical regions are only the tip of the iceberg of what
context-awareness means in this discipline. Standard technologies that
have emerged from this domain, such as client-server communication protocols, or user interfaces built from marked-up documents, are nowadays
also being used to build applications outside the traditional setting of
the Internet. This development adds to the importance of the notion of
context as it is defined by these researchers and makes the discussion of
these approaches indispensable.

2.2   Ubiquitous and Pervasive Computing

Within computer science, researchers working in ubiquitous and pervasive computing study the embedding of computer-based applications into our everyday life. Therefore, a major goal of ubiquitous and pervasive computing is to take a step beyond the paradigm of personal computing by integrating computing tasks and daily objects and artefacts. As a consequence of this vision of the future, the personal computer, as known today, would disappear from many households and be replaced by smaller, invisible computers that seamlessly support our life in the background. For example, instead of sitting in front of their personal computer to compose a message to a friend, a user could achieve this task by writing with a special pen on digitally augmented paper. The pen would then perform character recognition and transmit the text through the user's mobile phone to the recipient. In a way, the replacement of video recorders and DVD players with so-called media centres that integrate a part of the multimedia functionality of personal computers, can be seen a first step in that direction that already has a concrete and visible impact on our life today. According to experts in this area, this evolution will continue and will spawn new requirements to both hardware and software. In 1991, Weiser [289] coined to term "ubiquitous computing" to summarise all research efforts aiming at addressing these new requirements, be it through establishing general concepts and foundations that facilitate the development of applications or through the implementation of custom systems that lead to proof-of-concepts or new challenges. The term "pervasive computing" was later created by the industry to denote a less conceptual and more technological approach to these issues. However, this distinction has become less pronounced over the years and today the terms ubiquitous and pervasive computing are used almost interchangeably.

A major area of research within ubiquitous and pervasive computing are context-aware or sentient systems. As such applications are incorporated into the user's environment, they often require novel forms of interaction which are no longer based on a traditional interface consisting of a screen, keyboard and a mouse, as these devices are usually not available to the user. Therefore, these systems can neither be configured by setting options and preferences nor is it possible to control the state of the application by giving explicit commands through buttons or menu items. To compensate for this lack of information explicitly provided by the user, many systems found in ubiquitous and pervasive computing rely on context to influence the behaviour of an application. The scope of such applications is wide ranging, from setting user preferences based on context information to proactive and autonomous system behaviour through the execution of application functionality, whenever a certain context state is detected. Commonly accepted as the first of these context-aware systems in the field of ubiquitous and pervasive computing is the *Active Badge Location System* [284] developed in 1992, even though it was not until 1994 that the term "context-aware" was introduced [243] to denote the influence of context on ubiquitous and pervasive applications. Over the last decade, countless context-aware systems [10] that address a wide variety of requirements have been developed.

2.2.1   Location-Aware Systems

The first class of applications that integrated context-aware behaviour were the so-called "location-aware systems". These systems assumed a notion of context that seems somewhat limited from today's perspective, as they restricted adaptation to the location of a user only. Users of the previously mentioned Active Badge Location System wear identification badges, and sensors distributed throughout the rooms transmit their positions within the building to a central server. This context information is then used by an application supporting the telephone receptionist in forwarding calls to the phone nearest to the callee's position.

The *Chameleon* [108] system, a portable hand-held device capable of acting as both an input controller and output display, takes location-awareness into a slightly different direction. Instead of locating users through external sensors, the Chameleon device is itself aware of its position and orientation in a three-dimensional space. Including the system's orientation in the context along with its position represents the integration of a second context dimension that refines and broadens the notion of locational context. The notion of context as defined by Chameleon increases the number of possibilities in which applications can adapt. Instead of one single context dimension, Chameleon provides two independent dimensions as well as all their combinations. Several such applications have been developed, as, for example, "Active Maps and Paper" where the Chameleon device is used as an electronic information lens that provides additional information when used in conjunction with the printed documents. In the map example, weather information, travel itineraries and geographical points of interest are displayed on the hand-held device, depending on its position over the map and its orientation. Another application of the Chameleon system is a "Computer-Augmented Library" where the unit assists its user in finding the desired information, based on navigational information that is emitted by the books and the bookshelves. Additional information such as excerpts of a book or a table of contents are also available on the display or through headphones connected to the device. Finally, the bookshelves are equipped with lights that can be used to indicate related books by highlighting their position on the shelf. A third application, the "Portable Surrogate Office", that was proposed for the Chameleon system, uses the device to transport the office space of a user to another location. To root this virtual office in a physical environment, mediator objects serve as anchors that link into the information available from the original office. The portable unit detects the presence of these mediator objects based on their location and displays the associated data automatically. Based on a panoramic image of the office at work, the Chameleon unit is even capable of acting as a window into this room from a remote location such as the home of an employee. Again, location and orientation context information is used to display the correct section of the image.

A more intricate application of context is exhibited by the *LiteMinutes* multimedia meeting minutes system [67]. LiteMinutes is a room-aware application that can be used during a meeting to capture multimedia streams of the session and personal notes taken by the participants using their portable computers. Parallel to the capturing of this information, LiteMinutes also records a stream of contextual information containing the location of users and devices and timing information for certain events and actions. This contextual information is then used by the system to generate a web-based record of the meeting that includes links to the captured multimedia streams and textual notes taken during the meeting. LiteMinutes is implemented based on *Nibble* [52], a locator service that uses the wireless network technology IEEE 802.11 to determine the position of WiFi-enabled devices, such as laptops or PDAs.

Another special case of location-aware systems is the class of follow-me applications. The goal of a follow-me application is to use the context information of a user's location to provide the user with the data and programs required for work as the user moves through a building. Harter et al. [133] use sensor tags called Bats to track the position of a person within a building. This location information is then used to teleport the personal desktop to another computer when users come away from their personal workstation in their office. Whenever a user equipped with a Bat sensor tag approaches a context-aware workstation, their working environment is brought to that computer using the Virtual Network Computing (VNC) protocol which enables them to work at another machine as if it were their own. As location is often the only context considered by follow-me applications, the use of context in these systems has to be regarded as less elaborate than in some of the other approaches we presented. Nevertheless, this class of applications stresses again the omnipresence and importance of locational information as a dimension of context that needs to be addressed by every context-aware system.

2.2.2 Communication Tools

In comparison to a face-to-face meeting, electronic communication limits the amount of information that can be exchanged between the participants of a conversation. This lack of information can lead to a number of undesired effects, such as misunderstandings or interruptions at an inopportune moment. To compensate for this insufficiency, a number of context-aware communication tools have been proposed that endeavour to replace the missing information with adaptation of the application to the sensed context. For example in *Context-Call* [249], users can specify on their mobile phones in which context they currently are. Similar to ringing profiles known from most mobile phone models, the context can be set to general, meeting or sport. The Context-Call application provides information about this context of the callee to the caller using the Wireless Application Protocol (WAP). The caller can then decide whether their request is appropriate to the callee's context. Note that, in the Context-Call system, the application itself is not context-aware but only raises the awareness of the caller. Proposals to automate the negotiation of a phone call based on such context information have been made based on this application. Therefore it is also worthwhile to consider this form of context in the design of future systems.

Adaptation to the user, location awareness, non-intrusive user interfaces and minimising interruption have been recognised as requirements of "Everywhere Messaging". A survey [246] of four experimental communication tools—Clues, Active Messenger, Nomadic Radio and comMotion—has examined their capabilities to address these demands. As all of the surveyed prototype systems rely on context information to cater for these requirements, we will give a brief summary of the notion of context present in each of them. *Clues* [187] filters incoming messages

and prioritises them according to their importance. The motivation behind the project is to only forward a message to the user when it is
appropriate for them to receive it. If a user is busy or in a meeting, for
example, only messages of the highest priority are forwarded. As a source
of context information, Clues relies on the user's calendar and e-mail log
to determine in which circumstances the user currently is. Compared to
location-based systems, this notion of context is much broader, as it is
also based on historical information, such as the log of an e-mail exchange
between two people.

The idea of message prioritisation is taken one step further by *Active
Messenger*, a project that integrates the Clues engine in a more comprehensive application. Active Messenger provides a component registry
that serves two purposes. First, heterogeneous output channels such as
e-mail inboxes, fax machines, pagers and phones can be described there
and thus made known to the system. Second, the registry also serves
as an inventory of workstations used by people. With this information,
Active Messenger is able to determine the virtual position of users by
checking on which machine they are currently logged in. This virtual
position then serves as the basis to redirect messages to one of the registered output channels according to the priority the message was given
by Clues. As the technical capabilities and possibly the location of the
output channel have an influence on when they are triggered by Active
Messenger, this metadata has to be considered as context information
as well. It therefore presents another previously undiscussed dimension
that can play an important role.

Nomadic Radio [239] is a wearable messaging system that interacts
with its user through voice input and output and can thus be operated
without using one's hands. It is capable of delivering a variety of information to the user such as e-mail, calendar events and alerts, as well
as voice mails and hourly news broadcasts. In contrast to a traditional
radio set, the intention is not to provide a continuous service. Again, the
goal is to make the system as unobtrusive as possible by using various
contextual factors in the user environment. As this system is also based
on the Clues message filtering engine, it has access to the same context
information as described above. However, Nomadic Radio augments this
notion of context by relying on additional dimensions. One factor that
can have an impact on its decision whether to make a user aware of a
message or alert is the usage history of the device. A user that has not
been interacting with Nomadic Radio for a longer period of time is assumed to be concentrating on something else, while a user that has just

issued a command to the system is supposed to be focussing on the device. Another form of historical context is how the user has reacted in the past to the class of messages that Nomadic Radio is about to deliver. If they listened to these messages, the system reckons that the information was valuable. If they aborted the playback of the message prematurely, however, it assumes that the user was bothered by the interruption. Finally, Nomadic Radio is also able to analyse the background sounds in the user's environment. From this information, it infers various situations and locations, such as people having conversations, public places in a city, hallways and offices in a building and the outdoors. Although this context information is comparable to the phone profiles of Context-Call presented above, it is vital to note that Nomadic Radio is able to both acquire this information and adapt to it autonomously.

Not unlike Nomadic Radio, *comMotion* [186] is also a wearable platform that has been designed to deliver relevant information to users, based on their context. However, in contrast to Nomadic Radio that is only able to infer the general situation of a user, comMotion is equipped with a Global Positioning System (GPS) receiver and can thus determine the exact position of the user at most times. As we have shown, using location information as a basis for adaptive application behaviour is a very common form of context-awareness. However, comMotion extends this purely location-based notion of context by taking the location history of a user into consideration. Thus, not the position itself but also the behavioural pattern of the user becomes a context dimension to which the system can adapt. Based once more on Clues, all this additional context information is processed to trigger and send context-relevant information such as reminders, messages and content information to the user at the right place and the right time.

Family Intercom [197] has a similar goal as the Context-Call and comMotion projects. By taking the current circumstances of the recipient of an audio connection into consideration, the Family Intercom attempts to facilitate compliance with social protocols by controlling when it is advisable to interrupt a callee. As forms of context, the system is able to process the location and activities of users as well as the ambient sound levels in both the environment of the initiator and the recipient of the call. In contrast to Context-Call, where a user was required to define their own context using a set of predefined profiles, the Family Intercom is able to capture all required context using sensors. A caller using the Family Intercom is made aware of the context information regarding the location and the activity of the callee. As in Context-Call, they can then decide for themselves if an interruption of the recipient is appropriate or not. However, the Family Intercom is also capable of automatically blocking calls that it classifies as violations of social protocol, for instance if a recipient is sleeping in their bedroom with the door closed. Finally, the ambient sounds are used both as a context to adapt the initial volume of the Family Intercom headset and, through speech recognition, as a basis for changing the state of the device.

The *Context/Communication Information Agent (CIA)* [144] assesses the user's current condition in terms of a comprehensive set of context factors. These factors include traditional context dimensions, such as the identity of the user, their location, their activity and the current time. This information is gathered from environmental sensors and from software sensors that infer information from the user's calendar. Furthermore, the system also monitors all user communication. It records what they are writing with an electronic pen, the text messages they receive and their phone conversations which are converted to text using speech recognition. The objective of the agent is to use this context information to proactively fetch relevant information and deliver it to the user at an opportune moment. For example, while a user is talking on the phone about the shopping they are going to do later, the system will add a reminder of the phone call to the shopping list the user has written with the electronic pen earlier in the day. When the user finally arrives at the store the updated shopping list will be presented to them automatically. By integrating written documents and spoken conversation into their system, the creators of the Context/Communication Information Agent have further extended the notion of context and with it also the requirements to general context-aware systems.

ConChat [223], a context-aware chat program, uses context to accomplish two primary goals. First, ConChat, as many communication tools before, attempts to raise the awareness of its users by providing them with contextual information about their chat partners. This additional knowledge about the current situation of other participants has been found to lead to a more precise assessment of their context, and shown to reduce misunderstandings. Second, ConChat actively removes ambiguities from conversations by tagging certain statements that could lead to confusion. In order to do so, ConChat uses a set of rules to detect patterns in the text, such as date and currency values that are then transformed using a conversion table. To effectively fulfil its purpose, ConChat relies on a vast number of different context dimensions. These dimensions are the user's location, the number of other people in the room, their identities, the room temperature, light and sound, other applications running in the room, the user's mood, the user's status, as well as the activity that is going on in the room. Values for all those context dimensions can be queried and examined by the person talking to a user, by means of a special side channel that is designed to empower participants to share contextual information parallel to the main communication channel. As mentioned before, the main communication channel is also influenced by the context, as terms that can have different meaning according to a sender's context are disambiguated by the system by tagging them with the value as it would be in the recipient's context. Such terms are statements of times, units of measurements such as length, weight or currency, date formats and special words that are known to have context-dependent meaning.

The broad set of context dimensions used by ConChat concludes our presentation of context-aware communication systems. Of course, the list of systems discussed here is far from exhaustive and countless other systems have been proposed, implemented and surveyed [245] in this domain. However, in terms of the context information that they use, these systems are comparable to the ones described here. Since collecting challenging and extraordinary forms and uses of context is the primary goal of this chapter, we believe that little is lost by not discussing further approaches in detail and moving on to another class of applications.

2.2.3 Intelligent Environments

In contrast to the applications described so far where the focus was on capturing the context of a single user, intelligent environments take a more comprehensive view of our surroundings, as they consider spaces where groups of people interact with a ubiquitous or pervasive system. While early approaches such as the *Intelligent Room* [73] were intended to enhance the work experience of employees in an office environment, the focus of research shifted over time towards the private life of people at home. According to researchers working in this field, this change of direction was motivated by the fact that humans spend most of their life at home and hence this area should be favoured particularly and profit substantially from these technological advances.

According to its creators, *KidsRoom* [32] is believed to be the "first multi-person, fully automated, interactive, narrative environment". The intelligent environment consists of a single room that is furnished as a children's playground. Inside the room, children can follow a story

which is told using a series of output channels such as speakers, lights
and projections that are all controlled by KidsRoom. During the narrative, the children can interact with the story. To do so, the room is
equipped with a system of cameras and sensors that are able to track
objects and persons, detect their movement, and recognise the actions
of the children currently in the room. An important and novel aspect of
this intelligent environment is its use of a narrative to provide a room for
manoeuvre which defines the possible interactions at a given moment.
Hence, in addition to the sensed context factors, the current position
within the story line is also a dimension that is exploited by the system.
Maybe one of the most interesting contributions of KidsRoom in terms
of context-awareness is its ability to not only sense context, but to proactively control it by triggering sounds, images and lighting moods using
the featured output channels.

A maybe more serious application of intelligent environments is pursued by numerous approaches such as *Classroom 2000* [3, 1], *Smart Classroom* [257] and *eClass* [36], that propose to use ubiquitous and pervasive
computing in an educational setting. The issues addressed in such intelligent learning environments are manifold, raging from capturing lectures
for later access and review to providing a basis for tele-education. The
learning experience is captured using a number of sensors that are installed in the environment. For example, cameras and microphones are
used to record the image and speech of the teacher and the audience.
Additionally, whiteboards present in the classroom feature a tracking
system that locates the position of the pen on the board and transforms
it into images of what is being written. Finally, slide presentations are
recorded using special software sensors installed on the teacher's laptop.
In Classroom 2000 and eClass, context is predominantly used to facilitate
the automated postproduction of the captured material into a presentation that is then accessible to students who have either not attended or
wish to review the course again. To successfully process the recorded
data, the system needs to know what happened in the environment at
any point in time. Similar to the narrative in KidsRoom, this context
data also includes information about the current state of the lecture and
information about the activities of the people attending it. Based on this
contextual knowledge, the system can then decide, for instance, whether
to integrate the captured video of the teacher, the one of the audience,
an image of the writings on the whiteboard or a screenshot of the slide
show in the final video stream. Although the intention behind the Smart
Classroom is slightly different, it uses a very similar notion of context to

that of the other two approaches. The objective of the Smart Classroom is to integrate remote students into the learning experience. Therefore the system has to control which scenes are delivered to the remote students at any point in time. To make this decision, Smart Classroom relies on four contextual situations that are inferred from an array of sensors. In contrast to other systems that deal with context at a relatively low level, these four states are a rather advanced form of context, as they represent complex information such as whether the teacher is writing on the whiteboard, presenting a model, or interacting with physical and virtual students.

The *Ambient Wood* [286] is another example of an intelligent environment that is designed to help children with their learning experience. The system addresses the problem that pupils often show difficulties relating physical experiences gained on a field trip to the more formal scientific knowledge of the classroom. This gap is bridged by the system by logging all events during the children's visit to the mixed reality space environment. This space is a piece of woodland that has been augmented with hidden sensors, position beacons and speakers. The children explore this ambient wood equipped with a portable device that can be used to display information about objects in the environment as well as to take light and moisture measurements. Additionally, the pupils can also influence the virtual conditions of their environment using tangible objects that represent the introduction of a new species or a change in the climate. Every interaction with the environment causes a number of events to be sent to all components involved. When captured, these events can later be used to generate a journal that allows the students to relive their field trip in the classroom, which reduces the divide between experience and knowledge. Beside the location information that is used to trigger actions in the environment and the display of information, the Ambient Wood system also processes other contextual input. For instance the objects that are used to change the environment are equipped with Radio Frequency Identifier (RFID) tags that allow their detection if placed sufficiently close to an RFID antenna. This context is then used to adapt the content of the information that is delivered to the hand-held devices carried by the children.

Context-aware homes [188] are the most ambitious form of intelligent environments that has been proposed so far. Surpassing the capabilities of the approaches presented so far, context-aware homes aspire to provide support for every aspect of human life at home. At least two factors are mainly responsible for the fact that the task of designing a home environment to be truly intelligent is vastly more complex than building a context-aware classroom or children's playground. First, according to literature, people's behaviour is of a far more unstructured nature when they are at home as compared to them working at the office or in a classroom. Second, it is more challenging to determine the user context, due to the absence of a framework that limits the number of possible situations, such as the progression of a lecture or a predefined narrative. Nevertheless, many prototypes that address these requirements have been proposed over the last years. The most important and comprehensive approaches include systems such as the *Neural Network House* [194], the *Aware Home* [160], the *Gator Tech Smart House* [137] and *eHome* [162]. Most of these intelligent environments share a vision of the home of the future. These common goals envisioned by the researchers who have created these context-aware homes include facilitating in-house communication, optimisation of power and resource consumption, adaptation of the living space to its occupants and, last but not least, security, including burglar alarms, fire detection, or other emergencies. All of these features use context information that is captured from sensors installed throughout the house. The Gator Tech Smart House, for example, relies on an especially impressive number of context sources. Special sensors monitor the operation of appliances such as cookers, toasters or washing machines, or observe the use of everyday objects such as the mailbox, toilets or showers. Photometer and thermostats record environmental conditions and leak detectors measure if a room is flooded by a malfunctioning toilet, washing machine or dishwasher. Finally, a number of technologies have been installed that assess and measure the biometrics of the inhabitants such as their weight or temperature. Clearly, the use of as many context dimensions as demonstrated by this example produces an interesting requirement in terms of scalability. A system which relies on many contextual factors cannot design an action for every possible combination of context values as the number of such combinations grows exponentially. Hence, a system has to be capable of deciding which action is the most appropriate, based on the current context.

A special case of context-aware homes are intelligent environments that commit themselves to supporting the medical care of their inhabitants. In the case of the *Aging in Place* [196] project and the *House of Matilda* [136], the goal is to design a living space that provides the support that is required in order to spare elderly people from having to move to a specialised institution and giving them the chance to spend their life in a familiar environment. Through constant surveillance of its inhabitants, the context-aware home tries to detect possible health problems and, in the case of a suspicious finding, suggests preventive help or calls an emergency hotline. Another approach is taken by the interdisciplinary project *House_n* [147]. Based on the observation that people do not like to be patronised by an intelligent environment, House_n does not automatically execute the actions it believes to be appropriate. Rather, it merely suggests to the inhabitants what they should be doing, by using non-intrusive user interfaces such as small lights that are embedded in the frames of the windows and can be used to indicate that a window should be opened or closed. This proposal has a few advantages compared to systems that take complete control over the user. As the user is in control, they do not get frustrated with the decisions of the intelligent environment, which, in turn, leads to a higher acceptance of the system. Further, users have to perform the changes themselves which means that they have to be active and move around. Finally, the system can be seen as teaching its inhabitants how they should act in certain situations. The researchers who designed House_n believe that the last two factors are beneficial to the physical and mental health of the persons residing in such a context-aware home. While these intelligent environments rely on much the same contextual information as the conventional context-aware homes, there is another challenge associated with the use of context in these systems. While we have stated that an intelligent environment cannot be programmed to respond to every combination of sensed context, it is required to react in a well-defined and deterministic way in all possible situations, especially if lives are at stake.

2.2.4 Models, Frameworks and Infrastructures

Many of the systems just presented have led to the development of frameworks that provides support for requirements that are common to a number of context-aware applications. While the exact set of capabilities of a given context infrastructure is highly dependent on its initial purpose, the functionality offered by most of these frameworks includes models to represent context, abstractions from sensors acquiring context, facilities to manage and process context and techniques to adapt applications to context. A vast variety of context models has been proposed [272], originating from very different backgrounds. An approach that is very frequently used are simple ⟨*key, value*⟩ models, but other models based on mark-up languages, graphical notations, object-orientation, logic and ontologies have also been developed. Technologies to acquire context can be classified into at least three different categories [63]. The most simple one is to access the sensors directly and extract context values. A more advanced approach is represented by middleware solutions that provide a common interface to several types of context-aware applications. Finally, context servers gather context and redistribute the context information over the network, with the advantage of allowing applications and context infrastructure to be loosely coupled. Usually, in a context-aware system, multiple processes are involved in the generation and consumption of context information. To manage and coordinate these components, architectures based on widgets, networked services and the blackboard model have been designed [295]. Widgets abstract from the sensor implementation and encapsulate context information using a well-defined public interface. In contrast to this tightly coupled approach, networked services represent a more flexible and robust architecture by providing a set of standardised services and protocols in the style of today's Internet. The blackboard architecture puts the focus on the context information which is shared and managed through the metaphor of a blackboard where processes can publish information and subscribe to updates. To become context-aware, applications need to adapt to the current state of context, which is normally done in one of two ways [140]. A context infrastructure can trigger certain functions of an application when certain predefined events occur, or the application itself may branch to the desired functionality by analysing the context information through a series of conditional statements. These common factors—context modelling, gathering, management and adaptation—that we have introduced just now, will serve as the basis for the following discussion of some of the most well-known context infrastructures. For the purpose of the work presented in this thesis we will, however, place special emphasis on the adaptation capabilities of these frameworks, as we believe that this aspect is most related to context-aware data management.

A first framework that allowed context-triggered actions was developed for the *ParcTab* [244], a wireless, palm-sized computer. The system uses direct sensor access to acquire context information and processes it by evaluation of simple conditional rules that specify how context-aware systems should react when a certain context state is detected. Due to its simple approach and its entanglement with the ParcTab architecture itself, the framework has not been applied in other projects. However, the basic components that it was built from have since been refined and generalised and are still the building blocks of numerous platforms that support context-aware applications.

The *Context Toolkit* [237, 90] constitutes a very copious infrastructure to gather and manage context information. It introduces a layered approach that is built around the notion of context widgets that were inspired by graphical user interface widgets. These widgets reside on a layer above the physical sensors and hide complexity by providing an abstraction of the context information designed to meet the expectations of a context-aware application. Thus, the same context widgets can be used by many applications as they are reusable building blocks. Examples of predefined widgets include `IdentityPresence` and `NamePresence` that determine which users are interacting with an application, `Activity` to sense what they are doing or `PhoneUse` and `MachineUse` that indicate which devices people are using. Apart from predefined widgets, it is also possible to implement custom context widgets, which can later be integrated as widget libraries into the Context Toolkit. The architecture of the Context Toolkit is object-oriented, consisting of the various widgets, context servers capable of aggregating over multiple widgets, and interpreters which transform context information to an appropriate granularity. A communication infrastructure that is built into all of the components of the architecture through a common superclass `BaseObject` allows information represented using the Extensible Mark-up Language (XML) to be exchanged using several methods such as the Hypertext Transfer Protocol (HTTP), the Simple Mail Transfer Protocol (SMTP), the Common Object Request Broker Architecture (CORBA) and Remote Method Invocation (RMI).

While the Context Toolkit proposes an infrastructure based on widgets that are tightly coupled with the context-aware application, approaches based on a loosely coupled service architecture have also been proposed. For example the *MUSE* [51] project introduces the concept of a fusion service that gathers and derives context information from sensors. The specification of a fusion service is effected using a Bayesian network that describes the derivation of context information. Due to this representation, information theoretic algorithms can be used to compute the reliability of such fusion sensors in terms of a quality-of-information metric that has been defined for this purpose. In general, the loosely coupled nature of an architecture based on networked services has several advantages [145]. On the one hand, a context-aware application is not dependent on specific hardware and software such as operating systems or programming languages. On the other hand, maintenance, evolution and sharing of services is favoured by the clear separation between a context provider and a context consumer. With the Internet as a role model, the vision of many researchers advocating service-oriented architectures is to build a context platform based on a set of standardised protocols, formats and services. Fundamental building blocks including Automatic Path Creation (APC) to infer context information along a chain of services, or a discovery service detecting devices and people in proximity have already been identified. Apart from these advantages, loosely coupled approaches are, however, less suited to deal with the adaptation aspect of context-aware systems. As communication between the application and the infrastructure is limited to request and response messages, most of the processing needed to adapt to a context state will be done by the application. A possible solution to address this issue would be to extend this communication model to allow context information to be proactively pushed to a registered application when certain events are detected by the infrastructure.

A radically different approach is the underlying foundation of the *GAIA* [230, 222] context infrastructure. GAIA is built on the metaphor of a distributed meta-operating system that extends the operating system of a device with components that support context-aware processing. These components include an execution environment for applications, an I/O subsystem, the context file system, communication primitives, error detection and handling mechanisms, as well as resource allocation. Throughout the entire infrastructure, GAIA uses a unique context model that is based on first-order logic representing context values as Subject-Verb-Object (SVO) predicates. A context management component manipulates these predicates and can be accessed through queries, subscription or direct context serialisation. Context-sensitive application behaviour is effected by triggering rules which define the relationship between certain context states and methods representing the application functionality. Conflicts that arise when several rules are applicable are resolved by previously assigned values that govern the priority of a rule. This adaptation functionality is implemented by an event manager component that keeps track of context providers, context synthesisers and context consumers. The event manager also serves as a look-up service for context providers and maintains a history of context values. Finally, the context file system provides context-aware access to data. It is implemented as a virtual directory hierarchy that uses path components to represent context types and values. To access data in a given context, the application only needs to extend the path to the file with the appropriate context information and the file system deals with the retrieval of the corresponding data.

The framework for context-aware pervasive computing applications introduced in [140] proposes a layered architecture that addresses all aspects of a context architecture. The framework distinguishes seven layers—context gathering, context reception, context management, context querying, context-driven adaption, and application support. Those reside between the physical sensors and the context-aware application. The context gathering layer is in charge of the acquisition of sensed data from physical and logical sensors. It also contains various components which initially process context, such as aggregators and interpreters. The interface between context gathering and context management is implemented by the context reception layer that translates heterogeneous context information into a uniform representation, as expected by the context management layer. When different sensors deliver contradictory values for the same context, this layer also deals with conflict resolutions. Further, it maintains histories of previously sensed values. The context information supplied by the context reception layer is saved in a persistent store which resides within the context management layer. The data in this store is represented according to a uniform representation that adheres to a context model based on fact types. This context model also forms the basis of the query layer which offers an interface for applications to retrieve context information. The query layer supports three different types of queries. Simple fact queries can be used to retrieve the context value represented by the corresponding fact type. Situation queries combine fact queries with contextual situations that have been previously specified as a logical expression. Finally, event queries represent an asynchronous notification mechanism, and are triggered when a certain context state occurs. The situation specifications as well as preferences and triggers are managed in a repository on the adaptation layer which is also responsible for the evaluation of these preferences and triggers as well as for the generation of the appropriate notifications. In providing resources for query and notification mechanisms, the adaptation layer supports the implementation of the two adaptation models, branching and triggering, offered by the infrastructure. Finally, the topmost layer consists of a programming toolkit designed to facilitate the development of context-aware applications that interface with the context framework. Apart from utilities and support tools, this application layer supplies classes to access the lower layers of the framework as well as implementations of branching and triggering adaptation strategies.

An infrastructure for intelligent spaces based on the concept of independent agents supported by a context broker is represented by the

Context Broker Architecture (CoBrA) [62, 63]. The central component of the architecture, the context broker, is responsible for context gathering, storing and inference, as well as privacy management. Each of these tasks is performed by a dedicated module within the context broker. The context acquisition module provides a library of procedures that abstract from the physical and logical sensors, and offers a common interface. Derived context values are generated by a reactive inference engine that reasons over stored context and is located within the context inference module. A persistent context store is provided for the other module by the context knowledge base that manages the context information gathered by the context acquisition module. Although many infrastructures promise to deal with security and privacy aspects of context information, most of them do not offer concrete solutions. In contrast, CoBrA features a privacy management module that manages permissions and determines whether a given agent has sufficient rights to access a context value. Agents such as context-aware applications, devices, services and web services use the context broker to get context information. Based on the delivered context values, the agents adapt their behaviour. Thus, the context broker architecture provides no support for the adaptation process which is left entirely to the requesting agent.

An entirely different approach to building context-aware applications is taken by the *Smart-Its Platform* [258]. Services for this platform are implemented using the high-level Smart-Its Context Language (SICL) that describes the application. The SICL program is parsed by a pre-compiler that translates it into the implementation language of the execution platform. The generated code can then be compiled and linked with the standard compiler of this platform. Usually, a SICL program has four main blocks to specify sensor access, context recognition, adaptive behaviour and basic behaviour, respectively. Within the Smart-Its platform, context is represented as tuples with an arbitrary number of values. These context tuples are generated by the sensors and later processed during context recognition, using tuple transformation rules, to create new tuples. Finally, adaptation is specified in terms of rules that link the occurrence of a specific context tuple to the triggering of a function defined within the SICL program. As tuple transformation and adaptation rules can be specified in a reasonably natural way, this design not only supports the separation of application and adaptation logic but it also leads to readable programs. Beside this mechanism for specifying and implementing context-aware services, the Smart-Its platform also provides support for inter-object communication. Context-aware applications profit from this communication infrastructure in two ways. First, the collection of all context tuples stored within the different devices forms a tuple space used as a distributed information repository to share data, resources and context. Second, the communication services offered by the platform are also context-aware. Thus, a program running on a device does not have to handle the discovery of other devices, topology construction, establishing connection and data transfer as all of this functionality is already provided by the infrastructure.

The *Co-operating Real-time Sentient Objects: Architecture and Experimental Evaluation (CORTEX)* [109, 30] project is based on the sentient object model. A sentient object is an encapsulated entity as known from object-oriented systems. However, its interface is not a collection of arbitrary methods but is instead defined as a set of sensors for input and actuators for output. Sensors providing data for a sentient object call the part of its interface that represents its input channel. After processing this information, actuators are activated using the output channel part of the sentient object interface. The inner life of a sentient object that performs the processing is made up from three components. A sensory capture component deals with gathering of context values, performs context fusion over several input sources to eliminate uncertainty and translates the values to the higher context level used in the sentient object. Representing static knowledge about actions and possible future systems as contextual information is the task of the context hierarchy component. Finally, an inference engine performs context reasoning over Event-Condition-Action (ECA) rules and triggers context-aware behaviour based on these rules. Due to its general notion of context providers and consumers, a sentient object does not necessarily need to be connected to sensors and actuators but can instead also be a link in a chain of sentient objects. This feature of the sentient object framework allows complex contextual processes to be defined.

The approach of using a service middleware infrastructure based on distributed context aggregation is taken by *ConStruct* [271]. The creators of this middleware approach have identified four challenges—flexibility, maintainability, scalability and inter-operability—that they attempt to address with their infrastructure. Context in ConStruct is represented by sets of context entities that each represent context values. The execution environment used together with the middleware, the so-called range, is a platform that bundles together a set of basic components for context-aware computing. A range comprises a context server that is capable of managing context entities and provides interfaces to exchange this data with other ranges, as well as with context-aware applications. For the latter purpose, the context server provides a query interface that is also capable of constructing a directed acyclic graph of context entities to derive the information desired by the application. These graphs or context configurations are computed by an automatic path creation algorithm that uses a matching strategy to compare the required attributes specified in the application as $\langle name, value \rangle$ tuples to the attributes of context entities. The algorithm works recursively starting with the target entity and then selecting possible source entities according to its input requirements. During the matching process, the algorithm needs to handle situations where there is no match, a partial match, an over match or, ideally, an exact match. At first, the algorithm looks for context entities that match exactly. When no such entity is found, it considers partially matching entities, i.e. entities that specify a subset of the required $\langle name, value \rangle$ tuples. Should this also fail to yield a result, the algorithm resorts to entities that are over matching as they specify a superset of the requested attributes. Apart from the context server, a range also includes components designed to deal with the registration of services, mobility of users and the maintenance of the application system. Although the ConStruct infrastructure provides an elaborate mechanism that can query and derive context information, it does, however, not provide any support to applications for context adaptation.

2.3 Mobile Computing

Portable devices capable of performing simple computing tasks such as managing contacts and appointments have been around for quite some time now. While these devices have been small enough to merit the attribute "mobile", there has always been a trade-off in terms of their processing power. Laptops, Tablet PCs and subnotebooks, on the contrary, have put the emphasis on offering the processing power that is required to run complex applications and, in doing so, have traded it for mobility. It is only recently that devices have emerged capable of reconciling the conflict of processing power versus portability that exists between these two families of systems. On the one hand, devices such as mobile phones, media phones, digital music players or PDAs are outfitted with faster processors and larger amounts of memory. Portable computers, on the other hand, are subjected to a continuous process of miniaturisation that yields ever smaller and lighter devices. It is this hardware evolution that gave rise to the field of mobile computing which researches the challenges that arise when a user of an application, or application objects themselves, move around in space.

Clearly, the domain of mobile computing is closely related to the field of ubiquitous and pervasive computing and thus it is difficult to draw a clear separation between the two areas. There are many technologies and systems that cannot be attributed entirely to a single one of these disciplines as some of these approaches have started out in one domain and later have been found to have a beneficial influence on the other. For the purpose of this thesis, we will therefore apply the following distinction between the two fields as a criteria to classify an approach as belonging to ubiquitous and pervasive or to mobile computing. As mentioned before, the ultimate goal of ubiquitous and pervasive computing is to make the personal computer as we know it today disappear by embedding its functionality into everyday objects. As a consequence, ubiquitous and pervasive computing often also includes the development and use of non-standard devices and appliances. In contrast to that, research in the field of mobile computing does not make the assumption that computing devices will eventually no longer be recognisable as such. Developing special client hardware is therefore not considered to be a part of the mission of this field and many mobile computing applications are thus implemented using standard off-the-shelf hardware.

As an implication of the connection between the two disciplines, the forms of context used in mobile computing are similar to the ones found in ubiquitous and pervasive computing. A major difference is that while in ubiquitous and pervasive computing context is often used as an additional input channel to compensate for the lack of a traditional user interface, in mobile computing there is no such requirement. As user interaction based on keyboard input and display output is generally possible in mobile applications, context tends to be applied to the delivery of information rather than the adaptation of application behaviour. A mobile application needs to be able to supply a user with the appropriate information at the right place and time and in the correct format. Hence, context-aware data delivery assumes that context provides information that allows the fundamental questions *who, what, when, where* and *how?* to be answered, and thus enables the system to act accordingly. As context-aware data delivery is a major aspect of context-aware data management, the forms of context defined by applications in the domain of mobile computing are particularly relevant to the work presented in this thesis.

2.3.1   Location-Aware Information Access

A classic mobile application is the provision of location-aware access to information by overlaying the physical world with a virtual world that contains the electronic data. Usually, context information can be equated with location information in such applications. Such a use of spatial context can be found in the *Virtual Information Towers* [181]. This system augments the real world by providing information and support to users, based on their position in space. Mobile devices that are carried by the users are activated when a virtual information tower becomes visible, i.e. when the user is in its vicinity. As soon as the device is active, the virtual information tower can be used as a traditional help point in the real world. Virtual information towers are based on *Nexus* [143], an augmented world infrastructure. Nexus represents regions of the physical world using a spatial model. This representation is then used as the basis to augment the real world with digital artefacts, such as virtual information towers.

Another use of location-aware information access is to support *Social Navigation* [290]. The idea behind social navigation is that people can leave clues in the forms of Post-it notes, graffiti or posters, that can later be used by other persons. The fact that content is created by other system users and is not preauthored by a domain expert is the essential distinguishing feature of these systems. *E-Graffiti* [46, 47] is such an application that is capable of associating electronic notes with specific locations. Users carry with them a PDA that allows them to enter private or public notes. As context that is automatically bound to the note, the client device detects the user's identity and their location. User location is determined by the wireless network infrastructure. By analysing which access point is nearest to the client device in terms of signal strength, it can compute at which building a user is located. Additional context, such as a user's activity, is not captured explicitly but is reflected implicitly in the content of the notes associated with a position. Other users that find themselves at the same spatial position later are assumed to be in the same contextual situation and carrying out a similar activity, such as studying in a library or eating at a restaurant. Therefore, when other users later retrieve the previously entered notes, based on their physical location, the content accessible to them is expected to match their current task and interests.

GeoNotes [96, 218] builds on the concepts introduced in the E-Graffiti system and refines them in several ways. To realise the full potential of social navigation by exploiting user-to-user information dissemination, GeoNotes proposes the use of mass-annotations to augment existing content as an extension to the capability of E-Graffiti to publish and deliver notes based on user locations. The system offers two distinct modes of accessing the information created by its users, in addition to location-based retrieval. First, notes and comments can be retrieved based on their content, as is done in classic information retrieval. If a user chooses to do so, they will have access to the matching notes and comments augmented with the context information associated with their capture. Second, GeoNotes also supports the so-called socially-based access to information. This access method is based on matching the user's current social context, as captured by the dimensions discussed before, to the contexts of the stored notes and comments. This matching is achieved through techniques borrowed from collaborative filtering systems and based on the sharing of context information among the users. To provide this functionality, GeoNotes gathers a number of additional contextual values that are stored together with the notes, in addition to the user identity of authors or commentators, as well as their physical location. For example, when a note or a comment on a note is created, it also stores a timestamp that gives an indication of when this activity took place. Further, not only the writing of a note but also its reading defines the context of this piece of information. Whenever a user reads a note, the system records their identity and the current time in the form of a timestamp. This information can then be used in the filtering process as an indication of the popularity of a note or annotation. Finally, GeoNotes also provides the option for users to mark certain notes or comments as favourites. Whenever a user does so, their identity is also added to the context of the original content. Apart from these new context dimensions, GeoNotes also manages location context information that is gathered using wireless network positioning. Thus the system suffers from the same limitations in terms of granularity as E-Graffiti. To provide finer location resolution, a user can, however, select a predefined place label when entering a note which is then associated with it.

2.3.2 Electronic Guides

A great number of mobile systems have been developed in the area of electronic guide applications, with the goal of enhancing the environment of a user with digital information. Systems that take tourists on a tour of the visited city or guide them through an exhibition have been developed, as well as systems that just assist pedestrians with finding their way in an unknown part of a city. A very early example of such a mobile hand-held context-aware tour guide is *CyberGuide* [2]. The system runs on standard PDAs and PCs featuring pen-based input, such as Tablet PCs, and uses a combination of two systems to determine its position. If it is used indoor, positions are computed based on infrared beacons that are mounted in the environment and emit their own position. When used outdoors, CyberGuide uses a GPS signal to establish its position whenever there are no buildings that block the reception of the signal. Position information is, however, only one form of context that is applied to deliver information about attractions nearby or to make suggestions where to go next. Apart from location, CyberGuide also detects its orientation, keeps a history of previously visited attractions, knows the time of day and which events are currently available. The system is built from four main components that take this context into consideration when interacting with the user. A map component is responsible for visualising the current position of the tourist and assisting them with getting their bearings. Context-aware information delivery is the task of the content component that displays previously authored data about sights and events to the user. To find their way from one place to another, CyberGuide provides a navigation component to its users that plots a path from the current position to the target position and then guides the tourist accordingly. Finally, to exchange information between tourists, the guide system features a communication component that is context-aware in the sense that it knows which other users are nearby and on-line.

In contrast to CyberGuide, the *Context-aware Mobile Assistant Project (C-MAP)* [273] is targeted at visitors of art exhibitions. As this presents a rather controlled environment, establishing the position of a user is not as challenging as in a city. C-MAP uses an existing locator system, namely the Active Badge Location system. User interaction in this system is based on an animated life-like character that is designed to be a virtual assistant to the visitors and its main task is to give recommendations on what to see or where to go, based on the current context. C-MAP distinguishes between the physical context of the environment and the mental context of the user. The physical context is composed from temporal and spatial context information that is gathered using traditional hardware sensors. The mental context of visitors is sensed by monitoring their interaction with the mobile assistant. From this interaction, an interest vector that captures the preferences of the user is constructed and later used by the system's recommender component.

As part of the *ACTS OnTheMove* project, another example of a system designed to support tourists during city visits has been developed. Unlike other electronic guide systems, *City Guide* [175] does not display information that has been previously stored on the client device, but dynamically downloads the required content over a WaveLAN or Global System for Mobile Communication (GSM) connection. Both network technologies also provide the location data that makes up the spatial context information used by City Guide. Location is the only context information that is supported by the system and it is applied to provide location-dependent services, such as triggering the download and display of a map and highlighting the current position of the tourist. The user may then interact with the map through scrolling, browsing and zooming. All of these operations may trigger the download of another part of the displayed map or of a map with higher resolution. Interaction with City Guide is through voice commands that are processed using speech recognition and the system responds using text-to-speech technologies.

As a part of the *Hyper-Interaction within Physical Space (HIPS)* [26] project, the *Hippie* [210] exhibition guide was developed as a showcase application of a system for nomadic information access. In contrast to purely mobile systems, nomadic systems combine mobile client and stationary devices often called kiosks. The purpose of Hippie was to demonstrate aspects of adaptation to the Context of Use (CoU) which was defined to be the parameters of the physical environment, the geographical position of the user as well as their social partners, tasks, characteristics and preferences. To capture this broad notion of context, the system defines three models, the domain model, the space model and the user model. As with any other data-driven system, the domain model represents the information concepts that are relevant to the application. The space model provides information about the environment where the application will be used. Depending on the application, it might represent the rooms on a floor in a building or the streets in a city. Finally, the user model is used to define all aspects of a user, such as their knowledge, interest, movement and preferences. Based on these models, Hippie provides the user with location-dependent information based on their position. The system is also capable of generating multimodal presentations that adapt according to the type and capabilities of the device. Finally, the content of the presentation is adapted to user interest and knowledge. Apart from location-aware information delivery, Hippie also supports context-aware annotations, explanation in terms of a glossary and communication between nearby users.

GUIDE [66, 65] is another tourist guide, this time supporting visitors to the city of Lancaster and capable of creating personalised tours based on context. The notion of context used in the GUIDE system distinguishes between personal and environmental context. The personal context includes among other things the visitor's interests, their location and preferences, as well as a history of attractions that they have already visited. The environmental context captures dimensions such as the time of day or opening hours of attractions. Context is again used to adapt the presentation of information. However, in contrast to other systems, GUIDE moves a step ahead by allowing dimensions such as age, education and background to play a role in the adaptation process just as much as the nationality of users and the record of information that has already been displayed to them. Finally, by triggering the display of dynamic information, such as unforeseen changes in opening hours, GUIDE also supports context-driven proactive behaviour.

Helping pedestrians to navigate in an unknown part of a city by generating route descriptions is the ambition of the *REAL* [17] system. As this navigation system was not designed for a specific group of users, such as tourists, it also considers the type of user that it is advising. Depending on whether the user is a businessman in a hurry to get to the station or someone taking a stroll through a park, the system will plot different routes. REAL also adapts the presentation of these routes, based on contextual factors, such as the actual travelling speed of the user, their familiarity with the environment and the time pressure in the current situation. As mobile devices are often limited in the resources that they offer in terms of display and computing capabilities, the system supports another set of context dimensions that describe the device itself. These factors include information such as the screen size, resolution and colour capabilities of both mobile and stationary devices. Adaptation to this device resource context is achieved by supporting three different kinds of computing processes. Resource adapted processes have been optimised for a given device and are thus exploiting its capabilities optimally. Resource adaptive processes and resource adapting processes both feature adaptation strategies that allow them to adapt dynamically. While a resource adaptive process always uses the same strategy, a resource adapting process features multiple strategies. To select the best adaptation strategy, resource adapting processes use the device resource context which includes a history of performance statistics.

One of the few tourist guide systems that supports multiple users collaborating during their visit to an unknown city is the *George Square* [37] system. The system uses context to recommend places and sights to visit as well as to adapt the presentation of the map to the current activity of the tourist. As an example, the map representation might be changed to include symbols for cafés and restaurants at lunch time rather than those denoting bars and discos. Further, it offers functionality to cater for communication between tourists and for bringing the group together if people become separated from their colleagues during the visit. Apart from assisting tourists with these and other tasks that are important during travel, George Square also takes the previsit and the postvisit phase into consideration where some of the context information, such as location, has to be simulated as the tourist is not physically present at the visited destination. The project uses a pair of Tablet PCs with a comparatively large screen, rather than more portable devices, in order to support collaboration. As a consequence of using a pair of devices, George Square can employ the context data and history of both users to control recommendations and system adaptation and thus enhances the group awareness of tourists travelling together.

A central part of most electronic guide systems is the map component that serves a number of purposes depending on the system's functionality. In cartography, adaptive concepts [224, 225] for *Mobile Cartography* have been developed. Through a classification of user tasks into locator, proximity, navigation and events tasks, this research examines which context dimensions are important to mobile cartography systems and what forms of adaptation could be supported. Location, time, weather, medium of transport, as well as the user's profile, interest, knowledge and skill level have been identified as having an impact on how maps should be presented. Beside the physical and user context, there are a number of technological context elements such as network quality or device characteristics that describe what resources are currently available to the cartography system. The forms of adaptation that are suggested include changing the information content itself, encoding information using special data formats, adjusting to resources using techniques such as compression to reduce bandwidth use, rendering information according to device characteristics, and adapting to the users and their tasks. The visualisation of digital maps can be adapted in various ways. Simple techniques involve the highlighting of important locations or rotating the map to align with the user's point of view. Distorting maps or enlarging certain areas to guide the user's attention to the desired region are other more advanced examples of adaptation. Finally, maps can be rendered progressively to control the level of detail that is presented.

2.3.3   Mobile Fieldwork

Many ecological sciences such as geography, geology and biology, as well as disciplines such as archaeology, require researchers to do fieldwork in the outdoor environment. A lot of the work done in the field consists of collecting data and relating the findings gained from previous expeditions. The goal of the *Mobile Computing in a Fieldwork Environment (MCFE)* project is to provide tools that assist scientists with these tasks, using mobile computing technologies. During the course of the project, a series of context-aware tools for hand-held computers have been developed for archaeology [235], animal behaviour studies [215] and animal identification [216]. The experiences gained from having real fieldworkers using the device in their studies have influenced the development of the *FieldNote* [236] system, a general purpose tool for mobile fieldwork that can be customised for several domains. The central functionality of the system is the capture of textual and graphical notes using the hand-held device. By gathering information from the sensors installed on the device, the note is annotated with various context information such as location, attitude, time, temperature, humidity or wind speed, as well as logical context information that is authored explicitly by the user. Abstraction from sensors is achieved by modelling context in a hierarchy that extends from abstract context classes to concrete implementations. Later, the context values associated with a note are used to trigger the display of information that matches the current context best. A similar, yet more sophisticated use of context, is the retrieval of notes describing situations that have happened in the fieldworker's environment to predict situations that will happen in the future. For example, the system is able to identify an animal based on a measurement of a footprint or of its markings by comparing these values to context information stored in a history. Apart from producing a tool that has proven to be of great use to the intended users, the development of the FieldNote system has also yielded interesting insights about the nature of context itself. One such realisation is the fact that it is not always clear which information is application data and which is context, as for example temperature measurements. Two design choices in the development of FieldNote are a direct consequence of this peculiar nature of context. First, context values are modelled as attributes of the application objects themselves rather than being represented as an individual entity in the system. Second, the system does not distinguish between application attributes and context attributes but treats all data in the same way. Thus, information that is considered contextual in one situation can be application data under different circumstances. Another finding is that to query effectively for information based on context, it is important that, not only the query, but also the stored context information can be represented in the form of conditional expressions using Boolean operators. Finally, the genesis of FieldNote has led its developers to conclude that the richness of the functionality that can be provided by a system is directly related to the increase of available content information.

Instead of scientists conducting studies outdoors, field technicians operating inside a building are the target user group of the *NETMAN* [174] wearable computer system. NETMAN specifically supports computer technicians in charge of maintaining company-wide networks. Special attention is given to the collaboration between the mobile field technicians who repair or replace defective hardware components and stationary expert technicians that work at the workstation in their office. To this end, the wearable computer is equipped with a camera, headphones and a microphone, as well as a sensor array that detects the technician's location and the identity of objects nearby. The camera allows the expert technicians to see what the field technician sees, while the headphones and the microphone allows the two of them to have real-time conversations. Finally, a shared notebook application is used by the technicians to document their work and by the expert to make information available to their fellow workers. Similarly to the FieldNote system, while en route, the wearable notebook automatically displays a list with notebook entries that have been recorded near or at the present location of the technician. An interesting form of context exhibited by the NETMAN wearable computer is its ability to share the current situation of a field technician with the stationary expert. This exchange of contextual information is not limited to images captured by the camera but also extends to the sharing of the entire graphical user interface as seen by the fieldworker. Even though NETMAN does not use this information to adapt its behaviour, it is still an important factor in enhancing the collaboration through mutual awareness of the coworkers.

2.3.4   Models, Frameworks and Infrastructures

Similarly to ubiquitous and pervasive computing, a number of projects in mobile computing are targeted at providing comprehensive support for the kinds of mobile applications discussed in the previous sections in terms of system infrastructures and application frameworks. Most of these approaches gather, manage and provide context information to mobile applications. However, due to the importance of mobility, there are two notable differences to the approaches found in ubiquitous and pervasive computing. First, location information is considered to be far more important than any other context dimension, which often leads to it being treated in a special way. Second, resource limitations of many mobile and portable devices lead to a number of requirements that are not present in most ubiquitous and pervasive systems.

Mobile applications usually run in a very dynamic execution environment where services can appear, move around or disappear at any point in time. Providing information about the location of objects to mobile applications is therefore an important task of a supporting infrastructure. The *Active Map Service (AMS)* [243] uses the notion of located-objects to publish such location information for objects located in a certain region. Located-objects are virtual descriptions of anything that has an associated physical location. Examples of located-objects are persons, printers and workstations as well as location-dependent services. To organise the located-objects, AMS uses an active map that represents the position of an object as the containment of a located-object in a hierarchy of locations. The hierarchy of locations is used to model the concept of location at various levels of detail, such as rooms, buildings, streets, districts or cities. A mobile application can subscribe to a located-object and is then notified whenever a new position of the physical counterpart is published to AMS. Notification protocols using unicast and multicast have been implemented to support the delivery of updated location information to both individual devices and groups of clients.

The *Predator Location Service* [287] is another project that aims at a similar goal as AMS. Based on CORBA, it also provides a platform that allows mobile objects to be addressed. The location service manages a global domain of mobile objects that are also organised using a hierarchical location structure. In contrast to AMS however, Predator distinguishes between the notion of logical and physical location and manages a tree structure for each of these concepts. This has the advantage that applications can use a high-level view on location rather than being burdened with the exact position of a service. Both the querying and registering of location-based services is done with hierarchical path expressions that are evaluated by recursively mapping them to the tree-based location model.

In the scope of the *AROUND* project and the previously discussed *GUIDE* project, an architectural framework based on *Location-Based*

Services (LSB) [152] was developed to support applications such as mobile tourist guides. A location-based service is an ordinary Internet service with the additional property that its usage is defined by a scope
in terms of a geographical area. As location-based services are designed
as an extension of the traditional Internet environment, they represent a
very scalable and flexible concept. The framework imposes a location domain model that controls where a certain service is accessible. In contrast
to other approaches that model locations hierarchically as a tree, this approach uses a lattice to cater for the possibility that virtual locations may
be in many places at the same time. The location domain model is managed by an LBS server that also controls the registration information of
currently active location-based services. The position information sensed
by a device is translated using a simple mapping function to a location
context of the domain model. This location context is then used to dis-
cover the services required by the application. As soon as a service has
been discovered, the information it provides is downloaded to the mobile
device and displayed to the user.

Context-dependent information acquisition and delivery for mobile
applications is the focus of the *Stick-e* framework [38, 40, 213, 39]. It uses
a mark-up language to represent Stick-e notes containing both content
and context. Several of these notes can then be combined into a Stick-e
document which encapsulates the context-aware data of an application.
The model of context used in Stick-e distinguishes the dimensions of
location, time and adjacency. Further it allows triggers to be defined,
based on so-called critical and computer states which represent physical
and logical event conditions. Through the use of custom mark-up tags,
the model can be extended to suit any purpose required by an application.
An example of such an extension is the context dimension capturing
the presence of imaginary companions, such as historians or architects,
that was introduced in a context-aware guide system to express user
preferences about the displayed information and to control its depth.
Whenever a certain context state is reached, a matching algorithm is
triggered that selects the Stick-e note to be displayed to the user. As
the philosophy of the Stick-e framework is to give as much control as
possible to the user in order not to disturb them, the matching algorithm
is capable of processing so-called pretended values, i.e. simulated context
values that are not actually sensed, and are introduced to help filtering
the retrieved data. These properties made the Stick-e framework a good
foundation for the MCFE project where it is used in several applications
including the previously described FieldNote system.

The experiences gained from the FieldNote system and other applications in the domain of mobile fieldwork led to the development of the *Context Information Service (CIS)* [214, 216]. While the Stick-e framework was used in these projects to capture and retrieve data context-dependently, the Context Information Service is in charge of gathering, modelling and providing the contextual data that is used by the system to trigger Stick-e documents. Not unlike other infrastructures discussed before, CIS offers support for context sensing, adaptation and augmentation as well as contextual resource discovery. Context is represented using an object-oriented model that stores context information as special properties of application objects and thus provides support for extensibility and reusability. Multiple context-aware applications can connect in parallel to the Context Information Service to gain shared access to context information. Certain functionality, such as support for application semantics and adaptation, is not offered by the CIS itself. Since the CIS architecture was designed as a layered structure, other requirements can be addressed by building additional layers on top of CIS. This flexible architecture was chosen to address the need to develop a service which can scale over time when demands change. Finally, most parts of the CIS are platform independent and thus cater for the tremendous heterogeneity in execution platforms that is one of the hallmarks of mobile computing.

An extension and refinement of the Stick-e document framework is proposed by the *Context Document Framework (Condor)* [126]. As with the Stick-e framework, Condor is an application framework for mobility-based applications that focusses on the context-aware capturing and delivery of information. In Condor, the Stick-e note document is replaced by the notion of a context document that also integrates application data and context information into one concept. However, in addition to a Stick-e document that could only contain context information to control in which situation it will be triggered by the framework, a context document can also contain so-called post context information. Values stored as post context are sent back to the user along with the actual application data. On the mobile device, these values are integrated into the description of the user's contextual situation. In other words, when a context document is triggered, it can influence, change and extend the user's context, leading to different application behaviour or further triggering of documents. Context information is published and shared using the same central repository that also stores the context documents of an application. As Condor handles and represents context information and application data uniformly using context documents, an application that

wants to share its context only has to send a document to the central
repository.

A different approach to supporting mobile computing is taken by the
Cooltown [53, 161] project, as it is based on extended web technologies. Like other infrastructures presented here, the goal of Cooltown is
to provide location-specific services and information in the places that
people visit. To achieve this objective, the concept of a web presence
for people, places and things is introduced to bridge the gap between
the physical and virtual worlds. Technically, web presences are realised
in many different ways, depending on whether the object is a person,
a place or a thing. In the case of things, Cooltown uses an embedded
web server that is capable of delivering information about each object.
People are given a web presence through an ordinary home page that is
hosted on a traditional web server. Beside information about the owner
of the home page, their web presence also enables communication among
two people based on WebLink that redirects conversations to the appropriate locations of the participants. Similarly to people, places also have
a home page that provides information about the place. Additionally,
however, a PlaceManager manages a collection of web presences that are
present at that place and includes links to these objects on the home
page of the place. In this way, a PlaceManager captures information
about the physical and contextual organisation of a place and makes
it accessible to mobile clients. The dominant form of context used by
the Cooltown infrastructure is location information that is emitted by
beacons distributed in the environment. In contrast to other systems
where beacons send out information about their position, the beacons
in Cooltown send out a Universal Resource Locator (URL) to the web
presence of the object that is associated with the beacon. Client devices
support two modes of sensing location information. In the direct sensing
mode, a client connects to the web presence pointed to by the URL and
displays the available information. To cater for context-awareness, an indirect sensing mode is also available that resolves the URL in two steps.
First the client connects to the URL obtained from the beacon but it
does not download the information to display. Rather, it queries the web
server for another URL that is better suited to the current context of the
user and the device. With this second URL, it connects again, downloads
and displays the information from the location-dependent service.

Providing a solution to the problems of mobile devices such as limited
computing power and restricted memory is the central objective of the
Service-Oriented Context-Aware Middleware (SOCAM) [123]. The fact

that many portable clients are not capable of performing high-level context processing is addressed by a two-layered approach that separates the context model into a domain-specific low-level part and general high-level part that represents global concepts. The context model of SOCAM uses an ontology to define a vocabulary based on Subject-Predicate-Object tuples that represent context information. To relieve mobile devices from complex computing tasks, the middleware takes on the functions that require more processing power such as the acquisition, discovery, interpretation and access of various kinds of context information. Another advantage of the middleware approach is that, as a common component, it can also provide support for interoperability between different context-aware applications. All this functionality is implemented by a number of service components that are part of the middleware. Context provider services abstract from the source of context information, such as sensors, user profiles or explicit input whereas the context interpreter service is responsible for translating the low-level information gathered and delivered by the portable devices to match the ontology describing the global context concepts. The discovery of context providers and thus of context information is realised by the service location service that manages the locations of these services. All context information processed and managed by SOCAM is stored by the context database service together with rules expressed in first-order logic that describe context inference and adaptive application behaviour. Context-aware applications are also represented as services in the middleware. Such a context-aware mobile service can either query context providers or obtain context information by registering for it at a provider. When the context state in the repository changes, the stored adaptation rules are evaluated and the corresponding actions are triggered in the registered application services.

Like SOCAM, the *Context-Awareness Sub-Structure (CASS)* [100] is an example of an approach that provides support for context-aware applications on hand-held and other small mobile computers, by shifting memory and processor intensive tasks to a server-based middleware. Its main objective is to separate context-based inference and behaviour from the actual application code. Again, by using a high-level abstraction of context data that is shared throughout the middleware, the different components can interoperate and relieve limited devices of performing complex tasks. These components include a database that stores all context information gathered by the sensor listener components. An interpreter component translates context information into the representation expected by the context-aware applications that use the context retriever component to get answers to their queries for context information. An inference engine uses a rule engine to apply rules stored in a knowledge base to the context database, thereby inferring new context information. Rules describing context-aware application behaviour are also stored in the knowledge base and are evaluated to activate context-dependent behaviour in the client applications.

The same goal as SOCAM and CASS—coping with the technical limitations of portable devices, unreliable network connections and the characteristics of mobile users themselves—is also pursued by the *Hydrogen Context Framework* [142]. In contrast to SOCAM and CASS that address these issues by means of a middleware, Hydrogen proposes an application programming framework combined with a layered architecture that offers some basic components for context-aware computing. Support for a wide range of mobile clients and applications with a variety of requirements is provided through the framework's extensible nature. Context information, for example, is represented using a simple class hierarchy rooted at class `ContextObject` that contains all functionality required to exchange context information among components by serialising it to and deserialising it from XML. While this predefined notion of context may suffice for many applications, it can easily be extended by specialising any class that represents context information in Hydrogen. The layered architecture is another key factor in permitting extensibility. An adaptor layer is responsible for context gathering whereas a management layer contains a context server that can either be queried for context information or publish this data to subscribed clients automatically. Finally, the context-aware applications themselves reside on the application layer. Again, this simple three-layered architecture is intended and designed for standard applications but can easily be upgraded should more complex requirements arise.

The context framework presented in [173] has been developed specifically for the Symbian platform an operating system found in many mobile and media phones. To manage, process and deliver context information, the framework uses a blackboard-based approach that allows all components to publish and retrieve context through a shared information pool that is controlled by a context manager. Other components such as the resource server, the context recognition service or context-aware applications themselves all gain access to context information via the blackboard. For example, the context recognition service uses Bayesian reasoning to transform low-level context information found on the blackboard into high-level context values that are then published by placing them back on the blackboard. In order to establish a common under-standing of the meaning of the context information on the blackboard, a vocabulary defined by an ontology has been agreed upon that represents context by means of a type, a value, a confidence indication, a source and a timestamp. This vocabulary is known to all components of the framework allowing them to share context information and to interop-erate seamlessly. A number of context information sources have been integrated into the framework, either as part of the client device or as standalone sources. Sensors for time, sound, acceleration, light, temper-ature, humidity and touch have been realised as well as monitors for the state of the mobile device and its connectivity to the Internet or other networks. Further, user preferences, their social networks and the tasks at hand are also considered as context and managed by the framework. The context-aware applications that are then implemented for the Sym-bian platform can rely on an Application Programming Interface (API) that allows context to be added to and retrieved from the framework. As with most other infrastructures, two modes to obtain context infor-mation are supported. Applications can either retrieve context using a synchronous request and response protocol or by subscribing for notifi-cation whenever a certain context state changes.

2.4   Web Engineering

Over the last decade, the World Wide Web [29] has undergone a remark-able evolution. In the early 1990s, the web started out as a platform purely based on static documents distributed over a number of servers that were interconnected using hyperlinks. These so-called hypertexts were intended to provide a medium for information exchange to a very small group of scientists and researchers. In the years since, the web has rapidly grown into a resource that is used by millions of people on a daily basis for a vast variety of motives. Of course, the web of today still serves its original purpose as a virtually unlimited source of information, but dynamic applications such as electronic business, communication, entertainment, education or advertising, have long since become driv-ing forces behind its evolution. Recently, other developments have been witnessed that will shape the character of the web in future years. On the one hand, the initiative to transform the web into a platform that is capable of sustaining complex applications that will gradually replace the programs installed locally on a user's machine, is beginning to yield results in the form of early web-based office suites, such as the Zoho Office Suite or Google Docs & Spreadsheets. On the other hand, due to the collection of widely accepted standards that have emerged, web-based technologies are nowadays used for various purposes that are no longer directly associated with the web. For instance, the presentation and interaction capabilities of the Hypertext Mark-up Language (HTML) have made it a frequent choice as a technology to implement graphical user interfaces for arbitrary applications. Originally intended to advance the separation of content, structure, and presentation on the web, XML has already gone on to have a major impact on information systems and programming languages in general. Finally, another interesting example of a non-standard application of web technologies is their recent use as a basis for information dissemination in ubiquitous, pervasive and mobile systems.

The ever increasing number of ways in which the web is used, is also reflected in the systems that have been developed to address these new requirements. In the early days, when both the user community and the software used to access the web were still very homogeneous, adaptation of the hypertext structure based on user preferences and profiles was the only form of context-awareness that was taken into consideration. While at first this customisation was performed off-line using static context information, very soon a second generation of approaches was capable of adapting the hypertext dynamically based on profiling data collected from the user's interaction with the system. As the behaviour and choices of the user stand at the root of this form of adaptation, it has become known as personalisation and gained further importance with the advent of electronic commerce and portal sites. When the Internet began to spread around the globe, its users started to become more and more heterogeneous in terms of language and culture. It became necessary to support another facet of adaptation, commonly called internationalisation, to cater for web sites that are accessible to people from different countries. While providing content in different translations to match the language spoken in the target country is a primary requirement of international web sites, other more subtle issues have also to be addressed. Cultural influences such as the reading order, currency, measurement units, customs or local legislation, also affect how information is delivered. Advances in hardware have produced small and portable devices that are capable of accessing web sites while the user is on the move. This aspect of adaptation, mobilisation, is connected to a number of additional requirements that had to be taken into account in the design and implementation of web engineering solutions. Analogous to the user communities that became diverse with the global expansion of the Internet, client devices and software grew to be very different from one another in terms of processing power, display sizes and supported content formats. Apart from these device-specific adaptation requirements, user mobility has introduced similar needs to those discussed in the domain of mobile computing. It was only at this relatively late point in time that the term "context-awareness" itself actually emerged in the domain of web engineering to denote adaptivity.

As we will see in the discussion of example approaches, many systems developed in this research field were developed to provide one specific from of adaptation. The considerable knowledge of building flexible and adaptive web systems that has been gathered over the last decade has only recently been consolidated and become general enough to provide support for all discussed forms of adaptation. As a result of the almost interdisciplinary nature of the field of web engineering, the systems that have been developed in parallel to the technological and social advancement of the web come from a vast variety of backgrounds. While electrical engineers have had an influence on the web by designing its network protocols, content publishing experts, hypertext and hypermedia specialists have given the web its shape by defining how information is accessed and how it is interconnected. Finally, researches from the domains of software engineering and information systems have worked on providing infrastructures to support web sites and web applications. It is therefore not surprising that the proposed solutions also differ substantially in the kinds of approaches taken that range from methodologies and conceptual models to frameworks and infrastructures. As every approach distinguishes itself by the set of supported adaptation functionality and features, Kappel et al. [155] have developed a classification model that facilitates the analysis and comparison of such systems. On the requirements side, their approach differentiates three dimensions—levels, aspects and phases—that allow the systematic survey of web modelling methodologies. The levels dimension defines which parts of a web system can be customised in terms of content, hypertext and presentation. Whether an approach is capable of adapting structure or behaviour is expressed with the dimension of aspects. Finally, the third dimension focusses on the development phases of a web application and is divided into analysis, design and implementation. Another criterion to distinguish the different approaches is whether their customisation process handles context and adaptation statically or dynamically. Determining context and adaptation dynamically at run-time is assumed to lead to systems with a higher degree of customisability, as compared to systems that use a predefined static approach. Finally, the set of supported context dimensions is also taken into account in the comparison of different approaches. Here, the dimensions of user, device, network, location, as well as temporal context are considered to be the most discriminating.

2.4.1 Modelling Hypertext and Hypermedia Systems

An early form of representing the same content in different forms depending on a very simple notion of context found in the *Hypertext Design Model (HDM)* [117]. HDM can be considered either as a modelling device or as an implementation device, by serving as a basis for design tools that support application development. The main focus of the model is authoring-in-the-large, i.e. providing support to define the application's concepts and the navigation structure of a complex system without engaging in implementation issues. The information content of an application's concepts is modelled as entities that are each defined by an entity type. While the terminology and basic notion of entities have been adopted from the E/R model, the concept itself has been extended, as entities in HDM are not flat units but can have a complex inner structure. This structure is composed from components that are organised in a tree. The actual content of each component is represented by a set of units that provide variants of the same information in terms of formats, styles, languages etc. Which content variants exist at the component level is controlled by a set of supported perspectives for the corresponding entity. These perspectives both indicate which variants are available to the system and determine what content data needs to be provided by the developers of the application. To support navigation, HDM offers three different categories of links. Perspective links connect units to the corresponding component and thus govern the switching from one content representation to the next. Navigation within the component tree of an entity is implemented by structural links that allow a user to move from parent to child component and vice versa as well as among the siblings of a common parent. Finally, links realise navigation between different entities as required by the semantics of the application. When linking from one entity or component to another, it is not straightforward which content representation of the target object is presented to the user, as several representations might exist. To address this situation, all links that are defined in this manner are regarded as being abstract and need to be transformed into concrete links when they are actually traversed at run-time. The concept of a default perspective has been introduced into the system to resolve settings where the choice of an appropriate target is ambiguous.

As a further development of HDM, the *Object-Oriented Hypermedia Design Method (OOHDM)* [251, 250] introduces special purpose modelling primitives for the design of the navigation and the interface of a hypermedia application. Further, while the nature of the concepts used in HDM have been based on ideas coming from the domain of information systems, OOHDM uses an object-oriented approach that is inspired by models traditionally known from object-oriented software engineering. Based on these two advances, OOHDM gives more structure to the design process of hypermedia systems which it divides into the four phases conceptual modelling, navigation design, abstract interface definition and implementation. Three out of those are supported with a dedicated modelling language comprising concepts to specify all aspects of the hypertext. As in HDM, the conceptual model specifies the application domain, its concepts and the relationships between them using object-oriented modelling primitives from the Object Modelling Technique (OMT) [233] extended with domain-specific notions such as attribute perspectives or subsystems. As in HDM, perspectives capture content that has multiple representation variants. In OOHDM, however, these perspectives can be specified at the level of attributes, which leads to a finer modelling granularity than in HDM where perspectives are specified for entire entities. These class and instance schemas can be represented graphically using a notation close to the Unified Modelling Language (UML) [234]. In contrast to HDM where navigation was directly specified based on the entities defined in the conceptual model, OOHDM provides a dedicated navigation model that uses the technique of a view derived from the conceptual model similar to that of relational databases. The navigation model is composed from two submodels, the navigation class schema and the navigation context schema. In the class schema, application concepts are represented as nodes that will be accessible to the user of the hypermedia system. Further, links between nodes and access structures such as indices and guided tours are defined in this schema. The context schema structures the navigation space using the concept of navigational contexts, collections of nodes, links and other forms of context that share the same properties. While a context intentionally or extensionally specifies which objects belong together, special context classes, subclasses of the classes defined in the navigation class model, define how a concept is represented in a given context. Finally, the abstract interface model defines which concepts will appear and how they are represented to the user. We refrain, however, from discussing this third model in more detail as it neither offers further insight into the forms of adaptation supported in OOHDM nor is it required to understand them. Through the separation of the design process into four independent models, OOHDM supports predefined, static customisation as both different navigation views, and different user interfaces can be specified for one application. Based on context information about users, such as their identity, browsing history and preferences, OOHDM also offers dynamic customisation [231] that is effected at run-time. By introducing additional parameters into the definition of links and navigation nodes, link and content personalisation is achieved. Structure customisation is realised by augmenting the user objects with methods that return the modules a user has selected to be included on the web page. Finally, it is also possible to customise navigational contexts by extending the context definition with a field indicating which users can access objects in that context.

Adaptation based on a user model that stores context information about the people interacting with the hypermedia system has become the basis for a whole family of so-called adaptive hypermedia systems. The characteristics of such systems have been specified and formalised by Brusilovsky [41] who gives the following definition.

> "By adaptive hypermedia systems we mean all hypertext and hypermedia systems which reflect some features of the user in the user model and apply this model to adapt various visible aspects of the system to the user."

Brusilovsky partitions the set of possible adaptation methods into techniques for adaptive presentation and for adaptive navigation. Adaptive presentation allows information about a certain topic to be presented in different ways using techniques such as conditional content or content variants. Annotating, disabling, hiding or sorting links are examples of adaptive navigation designed to guide users to content that they will find interesting or to prevent them from accessing undesired information.

A number of hypertext systems [34, 42, 170, 191] have been developed that satisfy Brusilovsky's definition of adaptive hypermedia. While the exact set of supported adaptation methods and techniques varies from one approach to another, many of these systems are more or less equivalent when considered at the conceptual rather than at the implementation level. An important factor, however, which distinguishes these systems is how they represent user context. Since the goal of this thesis is not the modelling and management of context, we have decided to discuss an adaptive hypermedia system that leaves the definition of the user model to the application designer. Applications developed with the *Adaptive Hypermedia Architecture (AHA!)* [78, 80] are defined using a domain, adaptation and user model. The domain model captures the concepts that are important to the application and the relationships between them. Concepts are defined in terms of a name and a set of attributes that can be of type Boolean, numeric or string. The adaptation model governs the manipulation of the user models in terms of requirements and a set of generate rules that are defined for each concept. The requirements control under which circumstances AHA! modifies the user model, whereas the rules specify what modifications are performed. For each concept defined in the domain model, the user model stores the actual values of the attributes for the corresponding user. Apart from that data, the user model can also contain personal information about the user or their navigation history. As previously mentioned, AHA! does not assume that certain attributes of concepts exist, however practice has shown that attributes that capture whether a user is interested in a concept or has visited it before are common to most applications. On the implementation level, concepts are defined as Extensible Hypertext Mark-up Language (XHTML) pages or fragments. When such a page is requested, the AHA! adaptation engine is capable of performing adaptations of both categories defined by Brusilovsky. Adaptive presentation is performed by parsing the requested pages and scanning for tags representing conditional inclusion of concepts. If such a tag is found, the adaptation rules of the concept it references are evaluated and the corresponding fragment is included. Link hiding and annotation are the techniques that AHA! offers for adaptive navigation. Again, the requested page is parsed by the adaption engine and link anchor tags that are defined to be conditional are rendered in colours that indicate whether a link is desirable, visited or neutral.

A first effort to consolidate the various approaches to adaptive hypermedia systems has been proposed by the *Adaptive Hypermedia Application Model (AHAM)* [79] in the form of a reference model for such systems. AHAM is based on *Dexter* [132], a reference model that was previously defined for traditional, i.e. non-adaptive, hypermedia applications. The Dexter model partitions the architecture of a hypermedia system into three layers. The within-component layer contains the raw data constituting the information content of an application and is highly implementation specific. On top of this layer resides the storage layer which models the structure of the application in terms of components that represent the nodes of the hypertext and the links between them. Finally, the top-most layer is the run-time layer which is in charge of rendering the hypertext and interacting with the user. Based on the requirements for adaptive hypermedia formulated by Brusilovsky and the experiences gained from the development of AHA! and similar systems, AHAM augments the Dexter storage layer by introducing a user and teaching model. The original functionality of the storage layer is replaced by the domain model that uses concepts and concept relationships instead of components to represent the structure of the application domain. The user model persistently stores all information about users and their interaction with the hypermedia system. This knowledge is then used by the pedagogical rules contained in the teaching model to perform adaptation. As proposed by Brusilovsky, AHAM supports adaptive presentation and adaptive navigation, which are, however, called content adaptation and link adaptation, respectively.

Another approach that formalises hypermedia design is *UML-based Web Engineering (UWE)* [15, 139, 171]. All previously proposed models, such as HDM, OOHDM and AHAM have relied on proprietary extensions to conceptual models originating from the fields of information systems or object-oriented software design. In contrast to these custom approaches, UWE is entirely compliant with UML, as it is defined as a UML profile, i.e. all its modelling primitives are specified as extensions of classes defined by the UML metamodel. The concepts and models provided by UWE are directly based on concepts and models introduced in OOHDM. It is therefore not at all surprising that UWE structures the design process of a hypermedia application along the same models as OOHDM. First, a conceptual model representing the content of a web application is defined in terms of a UML diagram consisting of instances of class ≪conceptual class≫ which is itself a subclass of the UML class Class. As in OOHDM, the navigation model is composed from two submodels, the navigation space model and the navigation structure model, and acts as a view on the conceptual model. The nodes of the navigation space model are expressed using instances of ≪navigational class≫ and the links between them are modelled using directed associations. The navigation structure model provides the same access structure concepts as OOHDM in its context schema, namely indices, menus, guided tours and navigational contexts which are also realised as UML stereotypes. Finally, the presentation model defines several primitives that can be used to coarsely specify the static layout of the user interface. At the centre of these primitives is the ≪presentational class≫ which is used both to incorporate the nodes of the navigation model in the presentation and to provide a common ancestor for the hierarchy of user interface classes such as texts, images, buttons or forms. The dynamic aspects of the interface of the hypermedia application are defined in terms of UML state charts. Adaptation in UWE is based on the *Munich Reference Model* [172] for adaptive hypermedia applications. The architecture and concepts of this reference model are based entirely on the previously discussed Dexter and AHAM reference models. However, while Dexter has been described using the Z notation, a specification language that features no graphical representation, and AHAM has so far only been defined informally, the Munich Reference Model, being written in UML, offers both a graphical representation and a formal specification using the Object Constraint Language (OCL) [285]. The model uses the same layering as Dexter—within-component, storage, and run-time layer—and partitions the storage layer in the same way as AHAM into a domain, user and adaptation model. In contrast to the existing models, the Munich Reference Model distinguishes three forms of rule-based adaptation, instead of two. To match the three layers of the UWE methodology, these forms of adaptation are adaptive content, adaptive links and adaptive presentation. A shortcoming of this rule-based approach is that the rules exist outside the model and thus have no graphical representation. A possible solution to this problem has been proposed through the use of aspect-oriented modelling techniques [16]. As adaptation logic is orthogonal to the basic application logic, the cross-cutting nature of aspects provides a possible solution for separating the two. By introducing the concept of aspects, the UWE metamodel has been extended to support adaptive navigation capabilities such as adaptive link hiding, adaptive link annotation and adaptive link generation.

2.4.2   Designing and Managing Web Sites

In web engineering, the degree to which adaptive behaviour is possible is directly linked to how well the content, structure and presentation of the web site have been separated. While the separation of these aspects is the foundation of the design methodologies presented so far, it alone does not provide support for managing adaptive web sites. In order to implement such dynamic behaviour, the run-time environment needs to be able to rely on metadata about content, structure and presentation, as a basis for adaptation operations. The use of such metadata to optimise and customise web sites has been explored by a number of different approaches. One of the first web site management systems that featured a formal machine-readable specification of web sites is *Strudel* [101, 102, 103]. The content of a Strudel web site is stored as semi-structured data in the format of the Object Exchange Model (OEM) [212]. Mediators are used to translate arbitrary data sources, such as XML documents or relational databases, into the OEM format. Based on this content, the structure of a web site is specified in Strudel using the declarative query language StruQL that transforms the data graph into a site graph. Finally, presentation is effected by applying HTML or XML templates that render a browsable web site by inlining nodes from the site graph into the template. The metadata constituted by the StruQL specification has proven to be beneficial both as basis for verifying the integrity of a web site as well as in adapting it to different output channels. Nowadays, the StruQL and Strudel's template language have been superseded by their XML-based successors, XQuery and XML Stylesheet Language Transformations (XSLT) [68], that have been defined based on the same concepts. Therefore, the technologies developed for Strudel still represent the foundation for most existing platforms that implement and manage adaptive web sites.

While most of the design methods presented so far start with modelling and representing the content of a web site, the audience-driven *Web Site Design Method (WSDM)* [83] introduces an additional step at the beginning of the design process. In WSDM the development of a web site starts with the definition of a mission statement that declares the purpose, subject and target audience of the web site. Based on the mission statement, an audience classification is defined that identifies the different kinds of users of the web site. The properties and requirements of each audience class are specified in the audience class characterisation. Together, audience classification and audience class characterisation constitute the audience modelling, the first step of the design process. Audience modelling is followed by conceptual design, which is composed from object modelling and navigational design. The intention behind these two subprocesses is equivalent to the purpose of conceptual and navigational models, as known from other approaches. In WSDM, however, both models build on the audience classes defined in the first step to adapt the web site for different kinds of users. For each audience class, a view on the object model is defined, based on perspective variants modelled as subtypes of the basic entity types. The navigation model is enriched with custom navigation tracks that provide different access structures over the content, taking the specific requirements of certain user groups into consideration. Finally, the implementation design defines the presentation of the web site in terms of the look and feel. At a later stage in the project, WSDM was extended with support for adaptive behaviour [50], based on adaptation rules that are executed at run-time. These adaptation rules are specified using the proprietary Adaptation Specification Language (ASL) that is based on a formal specification of the navigational model. The rules follow the Condition-Action (CA) paradigm. Whenever a certain state is reached the corresponding action is executed. Using these rules, it is possible to influence the structure of the web sites by adding or deleting nodes and links, moving nodes closer or farther away from the root, as well as clustering related nodes into groups that are accessed through a newly created node. While these forms of adaptation are mainly based on context information such as the audience class to which a user belongs or the history of their interaction with the system, another extension of WSDM focusses on designing localised web sites [82] that consider the location from which a user accesses the site. In order to allow such sites to be specified, the audience modelling step has been extended with models that specify and characterise the localities in which the web site will be accessible. These localities can then be used in the consecutive models to label parts that are particular to a specific location. Although localised features can be specified quite easily at the conceptual level, things become complicated as the development process moves to the implementation design step. From the point of view of data modelling, the different localities have to be mapped onto a standard database schema. De Troyer and Casteleyn propose several approaches for achieving this mapping. For example, they discuss labelling the columns or tables of a relational database with the name of the corresponding locality. While such an approach might be sufficient if very few localities need to be supported, it scales poorly in the case of several potentially overlapping localities, and becomes infeasible if additional dimensions other than language are required.

In contrast to the design methodologies presented so far, that have focussed on the modelling of the audience, content, structure and presentation of a web site, *Context-Aware Web Information Systems* [31] take a more process-oriented approach and emphasise the interaction between the information system and its users. A web site is specified in terms

of a storyboard that is represented as a story space, which is formally
defined as a directed graph with scenes as nodes that are connected by
scene transitions. A user's interaction with the web information system is
represented by a path through the story space, called a story. Scene transitions can be annotated with pre and post conditions that control how
users can navigate through the story space. Each scene in the story space
is defined by an identifier, a Media Object [241] constituting the content,
presentation metadata and properties that describe for which context the
scene has been designed. A media object is a high-level concept that abstracts from the underlying database and is similar to an updatable view,
but is capable of adapting itself to a fixed set of context dimensions which
are given as query parameters. Similar to Strudel, web sites are defined
using a definition language. Whereas StruQL is based on the transformation of object graphs, the theoretical background of SiteLang [275]
are story algebras. All metadata expressed in SiteLang is stored in a
special web site database that serves as the basis for dynamic web site
generation. One advantage of storing web site metadata in a database
is the possibility of easily adapting web sites at run-time, by parametris-
ing the queries to the database with context information. Adaptation is
formally specified using Kleene Algebra with Tests (KAT) [242] over the
formal representation of the story space. Context information such as
user preferences is formulated as a set of conditional equations that are
then used to modify the story space accordingly.

The most comprehensive approach to model-based web site specification and generation is the *Web Modelling Language (WebML)* [54, 55, 33,
56]. The original motivation behind WebML was to provide a solution
for the generation of data-intensive web sites such as on-line stores or
knowledge bases. However, with the continuous evolution of the web and
ever new requirements, WebML has become an all-purpose modelling
language. In contrast to many other model-based solutions, WebML also
offers a variety of industrial strength tools, such as editors, to define web
sites graphically, and an implementation platform that can execute the
generated specification [288]. Similar to most of the previously presented
methodologies, WebML also divides the design process of a web site into
three steps. In the beginning, a data model is specified that defines the
entity and relationship types describing the content of the web site. The
data model is expressed using well-known E/R diagrams. The next phase
of the design process engages in the definition of the structure of the web
sites and results in the specification of a hypertext model. The hypertext
model uses a proprietary notation to express the overall organisation of

the web site in terms of site views, pages, page areas and units. Units are the basic building blocks of any WebML web site fulfilling a variety of functions. Content units such as **Data, Multi-Data, Index, Multi-Choice Index, Hierarchical Index, Scroller** and **Entry** units represent the data concepts specified in the data model at the hypertext level. Support for modifying and updating the underlying data is provided by operational units that model the creation, modification or deletion of data entities and the relationships between them. The hypertext structure is specified by either placing these units inside pages directly or grouping them in page areas and placing those on pages. Pages belonging to one user interface or device output channel are grouped together in a site view. The possibility of defining multiple site views for the same application caters for the fact that the hypertext may need to be restructured according to the capabilities of the devices from which it is accessed. Finally, units and pages can be interconnected with links which build the basis for navigation but also serve other purposes. WebML classifies links along two axes. First, depending on whether or not a link transmits parameters from the source to the target unit, it is termed to be either contextual or non-contextual. Second, the mode in which a link is traversed is also a distinguishing feature. Normally, a link is navigated interactively when a user clicks on the corresponding anchor. Alternatively, a link may also be traversed automatically without user interaction, based on heuristic rules. Finally, transport links are exclusively used to pass parameters between units or pages and are thus not represented with visible anchors. The last step of the development process is the presentation design. WebML does not define a conceptual presentation model, but rather relies on standard tools and technologies.

Recently, WebML has been extended with primitives that allow adaptive and context-aware sites to be modelled [57, 61]. To manage context information, the data model is extended with a context model that is specific to the application. To gather context information, two additional units, **Get URL Parameter** and **Get Data**, have been introduced. The first unit retrieves context information sent to the server by the client device, encoded in the URL. The second unit extracts context information, according to the context model, from the database on the server. Each page that is considered to be context-dependent is associated in the model with a context cloud that contains the adaptation operation chains. These operation chains can be built from the standard WebML operation units as well as from units that have been introduced to model conditional or switch statements in the specification of workflows. When

a context-aware page is requested, the corresponding operation chain is
executed and the content of the page adapted accordingly. However, in
order to adapt the content itself, the context-dependent entities in the
data model have to be associated with entities representing the relevant
context dimensions. Depending on the complexity of the application,
this can lead to a very cumbersome data model that is no longer true to
the orthogonal notion of context. Apart from such content adaptation,
it is also possible to adapt the navigation and the presentation. The
newly introduced **Change Site View** unit can be used to forward a client
from one site view to another, whereas the **Change Style** unit adapts the
web site in terms of colours and font properties. Other extensions to
WebML include support for client-side adaptation [58] and reactive web
applications [99, 59]. The former approach controls the user's navigation through the web site by interfacing with an adaptive hypermedia
engine based on UML state diagrams. The latter approach uses the Web
Behaviour Model (WBM) in combination with WebML to form a high-
level Event-Condition-Action (ECA) paradigm. WBM uses the notion of
timed finite state automata to specify scripts that track the users' navigation on the web site. When a WBM script reaches an accepting state,
the condition it represents is fulfilled and the corresponding actions in
form of a WebML operation chain are executed as soon as the associated event occurs. Based on this graphical ECA paradigm, applications
such as profiling which infers a user's interest or updating specific values
within the user model, as well as adapting to this information can be
specified and implemented automatically, based on an intuitive model.

2.4.3 Building the Semantic Web

Augmenting the web with machine-processable meaning is the goal of
the Semantic Web initiative. To this end, a number of technologies that
allow the semantics of documents to be captured have been developed.
Based on the notion of ⟨*subject, predicate, object*⟩ triples, the Resource
Description Framework (RDF) [18] allows concepts to be annotated with
other information. The RDF Schema (RDFS) [35] language provides the
possibility to specify which RDF annotations are possible or required
for a given resource. Finally, based on RDF and RDFS, the Web Ontology Language (OWL) [217] allows complex ontologies including their
formal semantics to be expressed and exchanged over the web. *OntoWebber* [150] is a model-driven web site management tool that uses
semantic web technologies to integrate information from heterogeneous

data sources, such as RDF, UML or HTML. The design methodology proposed by OntoWebber structures the development process into five steps. The specification of a web site begins with a requirement analysis that forms the basis for the domain ontology design. The content, navigation and presentation of the site are then specified in the site view design step. In the personalisation design step, adaptation for the content collection, navigation and presentation style is defined. Finally, the last step, maintenance design, captures the future of the web site in terms of anticipated changes or updates. Apart from the first step, each step is supported by one or more graphical models that are all defined by ontological metamodels. Personalisation is based on a user model that describes a user in terms of their capacities, interests and requests. The capacity of a user captures contextual information such as the user's age, preferred browser, client device or connection speed. The user interest allows special versions of the content, navigation and presentation models to be defined at design time that have been adapted to the user's requirements. The request property defines triggers that are fired as soon as certain conditions are fulfilled and that update the site dynamically by model rewriting.

The *Hera* methodology [280, 146, 279] is a model-driven approach that integrates concepts from adaptive hypermedia systems with semantic web technologies. In the same way as OntoWebber, it relies on both RDF and RDFS for data integration as well as for defining the conceptual models that guide the design process of semantic web information systems. As with most of the approaches presented so far, Hera also offers three models—the conceptual model, the application model and the presentation model—that govern the process of designing and deploying a web site. Further, the notion that a model from the current design step overlays or extends the model from the previous step is retained. The basis of a web information system is the conceptual model that defines the concepts, their attributes and the relationships in between them that are required by the application. At the same time, the conceptual model describes the heterogeneous data source by providing a uniform semantic view expressed in RDFS. The available basic data types are defined by a media model that offers text, image, audio and video formats. The content of a media item is referenced by a media URL that is common to all media types. Based on the concepts of slices and slice relationships, the application model residing on the layer above the conceptual model, defines both a view on the data schema as well as the structure and navigation of the site. Hence, a slice relationship can either express the inclusion of a slice within another slice or a navigational link between two slices. The final step of the design process in Hera is the definition of the presentation model. Using a hierarchy of nested regions representing rectangular areas on the client device, the spatial layout of the slices in the application model can be specified. To arrange two regions in relation to each other, the presentational model offers a series of spatial relationships that capture where a region will be displayed. Faithful to its background of adaptive hypermedia systems, the specification of adaptation has always been an integral part of the Hera methodology [13, 113]. Hera distinguishes between static design-time adaptation, called adaptability, and dynamic run-time adaptation, called adaptivity. The design artefacts of all three models used in the development process can be adapted by annotating them with appearance conditions. Depending on whether the condition specifies an adaptability or adaptivity rule, they are evaluated during the generation step or at run-time. If a condition evaluates to true, the corresponding artefact will be presented to the user, otherwise it is omitted. Thus, alternatives can be specified using a set of mutually exclusive appearance conditions.

Similar to the approach taken by WebML, web sites that have been designed with Hera are implemented by using the conceptual models to configure a run-time environment. The *Hera Presentation Generator (HPG)* [114, 112] is an example of such a platform that uses the XSLT to combine the data stored as RDF with the models represented in RDFS, and to generate an adapted presentation according to user preferences, as well as device capabilities. The presentation compiled by the Hera presentation generator is rendered as a set of static documents that contain the mark-up and the content for one particular class of clients. Hence, with this approach, it is only possible to implement appearance conditions that express design-time adaptability. To realise adaptivity, the conditions that specify dynamic behaviour are mapped to the previously discussed AHA! engine that evaluates these rules continuously at run-time and adapts the web site accordingly. More recently, an alternative implementation platform for Hera has been proposed, based on *AMACONT* [107, 106, 104]. Using a layered component-based XML document format [105], reusable elements of a web site can be defined at different levels of granularity. The document components that encapsulate adaptive content, navigation and presentation are then composed through aggregation and interlinkage into adaptive web applications. The proposed document format has three abstraction levels—media components, content unit components and document components—mirroring the iterative development process of most web sites. Media components in the first layer represent the raw data such as text, structured text, images, audio or video. Each media component is annotated with descriptors capturing technical properties and content management information. In the second layer, content unit components aggregate the media components from the layer below into semantically meaningful groupings. Within these collections, the spatial layout of the member components can be specified, using a set of properties that are independent of the client. Finally, in the top layer, document components define the structure of the web site in terms of hierarchical composition. A document component can either contain content unit components directly or be composed from other document components. Similar to the content unit components, the layout of the subcomponents can be expressed through the use of client-independent layout managers. The navigation structure in terms of hyperlinks is expressed orthogonally to the hierarchical component structure discussed so far. Using uni- and bi-directional typed links, components from all three layers can be connected. Adaptation is realised by allowing components of all granularities to have variants. A variant of a component specifies an arbitrarily complex selection condition as part of the metadata in its header. The decision as to whether a component is presented to the user is made by the XSLT stylesheet that generates the presentation according to the current context. AMACONT's publishing process is based on a pipeline that iteratively applies transformations to a set of input documents to obtain the fully rendered output documents. Through the caching of partial results, intermediate steps can be reused multiple times, leading to improved performance.

2.4.4 Models, Frameworks and Infrastructures

While some model-driven design methodologies, such as WebML or Hera, feature an implementation platform that allows context-aware web sites to be realised and generated from the models, several attempts have been made to build universal platforms addressing these requirements. An early approach to delivering content according to the device context of the client is known as distilling or transcoding [110, 111, 263]. In most transcoding set-ups, a client connects to the content server through a proxy server. When a request passes the proxy server, the server extracts information describing the capabilities of the client in terms of the used software and hardware platform from the request header. The proxy then uses this information to adapt the content delivered by the server before it is returned to the client. Common forms of adaptation include splitting of large documents into smaller fragments as well as changing the format, colour depth or size of an image. Usually, these transformations are effected on-line and thus result in reduced performance. Several solutions to this problem have been proposed, among them the caching of results of the distillation process and the precomputation of content variants. While Singh et al. [262] advocate the former, the approach presented by Mohan et al. [192] is an example of the latter. Their system uses a so-called InfoPyramid that defines which variants of content objects exist and organises them along multiple dimensions, such as resolution or modality. As the content variants defined by the InfoPyramid are precomputed, the performance penalty of transcoding them in response to a client request is eliminated. However, the system now needs to select the variant that best matches the capabilities of the client device. To do so, Mohan et al. propose a customiser that uses a resource allocation algorithm to deliver the optimal content variant, according to a predefined content value that captures the perceived value of the transcoded variant relative to the original. Since the customiser processes one content object at a time, the system may perform poorly when multiple objects on a web page are dependent on each other.

A major shortcoming of automatic approaches such as distilling and transcoding is their tendency to yield unsatisfactory results in some cases. As a response to this limitation, solutions have been proposed that allow content variants to be authored manually and then delivered context-dependently. An example of such a solution is the web authoring language *Intensional HTML (IHTML)* [283]. Based on version control mechanisms, IHTML supports web pages that have different variants and adapts them to a user-defined context. The concepts proposed by IHTML were later generalised to form the basis for the definition of *Multidimensional XML (MXML)* [268] which in turn provided the foundation for *Multidimensional Semistructured Data (MSSD)* [267]. Similar to semistructured data that is often modelled using the Object Exchange Model (OEM), MSSD is represented in terms of a graph model that extends OEM with multidimensional nodes and context edges. In the resulting Multidimensional Object Exchange Model (MOEM), multidimensional nodes capture entities that have multiple variants, by grouping the nodes representing the facets. These variants are connected to the multidimensional node using context edges. In contrast to the conventional edges used in OEM, the label of a context edge specifies in which context the variant it points to is appropriate. Using these specifiers, a MOEM graph can be reduced to a corresponding OEM graph in a given context. Based on this graph representation, a *Multidimensional Query Language (MQL)* [269] has been defined that allows the specification of context conditions. Thus, it can be used to formulate queries that process data across different contexts.

A general and extensible architecture that supports context-aware data access is proposed by De Virgilio and Torlone [84]. Their approach is based on profiles and configurations. Context is represented as a collection of profiles that each specify one aspect of the context, such as the user or the device. Each profile contains a set of dimensions that capture certain characteristics and are associated with attribute context values. Profiles are expressed according to the *General Profile Model (GPM)* [85] that provides a graphical notation and is general enough to capture a wide variety of formats currently in use, to transmit context information as well as to transform from one format to another [86]. While such profiles describe the context in which a request has been issued to the web information system, configurations express how the response should be generated. A configuration has three parts that match the architecture of web information systems in terms of content, structure and presentation. The content part of the configuration is represented by a query formulated in relational algebra. The definition of the structure part is expressed using WebML to define the hypertext. Finally, the presentation part is specified using the notion of a logical stylesheet which unifies languages such as Cascading Stylesheets (CSS). Configurations are stored in a repository on the server side and matched to the profiles submitted by the client as part of its request. The matching is done based on adaptation rules consisting of a parametrised profile, a condition and a parametrised configuration [87]. The profile allows parameters, instead of values, to be used that are then assigned the values specified in the client profile. The condition constrains the values that are valid for the rule to be applied by formulating a logical expression over the parameters. Finally, the configuration includes the parameter values that adapt content delivery. During the matching process, the client profile is compared to the adaptation rules. If the client profile matches the parametrised profile of the rule, and the specified values fulfil the condition, the parametrised configuration is instantiated and applied.

While GPM provides support to express context in multiple ways, Kaltz and Ziegler [153] propose a context model for web engineering that

attempts to provide a unified view of context. Based on an analysis of
the context parameters required by current context-aware web systems,
a context space has been defined. This context space consists of the user
and role factors, the processes and tasks, the locations, the time factors,
the device factors, the available information items as well as the available
services. The context defined by the model is then used to adapt context-
sensitive resources, such as the navigation, content and services of a web
application. The resulting context system delivers adapted resources as a
response to a request, specifying the current context state as parameters.
This communication paradigm facilitates the integration of the context
system into web applications as an independent model. Due to this
orthogonality, the application developer can freely decide which parts of
the web site will exhibit context-aware behaviour. While this approach
is self-contained in the sense that it defines all dimensions of context
that are considered to be relevant for web engineering, it suffers from
the limitation that a fixed notion of context cannot be influenced by the
web application. Therefore, the model is ill-equipped to cope with future
developments that might require the introduction of additional context
dimensions.

2.5   Analysis and Hypothesis

In this chapter, we have motivated the need for context-aware data management, based on a survey of systems developed in the domains of ubiquitous, pervasive and mobile computing as well as web engineering. In
each of these domains, both applications offering context-aware services
as well as frameworks and models providing support for such systems
have been examined. In the survey of applications, a number of characteristics and requirements of context-aware computing have been revealed.
One such characteristic is the fact that the use of context and therefore
the definition of what information is considered to be context are both
highly specific to the application at hand. This situation gives rise to
the requirement that a platform supporting context-aware applications
needs to be both general and configurable. Further, context information
can be represented based on a variety of models and at different levels of
granularity, which is a additional characteristic that has been observed in
our survey. The challenge that is coupled to this property is the ability
of a context-aware platform to cope with different models of context. Finally, the scope of the impact of context on the behaviour of a system is

also an important property of context-aware computing. Whereas some systems exploit context in a reactive manner to improve their responses to user requests, other systems implement proactive behaviour, based on contextual triggers.

All of these requirements have been addressed either partially or comprehensively by numerous context models, frameworks and infrastructures. Most of these approaches have also been presented in the course of our survey of context-aware computing. Many systems react to the discussed challenges by providing support for gathering, augmenting, processing and representing context as well as modifying application behaviour based on context. In general, the focus of these approaches lies in providing services that have been adapted or triggered based on context. With few exceptions, these solutions do not address the requirement of adapting the content itself but rather limit their context-awareness to selecting which information is displayed in a certain situation. Some systems that do address this requirement have been included in the discussion of mobile computing frameworks and, in particular, in the domain of web engineering. However, from the point of view of data management, it has to be emphasised that none of these solutions build on established concepts of information systems but rather maintain content stored in document files. This approach suffers from a number of disadvantages. Files usually represent information at a very coarse level and shroud the structure of content by capturing it implicitly. This limitation precludes the use of these systems as part of a model-based development process, as fine grained concepts and the relationships between them are very difficult to represent based on files. Furthermore, a collection of files is not capable of offering the benefits connected with a database management system, such as efficient storage, formal query languages, access control mechanism or consistency maintenance.

It is the hypothesis of this work that the requirements of context-aware data management should be addressed based on concepts that have proven themselves in the domain of information systems. As a consequence, database systems have to be empowered to evaluate queries, depending on the current context state. In this thesis, we present a solution that addresses this requirement on two different levels. First of all, we believe that a version model should be used to manage context-dependent variants of application data within a database system. Then, we propose a matching algorithm that is used to evaluate context-dependent queries over the version model. Many existing version models have been designed to support revisional versions to keep track of system evolution. In our version model, we have therefore decided to integrate context-aware variants, that are intended to enhance the run-time behaviour of a database system, with revisions to assist the development process at design-time. After giving an overview over existing version models and systems in the following chapter, we present the version model for context-aware data management that we have developed, in Chapter 4.

3

Version Models and Systems

One of the contributions of this thesis is relating the requirements of context-aware data management to the challenges that have been addressed in the past by temporal and engineering database systems as well as software configuration tools. Therefore, this chapter concentrates on the achievements contributed by the research in these domains. Version models have been used in the field of information systems time and again to meet the challenges raised by applications in various domains. Whereas very early approaches were simple in nature, later version models have grown in complexity. Over time, version models have become as heterogeneous as the issues that they addressed. Consequently there have been a number of efforts to unify versioning terminology and to develop generic models that can be customised to different needs.

Due to the vast number of models that have been proposed in the past, our survey will not be exhaustive but rather focus on well-known and significant contributions. Providing the basis for positioning our work in the area of versioning systems by showing how it has evolved from the generalisation of these existing systems is one of the goals of the discussion of existing systems that follows. At the same time, it also introduces the technical background required for the presentation of the version model for context-aware data management in the next chapter.

Finally, and maybe most importantly, these existing version models also constitute a motivation and a validation of the approach that we have taken in our work.

However, before launching into past models, we introduce the terminology that we use throughout this thesis to discuss existing work and to introduce our own version model. The rationale behind this terminology is not to define yet another unified set of terms that attempts to cover all imaginable approaches. Rather it is an attempt to avoid widespread confusion by defining what certain expressions mean to us.

3.1 Concepts and Terminology

At the heart of any version model is the fact that concepts can have a number of states associated with them in one sense or another. In the scope of this thesis, we will call these elements *versioned objects*. It is important to point out that when using the term "object", we do not intend to limit ourselves to referring to a concept within an inheritance hierarchy with both fields and methods, as known from object-oriented systems. Rather, we use the term in a broader sense to mean any item that can have versions. Hence, examples of versioned objects that can be found at any level of granularity include simple files, individual tuples of a relation, attributes of a class in an object-oriented program or entire objects in an object-oriented database system. While versioning individual attributes or tuples provides very fine-grained control, working with whole objects places the versioning at the level that is semantically meaningful to the application. Finally, approaches that version entire files are very coarse-grained, as the internal structure of these files is not taken into account by default. Depending on the application, however, all of these granularity levels have shown their merits in the past.

A versioned object, perceived at a conceptual level, consists of a number of versions that exist at the implementation level. Each *version* is a possible representation of the versioned object and corresponds directly to one of its states. Depending on the semantics of the version model, an object state can have a number of interpretations which will be discussed later. Another important feature that distinguishes a version model is its *organisation of versions* which governs how all versions of a versioned object are managed by the versioning system. Some systems simply represent a versioned object by using a set of unrelated version items. When versions are organised like this, the semantics of an individual version can

only be derived from descriptors that have been assigned to it. Other
systems use directed acyclic graphs to encode the relationships between
versions. This type of graph constitutes an appropriate concept to organise the genealogy of a version as it makes access to predecessor and
successor versions straightforward.

Depending on the organisation of versions used by a given versioning system, the *storage strategy* determines how versions are represented
at the lowest level of the implementation. Again, a number of strategies have been developed, all with different motivations and goals. The
straightforward approach of simply storing all materialisations of a versioned object separately was among the first strategies to be proposed.
To optimise space requirements, other strategies have been proposed that
only store the difference between versions. These so-called delta-based
approaches come in several variations offering a number of optimisations
regarding which version can be accessed in constant time. Depending on
the requirements of an application, differences can be stored based on
either the initial or the current version. While delta-based approaches
perform well when data changes little between versions, their applicability is limited if differences between versions are substantial or if versions
exist in parallel, rather than in a predecessor-successor relationship. To
store differences between versions, two major approaches have been proposed. State-based deltas compare the final state of two versions and
store the difference, while operation-based approaches capture the editing process and express the delta with a set of change operations.

Orthogonal to the storage strategy of a version model is the *set of
operations* it offers to control the evolution of versions. Some models
restrict the evolution of a versioned object to one axis. In such a scheme,
a version can have only one successor and the operation to *create* a new
version can only be invoked once on an existing version. Other models do
not impose such restrictions allowing versions to have as many successors
as required by the application. Systems that support this behaviour are
often said to support a *branch* operation as the versions do not evolve
linearly but along diverse branches. To combine two or more versions
that have existed along different branches, some version models offer
a *merge* operation that, depending on its implementation, unites the
versions into one. In such systems, it is possible for a version to have
more than one predecessor. While merging is an operation found in many
versioning systems, the *delete* operation is only offered by models that
address very special application needs. Supporting the removal of an
individual version from within a genealogy of versions raises a number of

conceptual and technical problems in terms of ensuring the consistency of the system.

Using these elementary operations as a basis, several version models have defined *interaction models* that facilitate working with such a system. Models supporting *automatic versioning*, for example, are completely transparent to the client. A user of a system of this kind does not need to specify which operations should be executed at what time. They can simply work on a versioned object and the system decides for them when a new version or branch should be created. Obviously, automatic interaction is not applicable in all versioning systems. For instance, if a version model supports multiple clients working concurrently, conflicts can arise that might require undoing a client's changes. Therefore, semi-automatic approaches have been developed that work mostly automatically but delegate control to the client when conflicts occur. The best-known semi-automatic approach is the *library model* which derives its name from the manner in which a library lends books to its clients. Following this analogy, the library model provides two high-level operations—check-out and check-in—that are constructed from the basic operations described above. When a client wants to work on a versioned object, they need to check it out. In some models, the check-out operation will lock the versioned objects, preventing other clients from working on the object at the same time. A system to which this restriction does not apply will simply create a branch of the current version of the object. After a client has finished modifying the object, they use the check-in operation to save their changes. If the object was previously locked, a new version is created reflecting the changes and the lock is removed. Otherwise, the branched version of the client might need to be merged with other versions to form a new version that reflects the changes of all users. Since the library model is semi-automatic, a system that supports this mode of interaction will prompt the user to manually resolve any conflict that arises during the check-in operation. Finally, there are applications that have requirements surpassing the capabilities of semi-automatic models. For such applications, there are versioning systems that offer a user-defined or customisable interaction model. These models can be tailored to the needs of an application by specifying policies that express, for example, which version has priority in case of a conflict.

The type of *references* supported by a version model are another possible dimension which can be used to classify such systems. Models that allow references to specific versions within a versioned object to be expressed are said to support *specific references*. Specific references are required when there is a dependency constraint between a versioned object and a certain version of another object that would be violated if another version of the referenced object was to be used. In contrast to specific references, a *generic reference* expresses a reference to the versioned object itself without requiring the actual version to be specified. Therefore generic references have to be dereferenced at a later time to denote an actual representation of the object. This kind of reference is used predominantly in cases where multiple versions are believed to be equivalent and where a metric is available to resolve the latest or most appropriate materialisation. Generic and specific references are concepts that can coexist alongside each other, and, therefore, any combination of the two can be found in existing version models.

To summarise the concepts introduced so far, Figure 3.1 shows an example of two versioned objects. The versioned objects o_1 and o_2 are depicted as rectangles, with dashed lines labelled with the corresponding identifier in the upper left corner. Inside these versioned objects, the set of versions that represents them is shown as a set of circles. Each version within a set is identified by a label v_0, v_1 etc. Note that these identifiers themselves do not bear any semantic meaning as to how the object evolved. To simplify matters, we have chosen to organise the versions of both objects in a graph. Although other possibilities are imaginable, the graph representation lends itself very well to graphical representation and is therefore used in this figure. The version organisation of an object captures the relationships between individual versions. For example, since v_0 is the source of the version graph of object o_1, it is the initial version of this object. Version v_0 is then followed by two successors v_1 and v_2. Finally, version v_2 is the predecessor of versions v_3 and v_4. References between objects o_1 and o_2 are shown as horizontal arrows pointing from one object to another. The upper arrow pointing from version v_0 inside object o_1 to the rectangle representing o_2 denotes a generic reference as it does not end at a specific version inside object o_2. This reference expresses that version v_0 of object o_1 has no constraints as to which version of o_2 it actually gets when the reference is traversed. When v_0 evolved into v_2 this situation has obviously changed. Version v_2 now uses a specific reference to point to version v_1 of object o_2 directly. By using a specific reference, version v_2 of object o_1 expects to deal with exactly version v_1 of object o_2, as no other representation of o_2 would satisfy its assumptions about the referenced object.

Building on these basic concepts, many versioning systems have defined mechanisms to build a concrete materialisation from a network of

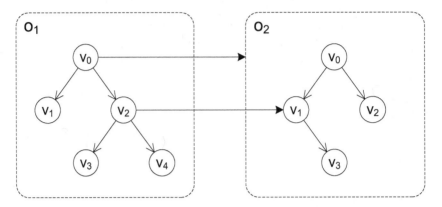

Figure 3.1: Two versioned objects

versioned objects. Taking a given specification as input, a so-called *con-figuration* determines the appropriate version to represent each of the objects involved. While some systems employ specific references to express which versions of the objects take part in a configuration, other models use a configuration algorithm that generates configuration from a set of constraints. This algorithm is, of course, highly dependent on both the version organisation and the types of references supported by the version model as these characteristics form the basis of computation. However, another aspect that has great influence on this algorithm is the use of the version model within an application. Since different use cases require different semantics, the algorithm is also specific to an application. Hence, a configuration algorithm can be seen as an intermediary between a given version model and a certain application system that cannot be specified entirely by either component.

To guide the construction of configurations, several additional concepts have been introduced in existing version models. Depending on the organisation of versions, situations can arise where the choice of an appropriate version to represent a versioned object is ambiguous. For example, if a version model allows multiple versions to coexist in parallel, the selection of the appropriate version is not always straightforward. To cater for this case, the notion of a *main derivation* has been defined by some models. The main derivation is a way of distinguishing the one version that should be selected in case of ambiguity among a set of coexisting versions. The systems that offer the notion of a main derivation can be further partitioned into those systems that expect the main derivation to be a static property of a collection of versions and those that allow it to be assigned dynamically to a version. Similar to the concept of the main derivation is the notion of an *active version*. In contrast to the main derivation that resolves ambiguity among parallel versions, the active version determines which version is selected if a collection of versions has evolved serially. Most systems define the active version to be the last version in a sequence of versions, but there are also models that support other scenarios, such as user-defined active versions.

In version organisations that allow objects to evolve in one dimension only, the concepts of main derivation and active version are essentially the same as only one or the other is meaningful anyway. However in version models that allow objects to evolve along multiple dimensions, the combination of these two concepts is a powerful instrument to eliminate uncertainty. Assume, for example, that a configuration algorithm needs to resolve the generic reference from object o_1 to object o_2, as presented in Figure 3.1. Without any additional constraints, the algorithm would be unable to select a version to represent o_2, as any version $v_0, \ldots, v_3$ could be a possible candidate. This ambiguity can only be resolved by introducing a main derivation and an active version. Suppose that the sequence $v_0 \rightarrow v_1 \rightarrow v_3$ has been designated as the main derivation of o_2. Suppose further, that the active version is always chosen to be the last in a series of sequential versions. In our example, this policy would define the set of active versions of o_2 to be $\{v_2, v_3\}$. Combining the two concepts, a configuration algorithm could select the active version of the main derivation, which leads to a single well-defined version of the object that is pointed to with a generic reference. Based on this procedure, version v_3 would be selected in our sample situation to represent object o_2 after the generic reference from o_1 to o_2 was resolved by the configuration algorithm.

At the implementation level, several technologies have been proposed to support the generation of configurations. Some versioning systems have introduced the notion of a *configurator* that constructs a configuration for a network of versioned objects by evaluating a collection of configuration rules against the version sets of each versioned object involved in the configuration. Most configurators distinguish between built-in rules that are hard-wired into a versioning system and user-defined rules that allow customisation of the configuration process. Rules are often specified as predicates that express which versions should be chosen to represent objects. Other approaches use the concept of a *declarative query* that expresses the constraints required by the application. In this case, the versioned objects managed by a version model are perceived to be a database that forms the basis for query evaluation. One major advantage of declarative approaches over other solutions clearly is the fact that the internal representation of objects and versions does not need to be known to the user who specifies the query. The same problem of decoupling the details of the version models from the specification of configuration is also addressed in systems that build on *logical unification* to configure a network of objects. Based on the theory of feature logic, feature terms are used to guide configuration of object networks.

3.2 Existing Systems

Having described the various concepts of version models at a very general level, we will now examine a number of actual approaches that have been proposed. While it has been the aim of this section so far to present those concepts as independently as possible of existing systems, some aspects are determined by how things are actually represented and implemented. Another matter of major impact on a version model, that has been neglected so far, is the actual application domain for which it has been developed. By focusing on a specific application domain, it is possible to introduce a terminology that is much more descriptive as it draws from the purpose of the versioning system. In the past, version models have been used to address the challenges of managing temporal data [229, 149] and product data [156], as well as for software configuration systems [74] and hypertext versioning [292]. With the advent of object-oriented programming languages and databases, versioning was also introduced in these object systems [220]. The desire to track the evolution of the content provided through the web and to make the distributed authoring of such content possible, versioning techniques have also been developed for hypertext documents. Over the years, each of these application domains has led to countless approaches that address the particular requirements of each field.

3.2.1 Temporal Databases

Among the first applications of versioning techniques are temporal databases that deal with different flavours of time-dependent data. Several approaches that address the problem of managing temporal data from very different angles have been proposed over the years. These solutions include conceptual models, data models, algebras, storage models, and query languages. In the following we present the most influential approaches from each of these fields and discuss a few interesting features of these solutions. In the past, a number of taxonomies and classifications for temporal data management have been proposed. These previous surveys have established useful criteria to examine systems capable of managing temporal data. As we will refer to some of these characteristics, it is necessary to introduce the ones that are most relevant.

Such a criterion is, for example, the distinction whether a given system uses tuple versioning or attribute versioning to represent time-dependent data. In the former case, a whole tuple is extended with additional information that captures the temporal aspects of the tuple. In the latter case, every attribute is extended with this information. In the relational model, tuple versioning can be realised without violating the first normal form, whereas approaches using attribute versioning often rely on systems that support relations in non-first normal form [148, 240]. Snodgrass and Ahn [265] distinguish three different types of time information that can be used to characterise temporal data. First, transaction time, sometimes also called registration or physical time, captures when a certain value was stored in the database. Valid or logical time is used to express when a value existed in the real world. Finally, user-defined time covers all aspects of time that do not fall into one of the two other notions of time. Based on these kinds of time information, Snodgrass and Ahn defined four different types of database. Static or snapshot databases are conventional databases that do not manage temporal data of any sort. Databases capable of keeping track of transaction time and supporting the AS-OF operation are termed static roll-back databases. In contrast to static roll-back databases, relations in historical databases evolve along the valid time axis and these databases therefore support the WHEN operation. Finally, temporal databases combine transaction and valid time and hence also support queries including both temporal operations.

Another characteristic of temporal systems is given by Gadia [115] who classifies temporal data models into homogeneous and heterogeneous models. According to Gadia's definition, a data model is homogeneous if the temporal domain does not vary from one attribute of a tuple to another. The time spans characterising attributes of different tuples are, however, not restricted by the homogeneity of a data model. Clearly, all models that use tuple versioning to capture time-related information are homogeneous by design and it is therefore only interesting to consider this property in approaches where attribute versioning is employed.

Gadia also introduced the notion of horizontal and vertical anomalies to quantify how the storage of a versioned data item is affected by a given data model. If a horizontal anomaly is present in a data model, a versioned data item is split across tuples in different relations. The reason for such a horizontal anomaly could be the fact that the data model uses tuple versioning and different attributes of the data item have different valid times. A vertical anomaly can be observed when a data item is spread over several tuples in the same relation. This condition arises if a given data model is unable to store more than one period of validity in a single tuple. It should be noted that both horizontal and vertical anomalies do not imply inconsistent data but rather provide a measure for the complexity of the representation of a data item in a given data model.

Conceptual models to represent temporal data were among the earliest approaches proposed for temporal databases. For example, Bubenko [43, 44] proposed a conceptual framework based on the relational model to incorporate time-related aspects into the development process of an information system. As Bubenko's approach uses an extra field in each tuple to capture temporal information, it has to be classified as an approach based on tuple versioning. The main focus of the proposed model is on versioning associations between entities rather than on versioning concept classes or entity sets. The model also forestalls the distinction of time into transaction and valid time by introducing the notion of intrinsic and extrinsic time. To express temporal aspects of data, the conceptual model integrates time as a first-order concept by providing a dedicated time model. In contrast to Bubenko, the conceptual model proposed by Klopprogge [166] is based on the E/R model. This *Temporal Entity-Relationship Model (TERM)* uses the notion of histories that are built from ⟨*time, value*⟩ tuples to represent time. Similar to Bubenko's approach, TERM recognises two notions of time by distinguishing between internal and external histories. These histories are then used to augment the concepts of the E/R model such as entities, relationships, existence constraints, data identification and data manipulation. As TERM recognises the fact that the modelling of time can be application-specific, it offers a language to define time and history structures, rather than predefining a fixed time model. A more recent approach is the *Bitemporal Conceptual Data Model (BCDM)* [149] that supports transaction and valid time. BCDM assumes tuple-versioning and timestamps each tuple with a set of ⟨*transaction time, valid time*⟩ pairs that capture when the corresponding tuple existed. Special UNTIL CHANGED and NOW values express that a tuple is current on the transaction and valid time axis, respectively. To represent BCDM within the relational model, two approaches have been proposed. Either relations are extended with four additional columns that store the start and end times of both transaction and valid time or non-first normal form relations are used to represent the sets of timestamp pairs directly. The conceptual model also proposes the query language TSQL2, an extension of SQL that introduces a VALIDTIME and WHILE clause. As SQL/Temporal, TSQL2 has been incorporated into the SQL3 standard.

Whereas conceptual models address the challenges of temporal data management from the point of view of modelling time-dependent information, data model approaches focus on the representation of such data. The *Historical Database* (HDB) [70] is based on Intensional Logic (IL_s) and uses tuple versioning to capture temporal aspects of data. The approach introduces the notion of completed relations that correspond to a snapshot of a historical database at a given point in time. The set of snapshots that together represent the entire lifespan of the historical database is called a cube. To ensure that all relations within a cube contain the same number of tuples, a completed relation also contains entries for tuples that have existed in the past or will exist in the future. Whether a tuple actually exists at a given point in time is indicated using a special EXISTS? attribute. As the model uses tuple versioning, it is homogeneous in the sense given above. While it has no horizontal anomaly, the vertical anomaly is substantial due to the fact that all tuples that ever existed are stored in each completed relation. A similar solution is the *Temporally Oriented Data Model (TODM)* [7] that is also based on tuple versioning. TODM introduces the notion of time-related attributes to describe attributes that contain values with some form of temporal semantics. A specialisation of time-related attributes are timestamp attributes that store a datum indicating when the tuple was recorded. Therefore, timestamp attributes correspond to transaction or physical time, whereas time-related attributes in general cover all types of time. A tuple containing a timestamp attribute is called a temporally anchored tuple and the concept of a cube is defined in TODM as a set of such temporally anchored tuples of a specific data type. Thus a cube represents a three-dimensional relation.

In contrast to the historical database and the temporally oriented data model, the *Temporal Data Model (TDM)* [256] is independent of any specific storage model such as the relational model. Therefore, the data model itself could be implemented on systems that use either tuple or attribute versioning. To represent temporal data of an object, TDM uses the notion of a time sequence consisting of a collection of temporal data values that are represented by ⟨*surrogate, time, value*⟩ triples. The surrogate field denotes the object to which this value belongs, the time field records the temporal dimension of the value and the value field contains the actual data. Because a time sequence only contains temporal values of one object, the surrogate field of all temporal values is the same and a time sequence can therefore be represented by ⟨*surrogate,* (*time, value*)*⟩. The time sequences of a class of objects are grouped together by the concept of time sequence collections, i.e. sets of time sequences. Over these time sequence collections, TDM defines a number of temporal operators such as a selection, aggregation, accumulation, restriction and composition.

Designed to satisfy the notion of homogeneity, the *Homogeneous Relational Data Model* [115] for temporal databases is a representative of the data models that use attribute versioning to record temporal data. Each attribute of a tuple can have multiple values for different periods of validity which are expressed as [*begin, end*] intervals. However, due to the criterion of homogeneity, all time periods of the attributes of a tuple must cover the same timespan. The concept of a snapshot is introduced to convert a temporal relation to a normal, non-temporal relation. Based on snapshots, the condition for weak equality between temporal relations is defined. Two temporal relations are weakly equal if their snapshots are identical in every instant in the interval [0, *now*]. The *Temporal Relational Model (TRM)* [198] is another approach that extends the relational model to represent temporal data. In contrast to the homogeneous relational model for temporal databases, it uses tuple rather than attribute versioning based on timestamps and time intervals. A time interval $[T_S, T_E]$ is built from two timestamps, one denoting the start and one the end time. TRM distinguishes between two types of time-varying attributes. Synchronous attributes are two or more time-varying attributes that are associated with the same time intervals, i.e. the values of synchronous attributes always change at the same time. Asynchronous attributes are attributes that are independent of other time-varying attributes, as their values change at different points in time.

Different from data models that address the challenges of temporal databases from the perspective of data representation, temporal algebras concentrate on the definition of operations over such data. Although the focus of a temporal algebra clearly lies on its operators, it is unavoidable to also make some assumptions about the underlying data model in order to define these operators. For example, an algebra and a temporal tuple relational calculus have been defined based on the previously discussed homogeneous relational data model for temporal databases. In Clifford and Tansel [69] each author presents his approach to specifying a temporal algebra based on attribute versioning. In his algebra, Clifford distinguished between constant, time-varying and temporal attributes. Whereas constant attributes are not affected by time, time-varying attributes are. Temporal attributes are used to store the time values that describe the time-varying attributes. The algebra defines two new operations, the TIME SLICE operation (τ) and the WHEN operation (Ω). To select tuples according to temporal attributes, the TIME SLICE operation is used and the WHEN operation returns a set of time intervals that satisfy a given condition. Finally, the existing operations of the relational algebra, PROJECTION (π), SELECTION (σ) and JOIN ($\bowtie$), are redefined to produce results annotated with temporal attributes. Tansel's temporal algebra differentiates between atomic, triplet and set-triplet values. Whereas atomic values are normal non-temporal values, $\langle begin,\ end,\ value \rangle$ triplets and sets of such triplets capture valid time values and histories. The model is also based on attribute versioning and can therefore be heterogeneous, as there is nothing to ensure that all attributes of a tuple cover the same timespan. In contrast to Clifford's algebra, Tansel's approach leaves most of the standard operations, PROJECTION (π), PRODUCT ($\times$), UNION ($\cup$) and MINUS ($-$), of the relational model intact. Only the SELECTION (σ) operation is adapted to handle the new temporal attribute types. Additionally, the algebra introduces a set of new operations to transform temporal relations to standard relations and vice versa. These non-temporal relations can then be manipulated with the existing operations. For example, the PACK and UNPACK operations convert to and from set values. Triplets are decomposed into three separate attributes using the T-DEC operation and constructed from such attributes by the T-FORM operation. The SLICE operation restricts the time of an attribute according to the time of another attribute. Finally, all time information can be discarded from triplets by applying the DROP-TIME operation to a temporal relation.

In contrast to Clifford and Tansel's approaches, the *Temporal Relational Algebra (TRA)* [183] assumes a data model that uses tuple versioning with two additional attributes S_{from} and S_{to} that denote the point of validity. As a time model, the algebra introduces two system relations CALENDAR and HOURS that contain all time points within the timespan referenced by the temporal data that is stored in the system. Similar to

Tansel's approach, TRA also introduces a number of new operations that aim at transforming temporal relations into relations that can be processed using traditional operators. The EXTEND operation, for instance, joins a temporal relation with the CALENDAR relation that contains an individual tuple for each time point in the time model. Based on the EXTEND operation, the UNFOLD operation is defined which returns the same results but removes the S_{from} and S_{to} columns by projection. Applying the FOLD operator to a previously unfolded relation reconstructs the original relation and restores the S_{from} and S_{to} columns. While these operations allow relations to be handled by standard operators, it has to be noted that intermediate relations can dramatically increase in size. Nevertheless, it is exactly this complete representation based on a tuple for each time point that enables the temporal relation algebra to handle queries with negation, a feature that is absent from most other approaches.

Below the data or logical model lies the physical model that organises the temporal data in terms of storage and access structures. An example of such a storage model for the relational data model has been proposed by Lum et al. [184]. The authors acknowledge that both logical and physical time are relevant to temporal applications. They argue, however, that on the implementation level only physical time needs to be supported. In their view, logical time can be expressed by taking physical time as a reference. The proposed storage model employs a single relation that only contains current tuples that are timestamped transparently to the user. The history of each tuple is then chained to the current tuple in reverse time order. To improve performance, the storage model provides indexes for both current and history tuples, as well as the possibility to use deltas to manage the storage consumption of history chains. As with most of the approaches presented so far, this storage model also assumes that a temporal database is append-only, i.e. data once entered can never be deleted entirely. However, Lum et al. also recognise the need for corrective database operations that are not recorded in terms of timestamps and thus provide support for such administrative interventions. Further, the proposed storage model is also capable of dealing with future time through an additional history chain for each tuple that contains the future versions of the data. Finally, schema evolution is supported by keeping versions of the system metadata. In Dadam et al. [77], some of the same authors present an analytical survey that motivates some of the choices made. They compare different version strategies and different units of versioning. In terms of strategies, storing complete versions, as well as the use of deltas in combination with forward and backward versioning, have been analysed. As for units or granularity levels of versioning, the authors examine versions at the physical level and the logical level, i.e. in terms of memory pages and tuples, respectively. The result reported by Dadam et al. is that the best choice to provide time versions in a relational database system is to use incremental backward versioning at the level of tuples based on timestamps, which corresponds to the solution presented in Lum et al. [184]. The survey by Dadam et al. closes with an analysis of possible applications of versioning mechanisms within a database management system and reaches the conclusion that time versions can be used for concurrency control but are not suitable for the implementation of recovery.

Similar to the work of Dadam et al., Ahn [5] compares five different structures to organise tuple versions in a two-level storage partitioned into primary and secondary storage. As in the previous storage model, primary storage is used to manage current data whereas secondary storage contains the data history. The first storage structure discussed by Ahn is reverse chaining, which is also used by Lum et al. to manage history lists. Accession lists, the second structure that is presented, introduce an indirection between the primary and secondary storage in the form of a list containing pointers to previous versions of the tuple that is referenced from the current tuple. Hence, an accession list functions as an index over the history of a tuple. The strategy on which the clustering storage structure is built, is to group all versions of a single tuple into the minimum number of pages. To control the space consumed by tuple histories, the stacked version structure has been defined. Each tuple is assigned a stack of a fixed size that contains the history tuples. To ensure that the stack does not exceed the allocated space, old tuples are deleted from the bottom of the stack whenever the memory limit is reached. Finally, the cellular chaining structure combines the concept of reverse chaining with stacked versions, as it collects several history tuples into a cell of a reverse chain. Based on these storage structures, Ahn and Snodgrass [6] introduce indexing techniques for temporal data. Two types of indexes over key attributes, i.e. primary indexes, are distinguished, namely partitioned and non-partitioned indexes. Whereas a partitioned index separates current entries from the collection of history entries, a non-partitioned index organises all entries in the same data structure. According to Ahn and Snodgrass, the design of secondary indexes that provide access to tuples through non-key attributes depends on the type of database such as snapshot, roll-back, historical and temporal database, for which the index structure is provided. Since a snapshot database does not manage temporal data, traditional index data structures can be used in this case. However, for roll-back and historical databases, the entries of the index have to be augmented with *begin* and *end* fields to capture transaction and valid time, respectively. As temporal databases support both transaction and valid time, index entries have to include four fields to represent the intervals that correspond to each notion of time.

An important component of every storage model are index structures that provide direct pointers to frequently used data and thus reduce the number of required access operations. As discussed above, indexes in temporal databases have to provide data access based on multiple search attributes, as both non-temporal and several types of temporal attributes may be involved in a query. *Multi-Dimensional File Partitioning (MDFP)* [232] is such an approach that allows data to be indexed by one ore more search criteria. MDFP organises data access into a three-level hierarchy. At the top-level, partitioning points are kept in fast storage such as the main memory. Partitioning points divide the data space into cells that are managed as a directory with an entry for each cell. Each cell points to one or more data pages that contain the tuples of the corresponding cell. Another temporal data access structure is the *Time Index* [95] which assumes a data model based on tuple versioning and is limited to append-only databases. Similar to multi-dimensional file partitioning, the time index also uses time points represented as [*start*, *end*] intervals to partition the data space. Based on these indexing points, the time index builds a B^+ tree to reduce the number of data access operations. Although the time index is not applicable to the evaluation of all algebraic operations, it has been shown to improve the performance of the WHEN operation, temporal aggregations functions, as well as the temporal variants of the SELECTION and JOIN operation.

To query temporal databases, a number of temporal query languages have been proposed. Several of these query languages have been defined, based on one of the data models or algebras presented above. For example, *Temporally Oriented SQL (TOSQL)* [7] is an extension of the Structured Query Language (SQL) specified within the scope of the temporally oriented data model. TOSQL extends SQL with a number of keywords, such as AT, DURING, WHILE, BEFORE, AFTER or AS-OF, to enable temporal queries. The same approach is taken by *TSQL* [198] for the temporal relational model that is also defined as a superset of SQL. Apart from temporal variants of the ORDER BY and GROUP BY operations, TSQL introduces MOVING WINDOW, TIME-SLICE and WHEN operations, as well as a series of comparators for time intervals. The MOVING WINDOW clause is used to define a time interval of a fixed length but with variable start and end points. The actual start and end point of the interval will then be evaluated by the query processor according to additional conditions specified in the query. To evaluate queries over a subinterval of the time interval covered by a temporal relation, the TIME-SLICE operation is applied to construct an intermediary relation by extracting the tuples contained in the given subinterval. Finally, the WHEN clause allows a temporal condition to be specified for the query by using the interval operators such as BEFORE, AFTER, OVERLAP or DURING.

Rather than extending an existing query language, the *Legally-Oriented Language (LEGOL 2.0)* [151] defines its own concepts and syntax. LEGOL is based on the relational model and assumes tuple versioning. Each relation is augmented with two additional attributes that store the start and the end timestamp of the validity period of a tuple. Either the end value or both values may be null to indicate temporal data that is current or non-temporal data, respectively. The attributes of a tuple that contain values expressing the temporal aspect of the data cannot be manipulated explicitly, as they are managed by the system. Rather, they are accessed implicitly, using one of the temporal operations of LEGOL such as the temporal join. As LEGOL, the *Temporal Query Language (TQuel)* [264] was also developed for the relational model, based on tuple versioning. However, instead of creating a whole new language, the syntax of TQuel is defined based on the Quel [138] query language. In addition to the concepts of Quel, TQuel introduces a WHEN and a VALID clause and is therefore a superset of Quel. TQuel can evaluate queries over two different kinds of temporal relations, event relations and interval relations. While event relations have an extra start column to capture time-related information, interval relations have both a start and an end column. Apart from the WHEN and VALID clauses, TQuel also defines a series of temporal operators that can be used in conjunction with the two clauses to form temporal predicates. TQuel was implemented within the Ingres database management system for which the Quel query language was originally defined.

3.2.2 Engineering Databases

The application domains of Computer-Aided Design (CAD) and Computer-Aided Manufacturing (CAM) strive to provide software tools that support the engineering of new products and the management of product

lifecycles. Engineering databases have been developed to store and process the product data that is generated by these applications during
the development and maintenance of products. Engineering applications
have two major requirements that need to be addressed by any component intended to manage product data. First, design objects can be very
complex, as they are often hierarchically composed from several smaller
objects. A data management system has, therefore, to provide concepts
to define and manipulate such complex objects in terms of data structure
and concurrency control. The second requirement—versioning of complex objects—stems from the fact that design tasks are iterative processes
where products are refined by trial-and-error or by experimenting with
alternative versions. The notion of revisional versions, to support the
refinement of complex objects, and the concept of alternative versions,
to cater for multiple variants of the same design object, have also to be
built into the data management system.

Whereas a temporal database capable of handling transaction time
could be used to manage the revisional aspect of versioning in an engineering application, the challenge of managing variants has never been
addressed by such systems. As discussed above, some temporal databases are capable of handling several kinds of time once, leading to multidimensional systems. Since the challenge of managing revisions and variants in parallel gives rise to a two-dimensional version model, it could
be assumed that a multi-dimensional temporal database could support
such a model. However, in contrast to the dimensions of time supported
by temporal systems, the dimension of object variance is non-linear and
has no order. Another substantial difference between temporal databases and engineering databases arises from the requirement of versioning
complex objects. In temporal databases, only simple objects such as
individual tuples have been versioned by augmenting them with time information. As a user of an engineering applications works with complex
objects that represent high-level concepts of the developed product, it
should be possible to control how the parts of such objects are versioned
and how changes are propagated within the component hierarchy.

Early work towards extending relational database systems with support for engineering applications was done by Haskin and Lorie [134].
Two new concepts, long fields and complex objects, were introduced into
the System R database management system developed by IBM. Long
fields can be used to store and retrieve unstructured or so-called non-
coded information of arbitrary length. Data is written to and read from
long fields with an extended cursor concept that allows iteration over a

stream representing the data of such a field. As the approach is based
on the relational model, complex objects are defined to manage several
tuples as one molecular object. Such an object consists of one root tuple
and a set of component tuples that are linked together using values of the
COMP_OF column type. This type is one of three new column types that
were defined in System R to represent and manage complex objects. The
IDENTIFIER column type is used to uniquely identify a complex object,
whereas values of the REF type are used to model references between
complex objects. The proposed model of complex objects supports references between two component tuples of the same molecular object, as
well as references from a component tuple of one object to the root tuple
of another. Concurrent access to complex objects is based on the check-
out/check-in model that creates a local writeable version of the object in
the user's workspace and synchronises it later with the database. Alternative versions are used to manage the working copies of different users,
and revisions keep track of engineering changes over time.

The data model of the *Version Server* [159, 157] distinguishes between
presentation objects and structural objects. Presentation objects are the
complex design objects that are visible to the user of the engineering application, whereas structural objects are used to organise design objects
in the same way as directories are used in file systems to organise files.
The version server defines three possible types of relationship between design objects, namely version histories, configurations and equivalences.
Revisional version histories keep track of the evolution of a design object
and are captured by the IS-A-DESCENDANT-OF and IS-A-ANCESTOR-OF
relationships. A special kind of structural object, the structural version
object, is used to group together a collection of version instances. The two
configuration relationships IS-A-COMPONENT-OF and IS-COMPOSED-OF
record how a complex object is built from smaller, but potentially also
complex, components. Alternative versions or variants are expressed by
the IS-EQUIVALENT-TO equivalence relationship. As with the approach
proposed by Haskin and Lorie, the version server also uses the workspace
model with check-out and check-in operations. In addition to these operations, group check-out and check-in operations are also available to
control change propagation and prevent version proliferation. In Katz
and Lehman [158], a possible implementation for the storage of such a
system is presented, based on the relational model. The storage model
manages revisions and alternatives by partitioning them into a current
file and a history file. An additional history index is then used to relate
the records in the history file to records in the current file. Operations

are provided to create revisions or alternatives and to control their evolution. For example, a freeze operation can be used on a version to indicate that it can no longer be changed. If a change is required, either a new revision has to be created or the version has to be thawed to make it modifiable again. Versions are transferred between the current and the history file using the archive and restore operations. Finally, the forget operation permanently removes a version from the storage.

In Klahold et al. [165], the authors present a general model for version management that introduces a layered approach to building an engineering database. The model consists of a four level stack. At the bottom, the version storage level manages all versions of an object independently, i.e. without assuming any semantic relationships between them. This layer provides basic operations to create, manipulate and delete object versions. On top of the storage level lies the version structures level that uses graphs and partitions to organise the versions of a design object. Time relations and the development history of an object are represented as a directed acyclic graph, whereas partitions are used to group together objects with the same properties, such as their state, within a development process. The next level, the version environment, provides the concepts of views, constraints and complex operations. Views are used to form virtual objects according to the requirements of a user or group of users. Multi-level transactions are used to represent complex operations as a sequence of simple operations or subtransactions. Finally, constraints can be defined to control the integrity and evolution of versions and version structures. The group oriented transaction model introduced by Klahold et al. [164] is a possible approach to using version environments to tailor a version system to the requirements of an application domain. It provides the notion of long transactions through the check-out/check-in model with locking. A two-layered transaction model consisting of group and user transactions is assumed. Group transactions transfer objects from a public database into a group database from where the objects are transferred to the personal workspace by user transactions. Hence, user transactions are subtransactions of group transactions. The transaction model manages versions in a directed acyclic graph that captures both revisions and variants. Alternative versions are simply represented as versions with a common ancestor. To control the evolution of version graphs, the concept of a derivation lock has been defined that controls whether a new version can be derived from an existing one.

While the approaches discussed so far have been focussing on data and storage models to manage engineering data, Batory and Kim [14] introduce a conceptual model to represent such data. Their approach is based on four modelling concepts, molecular objects, version generalisation, instantiation and parametrised versions. As the model does not provide the notion of revisional or temporal versions, all versions are purely alternatives. Molecular objects separate an object into its interface and its implementation. In their terminology, the interface is represented by an object type and the implementation by a number of object versions. Both the interface as well as the implementation level are modelled separately and are then integrated through molecular aggregation and correspondence. While molecular aggregation treats a set of heterogeneous entities as one single high-level entity, correspondence captures the identity of differently represented concepts across the two levels. The modelling concept of version generalisation is used to express the relationship between an object type and object versions, i.e. it captures which implementation alternatives have been defined for a given interface. Although all attributes defined by the type are inherited by its versions, a type may restrict a version from overriding an attribute by declaring it non-modifiable. To actually use an object type or an object version in product design, the corresponding elements are copied. In the terminology of Batory and Kim [14] this process of copying objects into a product design is referred to as instantiation. If an object type is instantiated and no implementation is specified, only the interface is copied. In this case, the last modelling concept, parametrised versions, comes into effect. Whenever an object type is instantiated, the unspecified implementation creates a "socket" that needs to be parametrised with an instance of a version which is called a "plug". Based on parametrised versions, a product can be designed to incorporate certain components without the need to specify which variant of the implementation will effectively be used.

Similar to the approaches already presented, the *Distributed Version Storage Server (DVSS)* [94] also organises an object as a set of versions in an acyclic directed graph. As new concept, however, DVSS introduces the notion of a principal version path that defines the main successor of an object that has multiple variants. The distributed version storage server also uses the check-out/check-in model to control the interaction between the database server and its clients. Within the framework of this model, DVSS offers three operations—refinement, derivation and consolidation—that can be applied to versions. Revisional versions are created through the refinement operations, whereas alternative versions can be defined using the derivation operation. In contrast to the refinement and derivation operations that are present in most engineering databases, systems that provide a consolidation operation are less common. Since the consolidation operation provides support for merging two alternative versions of an object into a single one, it is rather application specific and can normally not be implemented in a general way. References between objects can either be fixed or floating, representing the concepts of specific and generic references, respectively. DVSS has been implemented as a distributed platform that can cope with the partitioning and merging of sites.

The solution for version support for engineering database systems proposed by Dittrich and Lorie [91] identifies alternative and revisional versions as well as stages as key requirements of a computer-aided design process. While revisions and variants had already been introduced by other engineering databases, stages were a new concept to support the trial and error nature of development activities by allowing a user to easily go back to a previous state. Analogous to other systems, engineering data is represented as design objects that consist of a set of versions. However, in contrast to the solutions discussed before, that manage both revisions and variants uniformly in a directed acyclic graph, Dittrich and Lorie structure the version space using paths that connect an object to its versions. Such paths first lead from the design object to its alternatives. Then, each alternative is connected to its revisions, which finally point to the versions of the design object. This structure was very different from existing solutions as it distinguished the concepts of revisions and variants at a very low level. It was also the first model that takes the view that variants should be favoured over revisions in the data structure that links an object to its versions. The proposed solution also supports generic and specific references, where generic references are represented as references that do not specify version information. The novel concept of a design environment is introduced to provide a mechanism that controls how generic references are dereferenced into specific references. A design environment consists of three look-up tables that govern which version of a design object is used when it is accessed through a generic reference. The first look-up table contains direct entries that associate identifiers of design objects directly with the desired version number. Indirect entries delegate the decision which version to select to another design environment by linking a design object to the name of a design environment. Finally, inclusion entries incorporate an entire design environment into the current one while at the same time allowing a search priority to be specified for each included environment. When a generic reference is resolved, the dereferencing algorithm searches these three tables in the presented order until it finds a record specifying a version number for the references design object. To prevent ambiguous situations where no such entry is discovered by the search algorithm, each design environment may additionally specify a default version.

Another approach to version management of product data in computer-aided design applications is proposed by Ahmed and Navathe [4]. As in most other solutions, design objects are represented as complex objects, so-called composite objects, that consist of simpler objects. A speciality of the approach is that rather than organising the components of an object in a tree, as some of the solutions discussed above, it uses a directed acyclic graph, the composition graph, with a single source node. The leaf nodes of the graph, i.e. nodes that have only incoming edges, are called primitive objects or constituents. Based on their function, the attributes of a composite object are classified into two categories, external features and internal assembly. Within the class of external features, on the one hand, attributes that form the interface of the composite object are distinguished from descriptive attributes that are used to capture object properties. On the other hand, the attribute types composite aggregation, correspondence and interconnection are the subclasses of the internal assembly category. Attributes of type composite aggregation are used to capture the edges of the composition graph, whereas correspondence attributes establish a relation between the interface of the composite object and the interface of one of its constituent objects. Thus, the two attribute types are essentially equivalent to the concept of molecular aggregation and correspondence within the approach proposed by Batory and Kim. Finally, interconnection attributes are used to express relationships and references among constituent objects. In the proposed model versioning is realised based on three different types of objects. The trivial case of an object that does not go through an evolution process is handled with the concept of an unversioned object. Objects that do evolve during the development process are represented both through a generic object and through a set of versioned objects. Whereas the generic object contains all properties of the object that are common to all stages of its evolution, the versioned objects correspond to the versions of the object and are organised in a directed acyclic graph. Versioned objects can have invariant, version-significant and non-version-significant attributes. Invariant attributes cannot be modified at the version level, as they conceptually belong to the generic object. Whenever a version-significant attribute is updated, a new version of the object is created, whereas non-version-specific attributes can be changed without causing such a mutation. The evolution of object versions is controlled by a series of version states and a set of operations that convert versions between these states. All newly created or derived versions start out in the transient state. In this state, all non-invariant attributes can be modified but no new versions can be derived from this version. Using the promote operation, a transient version can be converted into a stable version. In this state, new versions can be derived from this version. While non-version-significant attributes can still be updated, version-significant attributes are no longer modifiable. Finally, a stable version can be transformed into a validated version. Any modification of the attributes of the version is now forbidden. References from the constituent objects of this version can only point to either unversioned or other validated objects. It is, however, still possible to derive new versions from a validated version of an object. The model also provides a mechanism to prevent version proliferation. The equivalence modification denotes a substitution of one versioned object through another without change propagation. This operation is the only permissible update operation for version-significant attributes of stable versions.

3.2.3   Software Configuration

Within computer-aided design and manufacturing, software applications are a special type of product with a unique set of characteristics. One such distinguishing property of software engineering is the fact that a system providing support for software development manages the product itself, whereas the computer-aided engineering systems presented above merely manage a representation of the product. In contrast to these systems that can only support the manufacturing process of product, a software development system is capable of fully automating the process of building the final product. After a software product has been assembled from the source code managed by the development system, the released products continue to be controlled by the systems. The requirements that arise from this additional functionality surpass the challenges that were addressed by the systems described above and gave rise to the application domains of Software Configuration Management (SCM) and Software Engineering Environments (SEE).

As these software engineering systems are related to computer-aided design and manufacturing, most of them have also been built around the concept of a design object. Depending on the actual system, a design object may be anything from a source code file to a module of a software program. In software engineering, however, the management of references and dependencies between design objects is somewhat more complicated. Whereas such connections have been modelled by engineering databases with external relationships that capture the semantics of the connection, the corresponding relationships in software engineering are often implicit, as they are, for example, embedded in the source code. As files are a natural representation of source code components, some software development systems use them to manage the product instead of a database as in most engineering systems. Managing versions based on files can either be achieved through version segregation or through single source versioning. Version segregation assigns a file to each version of the software component, whereas single source versioning manages all versions of a component in one file. Whether versions are managed by a database or in files is a choice at the storage level of a software engineering system. On the logical level, the evolution of a product can be represented either as a set of materialised object versions or as a set of changes that are applied to a base object to generate any required version.

To manufacture a software product for a specific target platform, configurations define which components and what version will be used in the build process. Configurations are either specified extensionally or intentionally, depending on whether the elements of the configuration are listed explicitly or defined by rules or goals. In this setting, the relationship between software configuration management and context-aware data management becomes apparent. Some software configuration tools are built on the notion of a context that characterises the target platform. The process of building a configuration of the software product is then seen as an adaptation of the system to this context by choosing the appropriate versions of its components. In the following we examine some of the approaches that have been proposed in the domains of software configuration management and software engineering environments. Of particular interest to the version model presented in this thesis are the mechanisms that these approaches introduced for both specifying configuration contexts and for adapting the objects of a software system to this concept of context.

The *Domain Software Engineering Environment (DSEE)* [180] is an early system that provides both revisional and alternative versions on top of a file repository. Its history manager provides revisional versions based on the reserve/replace model which is essentially equivalent to the check-out/check-in model presented above. For alternative versions, three different types—branch-merge, alternatives, and conditional compilation—are distinguished. Support for fixing software bugs in isolation is provided by the branch-merge type of variants that allow a parallel development process to be spawned off, which is later combined with the main line. Alternative versions cater for the fact that different hardware and software platforms may require different implementations of the same functionality. It also enables different flavours, such as a debugging variant or an optimised one, to be developed and managed. Finally, conditional compilation addresses variation that occurs within a file through the use of precompiler directives. Configurations are managed by the configuration manager of DSEE that uses a so-called configuration thread to specify revisions and branches explicitly or dynamically through wildcards. At build time, the configuration manager constructs a bound thread by binding these dynamic references to specific objects. Additionally, the system features a task manager that relates high-level design steps to source code changes throughout the network. An advice manager generalises task descriptions to be used as templates for similar tasks in the future. Finally, the monitor manager provides dependency management based on monitors that trigger notification updates in the user's task list.

Rather than building a software product for release to the end-users, the ambition of the *Gandalf* [131] project is the semi-automatic generation of entire development environments. Gandalf environments integrate the notions of both programming and system development environments by means of well-defined prerequisites that each environment has to meet. One of these characteristics is knowledge integration that demands the presence of a development database that provides support to share information between tasks. Other requirements are interactive user interfaces and application uniformity, in the sense that all commands of the development environment behave consistently. Finally, a well-defined system state has to be maintained by incorporating meta-information into the environment. A Gandalf environment can either be a programming or a system development environment, leading to additional criteria that have to be satisfied in each case. For example, Gandalf programming environments have to offer language-oriented editing systems, source-level debugging and incremental compilation as well as program interpretation. In contrast, Gandalf system development environments are additionally characterised by support for system version control as well as for project management in terms of tools to support cooperation, coordination, communication and version control. For system version control, Gandalf specifies that the software product has to be structured based on the concepts of boxes, modules, versions and revisions where boxes correspond to directories, modules to the interface of a component, versions to variants and revisions to the actual implementation. Thus, the organisation of the version space in Gandalf favours the variant concept over the notion of revisions, as a variant is a set of revisions. Also, a Gandalf system development environment has to support both specific and generic references between project components. Whereas generic references are resolved based on the concept of a standard variant and revision that can be updated, specific references are realised by storing the whole path to an implementation based on the hierarchical structure mentioned above. As with most other systems discussed so far, Gandalf uses a variant of the library model featuring a reserve, release and deposit operation to control how objects are checked out and locked for modification. Within the Gandalf project, an alternative approach to organising software products—the inverted approach to configuration management [189]—was developed. The inverted approach proposes to organise software based on variant, revision and transaction levels. The variants level is the lowest level and contains hierarchically structured collections of source code components. Each of these collection represents the entire software system with all its variants and common parts. Variants are labelled with *attribute* = ⟨*value tuple*⟩ properties, while common parts are not labelled and assumed to satisfy all values for a given attribute. One level above the variants level, revisions each contain such a collection of variants and common parts. Revisions are grouped into historical development paths that also support parallel lines through branching. The transaction level is the top level and contains long-term transactions based on the check-out/check-in model. Transactions are hierarchical, as child transactions are executed at each level and reserve locks are propagated down this hierarchy of transactions. All revisions that need to be accessed for modification in a certain development step are included in a transaction. In this inverted approach, transactions are said to be nested, as the root transaction corresponds to the entire development task, whereas nested transactions represent subtasks of the engineering process.

The *Adele* [20] software configuration management system represents versioned objects as an interface and a set of multiple implementations that correspond to alternative versions. Additionally, each implementation can have multiple revisions. Interfaces can be versioned as well in

Adele to provide support for complete system evolution. All objects are described using *name = value* attributes. Relationships between system objects are represented explicitly as, for example, the dependency relationship that is generated automatically by analysing the source code. Other relationships such as the SPECIFY relation between the documentation and a program or the MUST_DO relation between a plan or task and a programmer have to be recorded manually. Configurations are built based on a composition list that specifies the required implementations and is generated by a description of the target system. Adele supports multiple options to provide the specification of such a description. For example, a full description lists all implementations explicitly, whereas an empty description causes default implementations to be chosen. Additionally, a description can be expressed by specifying implementation constraints or by selecting implementations based on their attributes. In the latter case, several ways exist as to how this selection is performed. Imperative selection requires all attributes to match, whereas conditional selection is only applied if the attributes specified by the description exist for an implementation. Finally, default selection provides support to specify general preferences. In *Adele II* [98, 97], three-dimensional versioning was introduced to organise versions on historical, logical and cooperative axes. Historical versions represent revisions, logical versions correspond to alternatives, and cooperative versions are used in long-running transactions. To control system evolution, a historical version can have three different types of attributes. Immutable attributes trigger the creation of a new revision when updated, modifiable attributes contain object metadata and common attributes capture characteristics at the object level. The logical versioning axis supports multiple dimensions in which variants can differ, and introduces the notions of composite-versioned and composite-specified objects which roughly correspond to the concepts of generic and specific references, respectively. The process of deriving a so-called specified object from a versioned object is known as concretisation in Adele II. Finally, cooperative versioning is based on the workspace concept that is intended to increase parallelism while collaboration policies control the spawning and merging of versions.

The *Database Management System of Karlsruhe for Environments for Software Engineering (DAMOKLES)* [92] is built on a relational database management system. The system introduces the Design Object Data Model (DODM) that provides the concepts of structured complex objects, versions in terms of revisions and variants, relationships between objects or versions and attributes for both objects and relationships.

The data model distinguishes between simple objects that correspond to relational tuples and complex objects that are represented as a set of subobjects that may be recursive and overlapping. To support versioning, the notion of a generic object is supported that groups the versions of an object together. All of these versions have to have the same structure and the same attributes. The version graph that captures the predecessor-successor relationships can be linear, treelike or a directed acyclic graph. Additionally, DAMOKLES supports long transactions based on the check-out/check-in operational model as well as distribution of the schema and user access control.

Similar to the approach taken by DAMOKLES, the *Système pour l'Intégration d'Outils (SIO)* [28, 179] is also built on top of a relational database management system. This tool integration system represents each generic component or module as a relation with special attributes that capture version information such as NAME, DEFAULT, TIME, STATUS or TARGET. Each tuple represents a version, i.e. a revision or variant of the module. A default version is supported through the DEFAULT attribute. Relationships between components such as IS-USED-BY or IS-INCLUDED-IN are also represented as relations to enable change propagation and express compatibility constraints. Both generic and instantiated configurations are supported to denote the general structure of a product and one concrete materialisation, respectively. A generic configuration can either be instantiated extensionally, by listing all versions, or intentionally, by specifying conditions over the attribute values of the versions. Thus, the selection of a version is mapped to a database query problem [176] where both logical conditions and preferences are taken into consideration by minimising the distance between the specified and the available versions. In order to do so, the query language used in SIO is extended with a preference clause that allows simple and nested preferences as well as equally important preferences to be specified. Additionally, the query language has been augmented with second order constructs such as the ALL, MIN and MAX operators. Such queries are first processed without considering preferences that are only used at the end of the evaluation to reduce the cardinality of the result set. If the answer becomes void through the application of preferences, preferences are ignored and the whole result is returned.

In contrast to DAMOKLES and SIO that use relational databases to manage software objects, Winkler [294] proposes a decentralised, source-based approach that consists of so-called building blocks and external references to document relations between two blocks. To capture these concepts in a source-based manner, the programming language used to implement the software system is extended with several new statements. For example, the CONFIG keyword is used to describe a building block, USE to capture the required version of dependent components and BUILD to configure a given version. Versions can be both revisions and variants and are therefore uniquely identified by a ⟨*revision, variant*⟩ tuple. Dependent revisions of a building block are referenced through timestamps, whereas dependent variants are described using ⟨*name, value*⟩ tuples. To find the version that approximates such a description best, Winkler proposes to use a matching algorithm. While revision numbers match exactly, the values of variants can be specified to be either ignored, a list of values, a wildcard, or a special value such as ALL that selects the same version as the one containing the reference, or LAST to point to the latest, i.e. most recent version.

The *Multi-Version Personal Editor (MVPE)* [238] is a text editor supporting multi-version files and is therefore not an application that is limited to only software configuration management systems. In MVPE, the text contained in a file is broken down into fragments that are ordered into a sequence by a thread. A version of a text document is defined by such a thread that selects a sequence of fragments. A multi-version file as created by the editor is a collection of text fragments and threads linking them together in different ways for different versions. Variants of a text document can be defined using the concept of correspondence to mark a set of versions as alternatives. Dimensions partition the version space and at the same time describe the versions. For example, an operating system dimension could be used to group together those versions that have been developed for the same operating system. To edit a multi-version file, an edit set that contains the versions of interest has to be selected. Fragments that are contained in all versions in the edit set are called fixed fragments, whereas those that are only included in some or even in none are called unfixed and excluded fragments, respectively. An edit set can be constructed by explicitly selecting the versions it should contain or through Query-by-Example (QBE), by specifying a tabular scheme that lists for each dimension the values that describe the selected partitions of the version space.

In software configuration, the term "context" was first introduced in the *Software Project Management System (SPMS)* [199] that manages components at the level of source code files. Similar to the approaches presented so far, components are also described by properties. However, instead of simple ⟨*name, value*⟩ tuples to represent such a characteristic,

SPMS uses an *attribute(value)* function to capture the same information. For building configurations, a context model is provided that allows logical context expressions to be specified over these component attributes. Three-valued logic is then used to select the component that is appropriate in the current context. Attribute functions can also be redefined to implement a behaviour that is different from the default behaviour of using string comparison to match values. To realise required attributes, functions can be configured to return false, if the corresponding attribute is not defined for a component. Additionally, SPMS supports attributes with multiple prioritised values to realise fall-back behaviour in the case that no component contains the given attribute value directly. Although SPMS provides some mechanisms to increase the flexibility of its context matching process, it does not allow for approximate matches since it is based on Boolean truth values. To build the configuration given by a context expression, the software project management system provides the `pexec` utility that is similar to the `make` program.

Aide-de-Camp [76] was one of the first software configuration systems that did not follow the approach of tracking the evolution of a system as a sequence of versions but rather as the set of changes that have been made. Whereas the approaches discussed so far have all advocated the sequential change model, Aide-de-Camp introduces the selectable change model. In this model, change-sets are managed and versions are specified as a base version plus a collection of changes. These changes are then applied to the base version to create an actual version, the so-called change-set object. Similar to other systems, these changes can either be given extensionally by listing them explicitly or intentionally by specifying rules that select them implicitly. As a change does not necessarily have to represent the difference between two versions, they can be freely combined to create any desired version. Aide-de-Camp distinguishes between installed versions that are fixed and plastic versions that can be modified by adding or removing change-sets.

Similar to Aide-de-Camp, the approach proposed by *Change-Oriented Versioning (CoV)* [195] also favours the registering of changes instead of versions. Each logical change is represented as an option that can either be true or false depending on whether the corresponding change is included in a version or not. In CoV, the unit of versioning are so-called fragments that are managed in a repository database and characterised by a visibility in terms of a Boolean expression over options. To create a view consisting of versions for reading, a choice that assigns a Boolean value for each option is used. The view expressions specified by the

fragments are evaluated against the option values specified by the choice
to select the fragments that belong to the choice. Therefore, a choice
can be seen as a specification of a configuration. A so-called ambition is
used to record a physical change through writing to the database. As the
option, it also consists of a set of $\langle option, value \rangle$ bindings which specify
the version that will be modified. The concepts of choice and ambi-
tion together form the notion of a version context that is required for all
database accesses. Clearly, the change-sets of Aide-de-Camp and the version context introduced by change-oriented versioning are closely related
concepts. CoV was implemented in the *Expert System for Program and
System Development (EPOS)* [125] that refines the mechanisms available to describe versions. The technique to characterise versions based
on views, as originally proposed by change-oriented versioning, is still
supported in the form of explicit descriptions. Additionally, validities
representing a set of choices with *'?'* as a prefix for options that should
not be set are now supported. Further constraints such as *'at most one'*
to declare options as mutually exclusive, *'implication'* when an option
requires the presence of another option, or *'incompatible'*, can be specified. A preferred option or the wish to avoid an option can be expressed
by weighted option, and defaults allow values to be specified for options
that have no binding in the version context. Finally, aggregates allow
named version descriptors to be defined, and thus help reusability.

Lemur [221] is a programming environment for modular C programs
that uses source files to manage versions of software components. Each
version of a component is stored in a separate file with the metadata
about the version encoded in the file name. Both histories of versions
using incremental version numbers and subversions to represent variants
are supported. Lemur introduces an algebraic version language that is
used to manage versions and to build configurations. This algebraic
version language is based on a refinement relation for versions and a
dictionary order for subversions. The refinement relation ($\sqsubseteq$) establishes
a partial order over versions by defining that $V \sqsubseteq W$ holds if V is refined
by W. Under the refinement relation, the set of all possible versions
forms a lattice. For subversions, the dictionary order ($\ll$) introduces a
total order that is equivalent to the alphabetical order of the names of
the variants. Based on the lattice defined by the refinement relation, the
join operation ($+$) is defined as the lattice least upper bound. When
building a configuration to construct a version V of a system, the version
of each component gets chosen that approximates V most closely, based
on the refinement relation and the dictionary order.

Another approach that uses a program similar to **make** is the *Shape* utility [185] that abstracts from the mechanism and the implementation that is used to represent variants. Shape is configured using so-called shapefiles that specify variant definitions in terms of variable assignments that describe the variant as well as variant combinations and classes that are used to define compatibility among variants. Variants are activated or selected by the command line utility at build time. Based on the shapefile, it handles variant system compositions by controlling the search order of source directories, the set of files that are passed to the compiler and the linker, as well as preprocessor options and compiler flags. The *Attribute File System (AFS)* [178] has been proposed as a repository for source and derived objects within the Shape project. AFS can be implemented as an extension to a UNIX file system or any other data storage system. It is built around the notion of an object base that is essentially a hybrid between a file system and a database. A design object is represented as a group of successive versions that capture the revisional aspect of software evolution. Each version is an attributed software object, i.e. a data object that is described by metadata in the form of ⟨*name, value*⟩ tuples. Variants are supported by the attribute file system based on a special *variant* attribute which has to be interpreted by the application. Version histories are always linear and thus branching is not supported. To better support variants, however, parallel history lines can be managed in AFS. Although Lampen and Mahler do not describe this mechanism in detail, it can be assumed that a variant is created by duplicating the original object and creating a dedicated line of development for it. Again, the library model is used to interact with the system, providing check-out/check-in operations with locking. Each version is in a state that defines what can be done with the version. For example, the busy state indicates that a version is under development and can be modified. If it is in the proposed state, it has been submitted for publication and awaits formal approval. After approval has been given, the version passes into the published state and is now accessible to all. The accessed state denotes that a published version has been accessed, whereas the saved state marks a version for backup. A frozen version is part of a public release and must not be destroyed or changed. To build configurations, an exact matching over the attribute tuple keys within the metadata of the attributed software object is used.

The goal of orthogonal version organisation is to manage the evolution of the whole project rather than single components. This approach is implemented in the *Versions of Outdated Documents Organised*

Orthogonally (Voodoo) [226] project. Versioned objects are organised in an object pool along three dimensions represented by the component, variant and revision axis. The project tree models the structure of the project hierarchically in terms of structure nodes, component nodes, version group nodes and variant nodes. Structure nodes express the logical structure, component nodes are used to represent components of the project, version group nodes correspond to versions of a component and the named variant nodes capture variants of a version. Interestingly, the hierarchical structure of the project tree favours the concept of versions over variants by placing them at a higher level in the hierarchy which stands in contrast to the approaches already presented. Configurations are instantiated based on a filtering mechanism for revisions and variants. The filtering process uses exact matches over the revision numbers as well as variant names and does not provide support for predicates. Interaction with Voodoo is also based on the library model as the system provides a fetch operation to lock an object in the repository and obtain an editable local copy.

The approach to versioning proposed by *Incremental Configuration Environment (ICE)* [297] is remarkable in the sense that it notably distinguishes itself from the solutions presented above. In contrast to other approaches, ICE does not store versions in a graph structure. Its version set model rather manages an unstructured collection of versions that are simply annotated with feature terms, a concept proposed by feature logic. These feature terms uniformly capture the notions of revisions, variants and workspaces as well as configurations, and can thus be seen as a replacement for the ⟨*name, value*⟩ tuples that are commonly used by other approaches. Consequently, configurations are specified by Boolean expressions and feature logic unification—the binding of free variables—is used to instantiate the configuration. Feature terms can be used to support alternative properties and to express constraints which either identify or select versions. The version set is stored using the Featured File System (FFS) that uses the format of the C Preprocessor (CPP) to store multiple versions in one file and also provides support for versioned directories. As the incremental configuration environment can be used to implement a variety of software configuration management protocols, such as the check-out/check-in model, long transactions or change sets, it effectively unifies version-based and change-based approaches. Unfortunately, the algorithms to perform feature unification are NP complete, which leads to numerous complexity problems and performance issues in the operations that are defined by the interaction protocols.

3.2.4 Hypertext Versioning

Hypertext systems manage documents that are represented in terms of a collection of nodes and links that interconnect the nodes. Due to this link structure, a hypertext is essentially a non-linear text that has no sequential reading order. Depending on the system, nodes are either used to represent entire documents or fragments of a document. Nodes can contain a range of content formats, such as texts, images or videos. To reference pieces of a hypertext document, anchors can be defined that either identify a whole document, a node or a specific area within a node. The links that interconnect the document nodes then use these anchors as start and end points. Similar to engineering databases and software configuration management systems, the challenges of versioning a collection of hypertext documents arise from the fact that both nodes and links need to be versioned if the entire evolution of a document is to be captured. A second similarity is manifested by the capability of some hypertext systems to manage so-called composite objects that include other objects recursively and thus roughly correspond to the concept of a design object or a software component.

Neptune [88] is an early hypertext system that integrates the notion of versioning. The system is built on a transaction-based server called the Hypertext Abstract Machine (HAM) that maintains a complete version history of the hypergraph and gives fast access to any version of the graph. Additionally, HAM offers operations for creating, modifying and accessing nodes as well as links. Neptune supports the notion of generic and specific references by providing two mechanisms to associate links with a node. Based on these mechanisms, it is possible to either refer to a specific version or to the current version of a node in a time-based sense. Both nodes and links can be annotated with an unlimited number of ⟨*attribute, value*⟩ pairs. These pairs can then be used in predicates to determine which nodes or links satisfy a query. Neptune does not provide support for multiple version threads that would allow parallel development of a hypertext. This issue is addressed with the notion of contexts [89] that partition the hypertext. Thus, a context represents a user's private workspace or a view where an author can explore alternatives. The variant concept provided by these contexts is, however, rather intended to support collaboration than parallel alternatives. Contexts are managed using the derive and merge operations which are essentially equivalent to the check-out/check-in operational model. Neptune does not provide support for versioned links.

A slightly more complex model that offers more concepts than just nodes and links is introduced by the *Aalberg Hyperstructure Programming Environment (HyperPro)* [211]. Its basic model consists of entities, links, nodes, composites and atomic nodes. An entity provides attributes based on ⟨*name, value*⟩ pairs. Nodes are a subclass of entities and are versioned. They are used to store the content of the hypertext and thus are required to define a name and content attribute. Links are also modelled as a subclass of entity, but are not versioned. A link relates a source node to a destination node and can either be a generic version link or specific version link. A composite is a subclass of node that recursively contains a sequence of nodes and is also versioned. Atomic nodes are the leaf nodes of the tree structure that is imposed by a composite. A version history is also maintained for atomic nodes. To represent such histories of versioned concepts, the basic model has been extended with the notions of version groups and contexts. A version group is a specialisation of the composite class. It contains all versions of one entity and maintains the version history using revision links among the versions. As these revision links form a tree data structure, variants can be represented through branches. The version group concept itself is not versioned. The context concept is also a subclass of composite but is versioned. All entities are a member of at least one context and thus contexts can be used to define a hierarchical structure over them. Additionally, a context maintains selection criteria for resolving links, where the default behaviour is the selection of the latest version, i.e. time-based resolution.

CoVer [127, 129, 128] is a version server for hypertext applications that provides a hypertext model based on the concepts of nodes, links and composites, as well as a query language. CoVer differentiates between unversioned objects, so-called single-state objects and versioned objects that are called multi-state objects. Multi-state objects represent versioned objects based on a version set that is realised using a composite node. The individual states of a multi-state object are called versions and can be nodes, links or composites. Whereas the values of generic attributes of a multi-state object are the same in all of its states, the values of version specific attributes can vary between versions. Multi-state objects are references based on a two-step addressing mechanism. First, the object identifier is resolved leading to the generic part of the object. Then the version identifier, which can also be given in the form of a dynamic query, selects the corresponding version of the multi-state object. In this scheme, variants can be represented through queries that return several alternative versions. To preserve a state of a multi-state object, versions can be frozen, leading to a distinction between updatable and frozen versions. Automatic version creation and version identification is effected through task-tracking. Each time a version is created or accessed, meta-information about the current task is stored as contextual information. This information can later be used to retrieve all versions that are related to a given task.

The differentiation between the task description level and the change control level is a fundamental concept of the *VerSE* [130] approach. At the task description level, the tasks executed at the change control level are organised in terms of application workflows and through history documentation policies. The actual versioning related activities are performed at the change control level that preserves entire states of the hypertext network as snapshots. The basic unit of versioning is the change task which can either take the form of a linear change task or a parallel change task. Linear change tasks represent sequential updates that are stored using the difference between two values. Parallel change tasks are managed as directed acyclic graphs with the option to combine two branches using a merge operation. Both types of change tasks distinguish between active versions that can be modified and frozen versions that are read-only. From these change task types, a number of task-based versioning styles can be derived, such as linear versioning, hierarchical linear versioning and parallel versioning. VerSE is based on the assumption that versioning is applied to the entire hypertext network and that at most one version exists per object in each version of the application data space. Therefore its support for alternative versions or variants is somewhat limited.

The *Hypermedia Version Control Framework* [141] is based on the HURL process-based hypermedia model. In HURL, content is represented by components that can contain persistent selection and are edited and viewed by applications. Anchors and links are modelled as computational processes that are capable of arbitrary actions. Associations are defined between components to represent structure based on a set of links and anchors. All objects defined by the hypermedia model can either be referenced through their object identifier or based on a query over object attributes to enable static and dynamic references, respectively. A special type of objects are composite objects that group other objects by referencing them either statically or dynamically. A bridge is a triple of identifiers referencing a persistent selection, a component and an application. A side defines one side of an association as a collection of one or more bridge identifiers together with an anchor identifier.

Both bridges and sides are examples of composites referencing specific versions of the objects they contain. In the hypermedia version control framework, every object is associated with a version set history realised as a container that manages the revisions of the object. The version set history maintains the derivation history as a directed acyclic graph using a delta storage algorithm. As in other approaches, versioned objects can have two kinds of attributes, depending on whether they apply to the entire object or a single version. In HURL, these two classes of objects are called version set history level and individual revision level attributes. The hypermedia version control framework has been implemented within the SP3/HP3 hyperbase management system.

The Nested Context Model (NCM) is the basis of the *HyperProp* [266] hypertext versioning system. To manage a versioned hypertext, NCM defines a number of concepts such as entities, anchors, descriptors, links, nodes, content nodes, composite nodes, user context nodes, version context nodes, variant context nodes as well as a public hyperbase and a private base. All of these concepts are organised in an inheritance hierarchy rooted at the entity concept that is characterised by a unique identifier and an access control list. A node is a specialisation of the entity concepts and stores the content of a hypertext system, as well as a list of anchors and descriptors. Anchors and descriptors are also subclasses of type entity and represent marked information units with a node's content and information about the presentation of the node. The node concept is further specialised into content nodes and composite nodes. Content nodes store content that has an application-specific structure that is not transparent to the hypertext system, whereas composite nodes contain other nodes and links recursively. However, a composite node cannot be contained in itself. A perspective determines through which sequence of composite nodes a node is accessed or viewed. The fourth and last specialisation of the entity concept are links that define relations among nodes in a composition. Links may depend on the perspective in which a node is observed, leading to the notion of contextual links. In addition to these basic concepts, NCM also defines a series of specialisations of the composite node concept that are intended specifically for version management. The user context node can contain content nodes, other user context nodes and links, and is an example of such a subclass. Its purpose is to allow documents to be structured through the definition of multiple user-specific views on the same document. Other refinements of composite nodes are version and variant context nodes. A version context node groups nodes that represent data versions of the same entity.

Within the node, links capture the acyclic DERIVES FROM relation. Additionally, the version context node also maintains a reference to the current version using a special anchor. In contrast, the variant context node groups different representation versions of the same object. To support collaborative work on a hypertext document, NCM introduces a public hyperbase that contains all content nodes and user context nodes, as well as a private base that contains a subset of content nodes and user context nodes beside other private bases. Both the public hyperbase and the private base are also subclasses of the composite node. In NCM, only content nodes and user context nodes are versioned. The attributes of these nodes may be versionable or non-versionable, determining whether their modification will lead to the creation of a new version. Each version may either be in the committed, uncommitted or obsolete state, to express if a version is modifiable or ready to be deleted. HyperProp also uses an extended form of the basic library operational model. Versions can be created using the open or check-out operations which produce deep or shallow copies of the base object, respectively. The check-out and check-out-one operations are applied to an object to create a new variant. When a variant is being created, a descriptor has to be given that characterises the variant. In contrast to the check-out operation, the check-out-one operation will fail if a variant with this descriptor already exists. To move an object from the private base to the public hyperbase, the check-in operation is provided, whereas the delete operation allows objects to be removed from the private base.

The World Wide Web can also be seen as a global hypertext system and it is therefore not surprising that proposals have been made to empower the web to deal with versioned content. The *Delta-V* [291] standardisation effort is a project that intends to add full versioning capabilities to HTTP and the protocol for Web-based Distributed Authoring and Versioning (WebDAV). On the web, the basic unit of versioning is the resource which represents any object that can be accessed through HTTP. In order to do so, WebDAV has extended HTTP with methods to provide overwrite protection through the use of shared and exclusive locks, properties to store metadata on a resource and namespace management, by introducing the notion of collections of resources that can be maintained uniformly. The goals of the Delta-V initiative go beyond the simple mechanisms provided by WebDAV and aim at providing comprehensive versioning support in a transparent way. One of these goals is the requirement of being able to version arbitrary media and content types, while another is configuration management based on collections of specific versions of resources. Such configuration management facilities imply that the entire resource history has to be stored on the web server and made accessible through dedicated URLs that correspond to the concept of specific links, as encountered in the approaches already discussed. However, versioning should be transparent to the user and, therefore, it is important not to disrupt existing URLs by providing generic references that can be resolved to a possibly updatable default revision. Delta-V proposes two mechanisms to create versions. First, versions can be created automatically if a version-specific property is updated instead of a version-unspecific one. Second, workspaces based on the check-out/check-in model are a possible approach to create versions manually.

3.2.5   Object-Oriented Systems

The approaches presented so far have been mostly built as extensions of file systems or relational database management systems. However, the challenges of versioning have also been addressed in the domain of object-oriented systems such as object-oriented programming languages and databases. A number of researchers have even argued that object-oriented systems provide a more natural basis for implementing versioning in engineering applications than file systems or relational databases. This is due to the fact that object-oriented systems already provide the notion of complex objects and references between them. For example, Dittrich and Lorie [91] underline both the importance and the potential of object-orientation in the conclusion of their paper.

> *"Also, our emphasis is on structurally integrating versions in an object-oriented manner. [...] Object-orientation should also increase performance considerably."*

In the following, we therefore discuss some object-oriented approaches to versioning. It should be noted that these systems do not introduce new application domains that require versioning, but rather address the same challenges as the temporal and engineering databases or the software configuration management systems presented above. Nevertheless, we have decided to single out these systems, due to the fact that the version model for context-aware data management presented in this thesis has been defined in the setting of an object-oriented data model and implemented within an object-oriented database management system.

The *Personal Information Environment (PIE)* [118] is a software development environment that was implemented as an extension to the
programming language Smalltalk-79. PIE introduces the concepts of
multiple perspectives, metadescriptions, identification and context-sensitive descriptions. Object roles are introduced in Smalltalk-79 through
multiple inheritance to allow objects to be accessed in multiple perspectives. Each object is assigned so-called metadescriptions that consist
of constraints that allow the system to check attribute values and trigger procedures that can be used for change propagation and consistency
maintenance. Further, based on dependency lists, metadescriptions also
form the basis for user notification in the case of changes that need manual intervention by a developer. The personal information environment
features an identification mechanism that allows each node to be identified uniquely, even if the system spans multiple machines on a network.
Node attributes are stored as a map consisting of ⟨layer, value⟩ tuples.
Within PIE, layers are the central concept that enables context-sensitive
object descriptions. Each time an attribute value is stored, the current
layer is also recorded. Values are later retrieved, based on a search context which is expressed as a sequence of layers. PIE searches this sequence
of layers and returns the first value that is found. The personal information environment distinguishes itself by very fine grained versioning, as
the units of versioning are attributes and methods rather than objects.

Beech and Mahbod [19] propose an approach to versioning in Computer-Aided Software Engineering (CASE) applications that is based on
an extension of *Iris Object SQL (OSQL)*. In Iris, all objects including
system objects are uniquely identified by an object identifier and consist
of both attributes storing data and predicates representing the object's
functions. An object may possess multiple types reflecting its roles at
a given time. Design objects are represented as a set of versions that
can be derived from one another. The version set is organised through
object instances of two special types. Instances of type generic allow an
object to be associated with a version set and provide functions to query
the version graph by maintaining predecessor and successor relationships.
Instances of type version are only aware of their corresponding generic object, i.e. have a reference to that object. The approach provides support
for both generic and specific references based on the possibility to specify
object identifiers partially and have them completed by the system. So-
called contexts, a concept similar to the design environment introduced
by Dittrich and Lorie [91], are used as a declarative, rule-based method
to control the resolution of generic references. A context is represented

by a triple ⟨*trigger, predicate, action*⟩. Versions of an object can be created explicitly, based on the check-out/check-in operational model, or implicitly, through change propagation.

A data structure that is capable of recording the temporal evolution of an object class in terms of transaction time is presented in Tsotras and Gopinath [277]. The approach uses the history data structure to capture different temporal states of an object-oriented system that is represented as a directed evolving graph. In this graph, nodes represent object classes and edges denote inheritance relationships where multiple inheritance is allowed. The proposed graph history algorithm builds on the existing set history algorithm which is used as a module. History sets are used to keep track of the evolution of all parent nodes of each node, including so-called entry nodes that correspond to the root classes of the object system. The resulting graph history algorithm is capable of retrieving past versions of a graph in almost constant time.

Sciore [254, 255] examines the integration of multiple kinds of versioning in one object-oriented database system. The resulting system is based on an object model that is similar to the one of GemStone [48]. Each object belongs to a single class that defines its variables and methods. The variables and methods are called the scheme of a class. The model also provides support for multiple inheritance where, in the case of name conflicts, all methods are executed in the order of the priority of their class. Sciore introduces the concept of annotated variables that are used to express property annotations and active value annotations. While property annotations capture the default value or the range of allowed attribute values, active value annotations represent triggers that are executed when the variable is accessed. In the proposed system, variable annotations are the basis for the implementation of historical, revisional and alternative versions by keeping a set of previous or alternative values in a property annotation that is managed by an active value annotation. The approach to resolve name conflicts resulting from multiple inheritance by executing all inherited methods allows different versioning types to be combined elegantly without having them interfere with each other. To build configurations, the *EXCESS-V* query language is defined as a versioning-aware extension of EXCESS that was introduced for the EXTRA [49] data model. EXCESS-V supports data definition, generic and specific references, data manipulation and updates. Views can be defined and configurations can be frozen. During query evaluation, the default version of objects is chosen according to a context that is represented by a set of global variables. This global context can be overridden locally in a query using the INCONTEXT statement to control the values of the context variables.

Commercial object-oriented database management systems, such as *GemStone, Itasca, Ontos, O₂* [11], *Objectivity/DB* [208], *ObjectStore* [177] and *Versant* [281], all support versioned objects. However, the actual versioning functionality that is offered in terms of version set organisation, transactional models and configuration varies substantially from one system to another. As it is out of the scope of this thesis to discuss all commercial systems in detail, we have chosen to have a look at Objectivity/DB as well as ObjectStore and Versant. These systems are representatives of two different approaches to supporting versioning functionality in a commercial system. Objectivity/DB, for example, offers basic versioning facilities allowing objects to evolve linearly or with alternative branches. The version set is organised using `nextVers` and `prevVers` pointers in each version of a basic object. As Objectivity/DB does not allow a version to have multiple predecessors, it limits the genealogy of an object to a tree structure and has no support for version merging. Both specific and generic references are supported, depending on object genealogy, i.e. whether the generic object or one of its versions is referenced. To disambiguate generic references, the genealogy—represented by an instance of `ooGeneObj`—contains a field `defaultVers` that points to the default version of the generic object. Configurations in Objectivity/DB have to be created manually by the system developer using a composite object that contains the required versions of each object. Whereas Objectivity/DB offers basic building blocks to implement systems that require versioning functionality, ObjectStore and Versant provide more comprehensive support for versioning. Both system are capable of managing the versions of an object in a directed acyclic graph rather than a tree. They also support the library operational model with check-out and check-in as well as persistent private workspaces. In addition to these high-level operations, ObjectStore provides `new_version`, `branch` and `merge` operations as member functions at the object level. ObjectStore and Versant have automatic configurations facilities that allow the system to be configured by the developer, using policies. In comparison to the version models presented in previous sections of this chapter, it has to be noted that the solutions offered by commercial systems address versioning at a lower level. Instead of providing a system targeted at one application domain, commercial object-oriented databases rather offer a set of primitives that serve as a basis for the implementation of domain-specific version models.

3.3 Discussion

Motivated by our hypothesis that the requirements of context-aware data management should be addressed in terms of a version model, we have presented an analysis of existing version system in this chapter. Starting with the examination of early approaches in temporal databases, we have introduced several notions of time-based versions. The origin of alternative versions or variants lies in the domains of engineering databases and software configuration management where several parallel versions of a design object need to be maintained. Depending on the application domain, these variants are used to model a collection of alternatives, to support collaboration of multiple users or to allow the essence of an object to be represented in different formats.

The survey of existing version models also uncovered that an early notion of context has emerged in the domain of software configuration management. Of course, this concept of context is quite different from today's understanding of context in mobile, ubiquitous and pervasive computing as well as web engineering. Whereas context-aware computing sees context as optional information that can be used to refine the functionality of a system, its role in software configuration management is that of a mandatory specification. Nevertheless, the purpose of context, to adapt a version base of software components to a given specification is clearly related to adapting behaviour and content to a physical or logical context in modern applications. However, because of this different understanding of context, we believe that the algorithms proposed to compute software configurations that are specified by a context are not applicable in the setting of context-aware computing as presented in the previous chapter. We therefore see a need to revisit these approaches in the light of current requirements to generalise the proposed solutions for context-aware data management.

4

Context-Aware
Data Management

The necessity for context-aware computing is well documented by the existence of numerous applications that exhibit adaptive behaviour and by framework systems that attempt to provide comprehensive support for the challenges encountered in the realisation of such applications. Some examples of applications and systems in the domains of mobile, ubiquitous and pervasive computing as well as web engineering have been analysed in Chapter 2, in terms of their notion of context and their adaptation capabilities. As demonstrated by these approaches, context-awareness has been tackled on a large scale and in very different ways. Most solutions, however, focus on context representation or on enabling adaptation at the level of the application logic. The impact context-awareness has on information systems in terms of data management and querying is often neglected.

Many frameworks for context-awareness introduce the concepts of variants for aspects of a system that need to show adaptive behaviour under different context states. In contrast to context-aware data management in general, the management of alternative versions of data has been addressed by many solutions in the past. As presented in the previous chapter, these approaches were originally designed to cope with temporal and engineering data or with software configurations. Apart from alternative versions, most of these systems also provide revisional versions to manage the evolution of applications. The same requirement is also present in the domain of web engineering where keeping track of the development process of web-based systems has repeatedly been recognised as a key challenge. For example, in their paper introducing OOHDM, Schwabe et al. [251] state the following.

> "[...] *design decisions should be recorded and traced backward and forward in the development process.*"

Instead of proposing revisional versions, however, OOHDM addresses this requirement at a much coarser level by structuring the design process based on a sequence of models that build on each other and thus enable developers to move back and forth in the process. Nevertheless, documenting development and evolution is important in any complex system, regardless of the proposed solution.

Both alternative and revisional versions have been introduced to address specific requirements. Therefore, they have quite different properties in terms of how they are used and perceived. To illustrate this, assume that two kinds of actors interface with the data management system. Users with the developer role design the application and provide the content. In contrast, users with the client role query the content managed by the system. While we do not claim that this simple role model is of any relevance to real application scenarios, it is sufficient to exemplify the different nature of revisional and alternative versions. As revisional versions are intended to support the implementation of an application by keeping track of its evolution, they are usually visible to the developer only. Clients of an application are not aware of their existence as they will simply see the most recent data. Alternative versions cater for the management of variants of the same object. Therefore the definition of such default behaviour in analogy to revisions is often not straightforward and the system has to rely on the client to specify which variant they require. As a consequence, variants are not transparent to the users, as potentially they can witness how such objects change according to the specification they provide along with the query. Further, when users having the client role are given permission to create and update data in the system, the different perception of revisions and variants becomes even more obvious. Whereas revisions can be created automatically and behind-the-scenes, the creation of variants requires the client to specify a description that will later be used for retrieval. Another way of looking at the different characteristics of revisions and variants is the nature of queries that involve each kind of version. In contrast to revisions that are most likely to be used off-line to analyse the development of an application, variants are used in an on-line fashion as an integral and active part of the production system.

Many existing systems have managed to successfully integrate revisional and alternative versions and offer complete and comprehensive support for the domain for which they were developed. However, none of these systems have been developed to support context-aware data management based on alternative versions. As context-aware computing differs from existing domains in terms of the requirements in the area of data representation and query processing, the application of these systems in this field is not straightforward. In this chapter we present our approach to context-aware data management that builds on the existing version models and extends them to cope with these new requirements. As motivated earlier, object-oriented systems are better suited for the implementation of version models and our version model has therefore been defined as a refinement of an object-oriented data model. To provide an understanding of this object-oriented data model and its functionality, it will be introduced based on a metamodel detailing how the objects defined by it are represented. As a part of the work presented in this thesis, this metamodel has been extended to allow revisional and alternative versions of objects to be managed. In combining revisional and alternative versions into one model, our approach reflects the convictions that we have set forth in Section 2.5. Even so, it has to be accepted that revisional versioning is an already well researched area and little is to be gained from a repeated discussion of this subject. Rather than expanding these concepts that have been put forward in existing systems, our version model uses and integrates them. We have therefore decided to place the emphasis of the following presentation and examples on the concept of context-dependent variants and how they have been combined with revisions. As a consequence, it is in this part of our version model for context-aware data management where we see the original contribution of our work.

In this chapter, we also introduce the notion and representation of context that is assumed in the scope of this thesis. Based on this representation of context, we show how data objects are annotated to characterise the situation in which they are appropriate. These characterisations are then used by the query processor when evaluating queries in a given context. For each object, the version graph is analysed and the variant that best matches the current context is used for subsequent query processing. The properties and functioning of this matching algorithm are also be discussed in detail, as it is a major element of context-aware data management. Finally, the implementation within the framework of an object-oriented database management system is presented. The chapter concludes with a discussion of our version model relating it to the requirements of context-awareness and comparing it to previously defined models.

4.1   Context, Context Space and Context State

In recent years, a multitude of models has been proposed that address the management and representation of context. Typically, these systems suffer from limitations that are rooted in either of two design decisions in the development of the context model. On the one hand, many models have evolved from specific application domains and therefore assume a notion of context that is relevant to that field. Targeting a context model to a specific application domain often leads to a reduced generality, as such models tend to restrict themselves to a fixed set of context dimensions. For example, a common characteristic of the models discussed in the preceding chapter is that most of them classify context into user, device and environmental factors and predefine the dimensions that are required for each of those classes. On the other hand, some models dictate how context is represented and stored, as a consequence of the technologies that have been used to implement them. Hence, representation of context is often tightly coupled to the platform that is used to store and process contextual information. Solutions range from collections of simple attribute values to complex approaches that represent context data in terms of database objects, or are based on class hierarchies in an object-oriented programming language. The integration of a context model into a general-purpose database management system can only be justified if the model is free from these two limitations. Therefore, it is our goal to establish a set of universal primitives that will serve the purposes of several different usage scenarios.

The first challenge that has to be addressed when defining such a general context representation is taking care not to impose a specific notion of context onto client applications. There have been many approaches that have proposed models that are general in the sense that they can be configured by the client application to use its notion of context, i.e. these models expect the application to define what context is. While these models can be configured by the client, most of them still have some built-in assumption about the meaning of certain context dimensions in terms of context classifications or ontologies. Often these factors lead to situations where different context dimensions are implicitly treated quite differently. Clearly, this is not desirable for a general context representation which needs to refrain from any predefined assumption about the notion of context used. Therefore, it is even necessary to go one step beyond the current approaches and completely abandon any presumptions about the meaning of context.

As a consequence, context in our approach is defined in terms of its effect rather than its meaning, to guarantee that the system built on top of it is free from any hidden or implicit assumptions. Applied to the situation of a data management system, this means that the effect of context on query evaluation needs to be specified. Thus, in our system context is seen as a set of additional parameters that in combination with the set of parameters specified by the query determines the result computed by the query processor. However, the roles of these two sets of parameters are quite different. Query parameters are explicit parameters in the sense that they were defined by the client of the data management system. Therefore, these parameters constitute a specification that the query processor has to follow exactly. In contrast, context parameters are implicit parameters as they are not specified by the client as part of the query but rather defined by the situation in which the query is sent to that data management system. As an implication of this, the role of context is not specification but rather a factor that is used to refine the results of query evaluation. Due to this notion of context, implicit parameters have to be considered as optional since they refine the functioning of the query processor rather than providing a specification for it to follow. Even in the absence of context information, query evaluation will return a fully defined result that is computed using a previously specified default representation of each object involved. An overview of this notion of context and its impact on the database system is presented in Figure 4.1.

As shown, a query can be abstracted in terms of an n-ary function q that is given as input to the query processor of the data management system. In a traditional database system, the result r of the query evaluation only depends on the set of parameters $\{x_1, x_2, \ldots, x_n\}$ that are specified in the query. As an extension, a context-aware query processor additionally considers a context $c(c_1, c_2, \ldots, c_m)$ during the evaluation of the query. Later in this section, we will come back to how this notion of context is represented exactly.

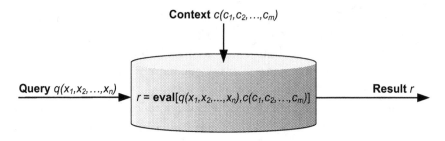

Figure 4.1: The role of context

The open notion of context introduced by our approach successfully avoids the first of the two pitfalls discussed at the beginning of this section. As it defines context in terms of its effect rather than is meaning, it is free from any assumptions that are specific to a given application domain. Nevertheless, it is important to establish a common understanding between the client application and the data management systems which context dimensions have to be handled in a given application domain. Context data may come from a variety of sources such as direct sensor access as well as context reasoning, inference or augmentation. As presented in Chapter 2, numerous powerful solutions for context processing exist already and the data management system presented in this thesis does therefore not offer any functionality to address these concerns. Instead, it is assumed that context processing is done outside the system by a context component specific to the application in question. In the following, we assume that a given set **NAMES** exists that contains the names of all valid context dimensions. Based on this given set, the number of possible dimensions for context values is limited by the concept of a *context space* as specified in Definition 1.

Definition 1 (Context Space). A *context space* represented by S denotes which context dimensions are relevant to an application of the version model for context-aware data management. It is defined as

$$S \;=\; \{name_1, name_2, \ldots, name_n\}$$

such that $\forall\, i : 1 \leq i \leq n \Rightarrow name_i \in$ **NAMES** and therefore $S \subseteq$ **NAMES**.

Note that a context space does not define a domain for the data value of the corresponding context dimension. As we see later, the decision to have a loosely typed context representation is motivated by the fact that it permits more flexibility in query evaluation.

Although a context space expresses a shared understanding about the context dimensions that exist in an application domain, it is of equal importance to also share a common representation of context. There are two possible solutions to address the problem of an application-specific representation of context. The first solution would be to define a comprehensive representation of context that embraces all possible notions of context that any current or future applications require. The other solution would be to build such a context representation based on an elementary approach that only provides the basic building blocks necessary to ensure that all existing solutions can be mapped to it. For several reasons, we have decided to follow the latter approach and rely on an elementary context representation. Our survey of existing context-aware applications has shown that most of these systems do not employ sophisticated context models but rather rely on collections of attribute values to capture context. Further, we believe that a basic yet flexible context representation is a better candidate for integration into a database management system. While a comprehensive representation would be constructed as a unification of existing approaches, an elementary representation is defined based on a metamodel of the concepts that are common to all known solutions. Hence, the comprehensive representation cannot cope with requirements that have not yet surfaced, whereas the basic representation is better equipped to do so.

In our version model, we have decided to use a context representation that is based on $\langle name, value \rangle$ pairs. Even though such tuple values constitute a very simple technique to capture context, most of the context models presented in Chapters 2 and 3 use this representation. This simple solution both fulfils the requirement of a basic representation and, at the same time, is already widely used. Again, we assume the existence of a given set VALUES that contains all possible values for the context dimensions defined by the NAMES given set. Based on these given sets, *context values*, as specified by Definition 2, form the basic building blocks.

Definition 2 (Context Value). A *context value* denoted by c is defined as a tuple $c = \langle name, value \rangle$ where $name \in$ NAMES and $value \in$ VALUES.

The equality of two context values c_i and c_j is defined as $c_i = c_j \Leftrightarrow name_i = name_j \wedge value_i = value_j$. Each context value captures one context dimension by associating it with a data point. A *context* as specified in Definition 3 aggregates individual context values into a collection of context values. Within a context, every dimension of the context space can be associated with at most one value, i.e. a context that contains multiple context values for the same dimension is not valid.

Definition 3 (Context). $C(S)$ denotes a *context* for a context space S and is represented as a set of context values

$$\begin{aligned} C(S) &= \{\langle name_1, value_1\rangle, \langle name_2, value_2\rangle, \ldots, \langle name_m, value_m\rangle\} \\ &= \{c_1, c_2, \ldots, c_m\} \end{aligned}$$

such that $\forall\, i : 1 \leq i \leq m \Rightarrow name_i \in S$ and $\forall\, c_i, c_j \in C : c_i \neq c_j \Rightarrow name_i \neq name_j$.

Based on this definition of context, it is now possible to revisit the role of context illustrated in Figure 4.1 and specify how context is handled and represented in our approach. In contrast to traditional data management systems that do not feature a system state to influence the operation of the system, a context-aware data management system is not stateless. As mentioned above, in such systems, context information is considered during the evaluation of context-aware queries. In order to fully support context-aware data management, it is therefore necessary to extend the information system with the notion of a context state. From a general point of view, this integration of context into the information system itself represents a move away from the paradigm of a stateless towards a stateful data management system. Definition 4 explains the understanding of the term as used in our approach.

Definition 4 (Context State). A *context state* denoted by $C_\star(S)$ is a special context, where $\forall\, name \in S : \exists\, \langle name, value\rangle \in C_\star(S)$.

In contrast to the concept of a context, a context state $C_\star(S)$ requires the presence of a context value for each dimension of S. However, if the value of a context dimension is unknown this can be expressed by a context value containing $\bot$ as value. Later in this section, we discuss how the context state can be influenced to reflect the current context of the client application. However, before going into these details of dynamic query processing, we continue with presenting the static organisation of our version model first.

4.2 An Object-Oriented Version Model

The version model for context-aware data management has been developed based on *OM* [200, 201], an extended E/R model for object-oriented data management. Even though the concepts introduced by our version model are universal and could also be applied to other data models such as the relational model, we have chosen to base it on one concrete model. The choice of the object-oriented OM model is motivated by the following reasons. OM has been designed to be semantically expressive, making it a powerful tool for database development. In order to do so, it features concepts that are absent in other models. Therefore, OM can encompass less expressive models. Such models can either be represented in OM based on their metamodels or by limiting OM to a subset of its concepts to obtain a model with equivalent semantics. Finally, OM itself has been specified completely in terms of metamodels expressed in OM. These metamodels constitute a firm basis for specification of the extension of OM for context-aware data management. Further, since most data management systems that provide support for OM are implemented based on these metamodels, they also serve as the starting point of the integration of the version model into one of these systems. It is therefore useful to give a brief overview of the main distinguishing features of OM before presenting how it was extended to support both revisional and alternative versions.

4.2.1 The OM Data Model

As the OM data model is an integration of object-oriented concepts into the well-known E/R model, it also builds on the notions of application entities and the relationships that exist between them. However, in contrast to the E/R model where there is some dispute whether entities represent entity types or entity sets, OM introduces a clear separation between the typing and the classification of entities. This distinction is achieved using a two-layered model. On the lower level, types describe the representation of entities, whereas the upper level captures the semantics of entities, based on the concept of collections. As OM is an object-oriented data model, all data and metadata is represented in terms of objects. Each object is defined by at least one object type that specifies the attributes and methods that its instances will have. Object types can form type hierarchies that are built using inheritance between supertypes and subtypes. In contrast to most existing object-oriented systems, OM supports the concept of multiple inheritance, i.e. a subtype may be defined as a specialisation of two or more direct supertypes. Apart from multiple inheritance that is defined statically, OM also features multiple instantiation enabling objects to dynamically gain or lose types that have either been defined along parallel inheritance paths in a type hierarchy or are not related through inheritance at all.

Based on the type model, a classification model uses collections to define flexible semantic groupings. Each collection has a member type that governs which objects can be contained in the corresponding collection. As it is not required to define a collection for each type, and it is possible to have multiple collections with the same member type, the typing layer and the classification layer are almost independent of each other. Similar to types, collections can build collection hierarchies based on the notion of supercollections and subcollections, to represent specialisations and generalisations of classification concepts. Again, a subcollection can have multiple supercollections and, vice versa, a supercollection can have multiple subcollections. Collections can either be sets, bags, rankings or sequences, depending on whether they can contain duplicates and if they are ordered or unordered. For example, a set is an unordered collection with no duplicates in the algebraic sense, whereas a sequence is an ordered collection that can contain duplicates. In contrast to a ranking that has an order but cannot contain duplicates, a bag is defined to be unordered with duplicates. Similar to multiple instantiation on the typing level, multiple classification permits an object to be a member of any collection that matches one of its types or a supertype of its types.

So far we have only described the concepts provided by the OM model to represent and classify entities, so-called objects. However, OM also features a relationship concept that is more powerful than the one known from the classical E/R model. Relationships in OM are represented by bi-directional associations defined in terms of a source and a target collection. Associations are a first-order concept and are defined as n-ary collections with $n > 1$. Much of the expressiveness of OM stems from the set of constraints it provides to control several aspects of a data model. Some constraints such as the relationships between subtypes and supertypes as well as subcollections and supercollections have already been discussed. In addition, the OM model also features cardinality constraints that govern the participation of objects as the source or target of an association. As in other extended E/R models, these cardinalities are specified in terms of a minimum and maximum value that expresses the number of objects to which an object can be linked. These so-called integrity constraints are complemented by classification constraints that control the membership of objects in collections. For example, the subcollection relationship between two collections can be declared to be either equal, strict or total. An equal constraint ensures that both collections contain the same elements in the same number and order. To assure that a sequence collection is a subsequence in terms of a segment of its super-collection it can be declared as a strict subcollection. Finally, when a bag must contain all occurrences of elements contained in its supercollection, it is defined to be a total subcollection. Additional classification con-straints deal with collection families, i.e. a collection with either multiple supercollections or subcollections. For example two or more subcollec-tions of a collection can be defined to be disjoint or to form a cover or a partition of their supercollection. Vice versa, if a collection has two or more supercollections, it can be defined to be the intersection of those collections. Finally, the last class of constraints, evolution constraints, monitor how a database grows and changes over time. It is, for example, possible to specify which types an object can gain and lose in the future, to limit the scope of object evolution.

Data models are specified in OM either by using its graphical notation or the textual data definition language. This data definition language is a subset of the *Object Model Language (OML)* [182] which also contains a data manipulation and a query language. The query language is based on a collection algebra that defines a set of operators that manipulate and process collections as well as associations. Apart from being used for data definition, manipulation and querying, the union of the three languages contained in OML also serves as a declarative object-oriented implemen-tation language for object methods, triggers and database macros. While many conceptual models have no direct platform support, a family of data management systems [168, 296, 167] has been built that allow OM data models to be implemented directly. These platforms cover a wide variety of requirements, such as rapid prototyping, as well as productive oper-ation both as light-weight in-memory and server databases. During its existence, the OM model has been extended a number of times to address the requirements of special application domains. These projects have led to a temporal data management system [270], a next-generation file sys-tem [228], and an extension of the model that is capable of role-based modelling of interactions in databases [219] to capture access control, context-aware and proactive operations.

As mentioned before, one reason for choosing the OM data model is the fact that it is capable of capturing its complete specification in terms of metamodels. This level of expressiveness has been the reason why most of the systems providing support for OM have been built based on this metamodel. As a consequence, they also represent and manage the entire metadata of a database in terms of objects, collections and associations. One advantage of this approach is the fact that the same language can be used to define, manipulate and query both data and metadata. Another benefit is that the implementation of extensions to these systems is relatively straightforward, as new system objects can be introduced at any time. An example of such a metamodel is given in Figure 4.2 using the graphical notation of the OM data model.

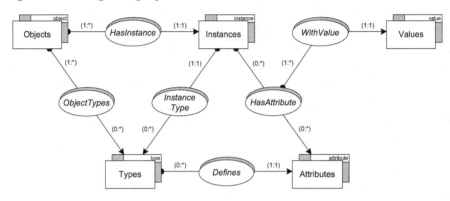

Figure 4.2: Metamodel of an object in OM

The model shows the definition of an object in OM. In the upper left-hand corner the collection **Objects** with member type **object** is depicted. It contains all objects that exist in a database at any point in time. The fact that OM supports multiple instantiation is captured by the fact that each object is linked to one or more instances through the *HasInstance* association. Both objects and instances are related to the **Types** collection through associations *ObjectTypes* and *InstanceType*, respectively. Whereas an object can be linked to one or more types as expressed by the cardinality (1:*) as a consequence of multiple instantiation, an instance is bound to exactly one type as indicated by the (1:1) constraint. However, not all constraints that are required to ensure the validity of an object can be expressed in the graphical notation. For instance, all types referenced by the instances of an object have to be referenced by the object itself. Also, an object has to be linked to an instance of each type with which it is associated. Hence, the number of associated types and instances has to be the same. These additional constraints are captured by the following condition given in OM collection algebra.

$$ObjectTypes = HasInstance \circ InstanceType$$

The left-hand side of the condition represents all links between objects and their types as a set of pairs. Analogously, the expression given on the right-hand side is also a set of pairs consisting of an object and a type. However, it relates objects to all types of the instances of these objects. As bi-directional associations are relations in the mathematical sense, this is achieved by using the composition (○) of the *HasInstance* and *InstanceType* association.

As can be seen in the figure, each type contained in collection Types defines a set of zero or more attributes. Type attribute specifies how attributes are represented in the system. For each attribute defined by a type, an instance of that type has to specify a value. This relationship is captured by the *HasAttribute* association between collections Instances and Attributes. While it is not possible in OM to attach attributes to relationships, it is possible to define complex n-ary relationships by combining multiple binary associations. In contrast to other proposals for relationships of a higher degree, this approach has the advantage that it defines an order among the associations. In the given model, *HasAttribute* is the primary relationship, while the *WithValue* association, that links a value to a pair of an instance and an attribute, depends on it. As with objects, instances and types, the constraints between instances, types and attributes cannot be completely specified in the graphical model. To express that an instance has to specify a value for each attribute defined by its type, the condition given below is necessary.

$$HasAttribute = InstanceType \circ Defines$$

Again, the condition is expressed using a composition of two associations.

4.2.2 Integrating Revisions and Variants

To support revisional and context-aware data, the metamodel presented in Figure 4.2 has been extended with concepts that allow objects to be versioned. Inspired by the version models discussed in the previous chapter, the notion of a version has been refined to be either a revision or a variant of an object. Each of the new concepts represents one dimension of our version model. Revisions capture the evolution of the database over time. While they document how an object has been updated and revised, they are not intended to represent temporal data. From the three notions of time—transaction, valid and user-defined time—presented earlier, only transaction time is supported. Each time a revision of an object is created, it is marked with a timestamp ts representing the current logical or physical time. Therefore, revisions capture the time when a change has been recorded in the database. As the sequence of times-tamps $T_{obj} = \{ts_1, ts_2, \ldots, ts_n\}$ assigned to the revisions of an object grows monotonically, it imposes a total order on the set of revisions. Revisional versions of an object o can therefore be identified based on a tuple $\langle oid, ts \rangle$ consisting of an object identifier and a timestamp that indicates when the corresponding version was created. The revision selected by the given tuple is a revision of the object with identifier $oid_o = oid$ that has the timestamp satisfying $max(\{ts_o | ts_o \in T_{obj} \text{ and } ts_o \leq ts\})$. As most queries to a database management system will request current data, a special revision is the one with the timestamp $ts = max(T_{obj})$. We will refer to this revision as the latest revision of an object. Note that the status of latest version will be assigned to different revisions over time as the database is updated. The concept of latest revision is therefore only meaningful at a fixed point in time.

The second dimension of our version model provides support for context-dependent data. Similar to the engineering databases and software configuration systems presented in the previous chapter, our model relies on variants to represent context-dependent alternatives of the same data. Different variants of an object are distinguished using the concept of a variant context as given in Definition 5 that describes in which situation the corresponding variant is an appropriate representation of the object.

Definition 5 (Variant Context). A *variant context* for the context space S is a special context denoted by $C_v(S)$.

In the following, the context values contained in $C_v(S)$ are also called either the properties or the characteristics of a variant. Whenever a variant of an object is created, a set of context values characterising the new variant has to be given explicitly by the creator. The context defined by these properties has to be different from all variant contexts of existing variants of the same object.

In contrast to revisions, addressing a specific variant of an object is not straightforward. Not unlike revisions, variants are also identified by a tuple $\langle oid, C(S) \rangle$, but in this case, it consists of an object identifier and a context. While the mathematical properties of the timestamp sequence used to describe revisions have rendered the selection of the desired revision trivial, there is no order relation between the properties of two variants. To select the desired variant, the system has to match the given context $C(S)$ to the variant context $C_v(S)$ specified by each variant of the object. As this process is rather complex, we defer the detailed presentation of this matching algorithm to Section 4.3 that discusses query processing. A concept similar to the one of latest revision for revisional data is the notion of the main derivation as presented in the previous chapter. As shown in existing systems, it is useful to designate one variant of an object as its default variant to cope with the situation where the matching of a variant specification to the variant descriptions leads to ambiguous results or no context information is available. In some systems, the status of default variant can be reassigned to different variants of an object during system evolution. In our model, we have however decided not to offer this functionality, as we believe it should be the developer's choice at design-time to specify the default representation of the created data.

If both revisional and alternative versions are to be supported by the version model, both dimensions characterised above have to be combined. It is important to note that the two dimensions are independent of each other as it would be possible to construct systems that only support one of them. This orthogonality is further supported by the fact that both dimensions evolve along different axes. While revisions progress along the time axis, alternatives grow along the variation axis. Taken alone, both axes are one-dimensional, and, consequently, a two-dimensional version space will result when they are combined. Identical to most existing approaches, our model uses a version graph to organise this two-dimensional version space. Although, in principle, there are several different possibilities as to how this version graph can be defined, it is the requirements of an application domain that finally shape the concrete layout of the graph. For the following reasons, we believe that existing solutions cannot be applied unaltered to the domain of context-aware data management. First, the internal organisation of the version graph depends directly on the nature of the expected queries, as certain graph structures will favour some types of queries over others. Further, some conditions presented above, such as the uniqueness of properties among the variants of an object, are closely related to the intended use of the model. Ensuring such constraints can be simple in one graph structure while cumbersome and difficult in another. Finally, there are some questions arising from the combination of revisions and variants that need to be addressed based on the requirements of the application domain. For instance, the scope of revisions and variants has to be clearly defined. While in the one-dimensional case the scope of a version was the entire object, in the combined case there is a choice. A revision could either be a version of the entire object or of a variant of the object. Vice versa, alternatives could be defined in the scope of a single revision or of the entire object.

In the following, we will discuss the advantages and disadvantages of defining the scope of revisions and variants one way or the other. At the same time, this discussion of possible graph structures will also serve as a motivation for the approach that we have chosen for our model. As shown in Figure 4.3, three candidate solutions to organise the version graph can be obtained by simply enumerating all possible definitions of the scope of revisions and variants. The version graph resulting if both revisions and variants are defined to have the entire object as their scope is depicted in Figure 4.3(a). As can be seen in the figure, the object is linked to a set of round nodes representing the revisions and a set of triangular nodes representing the variants. The different versions of the object are in turn associated with its instances shown as small circles at the bottom of the figure. Instead of linking each version with each instance, we have chosen to introduce the artificial concept of an instance group, represented as a dashed oval, to render the figure more legible. The concept of the latest revision and the default variant are illustrated in the figure using bold arrows linking the object to revision ts_3 and to variant P_2. The labels of revisions and variants are meant to suggest that they are distinguished based on timestamps and properties, respectively. This organisation of the version graph provides direct access to both revisions and variants. However, there are also several limitations implied by structuring the graph in this way. Consider, for example, a query requesting the latest revision of variant P_3. To answer this query, both instance groups linked to P_3 first have to be retrieved. Then, starting from ts_3, the sequence of revisions has to be accessed backwards until one of the two previously retrieved instance groups is encountered along this path. In other words, the query is evaluated by computing the intersection of the revision and the variant dimension. Another difficulty arises from queries that need to find out what variants of an object exist for a given revision. Such queries occur when an application wants the variant of an object that matches context $C(S)$ at time $t < ts_2$. To find the set of variants that are eligible at time t, the sequence of revisions has to be traversed in forward order until $t \geq ts_2$, to collect all instance groups that have been created up to that point in time. Then, as before, these instance groups have to be cross-referenced with the variant dimension to find the variants P_1 and P_2.

The problem of having to search all revisions or variants to find the one that matches a version group retrieved through the other access

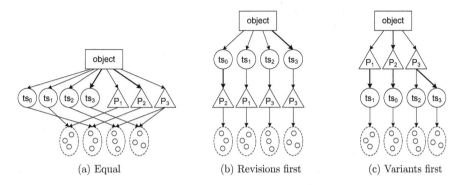

(a) Equal   (b) Revisions first   (c) Variants first

Figure 4.3: Different organisations of the version graph

path can be remedied by setting the equal status of both concepts aside. This implies, however, that one of the two concepts is dependent on the other and thus such a version graph organisation will only favour certain queries. Figure 4.3(b) depicts the same object as Figure 4.3(a) structured in a graph that gives priority to versions over variants. As can be seen from the figure, the processing of the query for the variants of the object at time $t < ts_2$ is now straightforward as the variants are directly linked to the revisions. However, computing which variant of the object matches a specified context $C(S)$ is now far more complex, as the set of variants is no longer accessible directly and has to be constructed first. Another issue that arises from this organisation of the version graph is the fact that a single variant can now be represented by more than one node, as has happened with variant P_3 in the figure. As the properties describing the variant would typically be stored in this node, the question whether these characteristics of a variant can also change over time has to be addressed. We believe that such functionality is not required, as properties are essentially metadata that is used exclusively by the system. However, analogous to temporal databases, where minor errors can be corrected without changing the history of an object, our model should provide the possibility for system administrators to edit property sets, if required. In such a scenario, the properties of the individual variants would have to be kept consistent at all times either through managing their redundancy or through a more complex graph structure.

A further question posed by both the graph structure presented in Figures 4.3(a) and (b) is when an object can gain variants. One possible solution is to define all variants when the object is created, while another would be to have the possibility that an object can gain variants over time. Additionally, if the second approach is chosen, it has to be decided whether capturing the times when such an operation happens is important. Defining the evolution of an object to include the creation of new variants is useful to cope with the advent of new requirements at a later stage of the lifetime of an application. However, similar to the latest revision that provides access to the most up-to-date version of an object, the current set of variants should be favoured over the management of historical states of an object. Figure 4.3(c) therefore shows a version graph where variants are given priority over revisions. Due to the on-line nature of variants, we believe that it is important to optimise the version graph towards queries involving mainly alternative versions. As can be seen from the figure, the currently existing variants are linked to the object and can thus be accessed directly. Each variant is linked to its revisions that have been made over time. As indicated by the bold arrow, again the latest revision is marked specially to enable faster look-ups. Although off-line queries discussed above are supported by this version graph, their evaluation is burdened with a performance penalty resulting from the fact that the history of objects has to be computed. Nevertheless, we have chosen to base our version model on this third approach of organising the version graph. In Figure 4.4, we show how the metamodel of an OM object has been extended to accommodate revisions and variants in the discussed manner.

In contrast to the metamodel of the traditional OM object presented in Figure 4.2, the metamodel of the versioned object does not link objects to their instances directly. Instead, the model has been extended to include two additional collections, **Revisions** and **Variants**. True to the intention of favouring variants over revisions motivated above, the path connecting the **Objects** collection with the **Instances** collection goes to variants first before following revisions. Hence, an object is linked to one or more variants through the *HasVariants* association. As indicated by the dashed arrow, association *DefaultVariant* is a subcollection of *HasVariants*, capturing the fact that every object has exactly one default variant. The same design has been used to connect a variant to a non-empty set of revisions. Again the association *LatestRevision* is modelled as a subcollection of the |*HasRevisions*| association, denoting one revision as the most recent version of the object. To establish an order among the revisions of a variant, association |*HasRevisions*| has been declared to be a ranking represented graphically by vertical bars surrounding the name of the association. While this ranking orders the revisions within the scope of a variant, it does not guarantee a complete order over all revisions of an

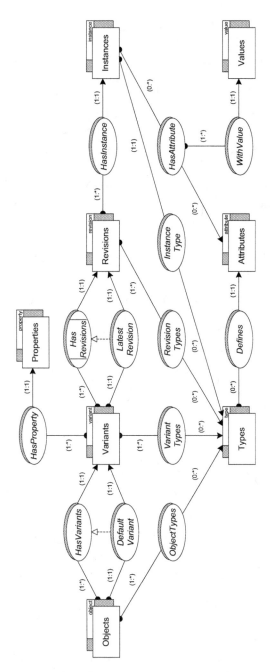

Figure 4.4: Metamodel of an extended object in OM

object. Therefore, type revision still defines a timestamp attribute that is used to capture the sequence of revisional versions of the entire object.

Each variant contained in collection Variants is associated with one or more properties through the *HasProperty* association. The condition that variant properties do not partake in the revisional evolution of an object is ensured by linking them directly to the variant concept itself. As the revisions of an object are referenced through one of its variants, this model ensures that they all share the same properties. The additional condition that it is illegal for an object to have two or more variants with the same set of properties cannot be expressed using the graphical notation. We use the algebraic expression below to specify this characteristic of our version model.

$$\forall\, o \in \mathsf{Objects},\ \forall\, v_1, v_2 \in rng(\mathit{HasVariants}\ dr(\{o\})) :$$
$$v_1 \neq v_2 \Rightarrow rng(\mathit{HasProperty}\ dr(\{v_1\})) \neq rng(\mathit{HasProperty}\ dr(\{v_2\}))$$

The expression defines v_1 and v_2 to be variants of an object o by first restricting the domain of the *HasVariants* association to only occurrences of o. The domain restriction operation dr constructs an intermediate association that only includes links that have one of the objects contained in the given set as their source. Then, the range operation rng traverses the links expressed by an association and returns the target objects only. In the above condition, the result of this algebraic expression will be the set of all variants of the object o. The same construct is used in the implication stating that if two variants of the same object are different then the set of properties defined by them is also different. Here *HasProperty* is restricted to v_1 and v_2, respectively. The set of property values is then obtained by applying the rng operation to the resulting intermediate association.

The *ObjectTypes* and *InstanceType* associations that capture which types are defined for an object and its instances have been taken on from the original metamodel. However, in the metamodel describing the versioned object, they are complemented with two additional associations, *VariantTypes* and *RevisionTypes*. Although an object can have multiple instances in OM, versions of an object are always defined for the entire object including all its instances. As a consequence, this means that our version model will not be able to track if an object evolves in terms of gaining or losing instances. Although this is a serious disadvantage, if the model were to be used to support the versioning of the database schema, we have decided not to offer this functionality for the time being. Therefore, the new associations that capture which types are defined for a revision and for a variant have to specify the same set of types as the object through association *ObjectTypes*. Again, this condition cannot be expressed graphically and is therefore given in algebraic form below.

$$\forall\, o \in \mathsf{Objects},\ \forall\, v \in rng(\mathit{HasVariants}\ dr(\{o\})) :$$
$$rng(\mathit{ObjectTypes}\ dr(\{o\})) = rng(\mathit{VariantTypes}\ dr(\{v\}))$$

$$\forall\, o \in \mathsf{Objects},\ \forall\, r \in rng(\mathit{HasVariants}\ dr(\{o\}) \circ \mathit{HasRevisions}) :$$
$$rng(\mathit{ObjectTypes}\ dr(\{o\})) = rng(\mathit{RevisionTypes}\ dr(\{r\}))$$
$$\wedge\ rng(\mathit{ObjectTypes}\ dr(\{o\})) = rng(\mathit{HasInstance}\ dr(\{r\}) \circ \mathit{InstanceType})$$

The first expression ensures that all variants of an object o define the same set of types as the object itself. Similar to the expression discussed before, this is achieved by restricting the domain of association *Variant-Types* once to each variant v of o and then comparing the range of the intermediate association to the set of types associated to o through *ObjectTypes*. The second expression contains two conditions. On the one hand, it uses the same approach as the first expression to check that all revisions of an object specify the same set of types as the object o itself. On the other hand, the second clause of the conjunction additionally controls that all instances associated with a revision r of object o also define this set of types. This part of the expression replaces the condition presented in the traditional model, ensuring that the types of the instances of an object match the types defined for the object.

Compared to the original metamodel of an object in OM, collections Revisions and Variants and a few associations linking them to other collections are the only additional concepts introduced in the extended meta-model. The rest of the collections and associations remains unchanged, which means that just the path connecting an object to its instances is now more complex than before. Both members of collections Types and Instances continue to be associated with attribute metadata represented by objects belonging to collection Attributes. Also, data is still linked to an attribute of an instance using the concept of the ternary association *WithValue* that has the *HasAttribute* as its source.

4.2.3   Identifying and Referencing Objects

Having discussed the internal structure of a single object in terms of its version graph, it is important to specify how the different parts of an object can be identified and referenced from the outside. As with any other object-oriented systems, platforms built to support the OM data model use the notion of object identifiers to reference a database object. An object defined by the original model presented in the previous section is completely identified using a simple identifier of the form o927. However, as an object can have multiple instances of types that have been defined along different paths of an inheritance hierarchy, access to data can still be ambiguous. For instance, if two parallel types define an attribute with the same name, there is no way of knowing which instance of the referenced object should be accessed. Therefore, to unambiguously access the data stored in an object, both an object identifier and a so-called browsing type that defines in which role the object is accessed must be given.

Although a goal of our version model is to retain this interpretation of object identifier to ensure its compatibility with the OM data model as originally specified, an extension of the format of object identifiers is inevitable. In the extended metamodel of an OM object, instances are associated with revisions and it is therefore necessary that each revision can be addressed directly. Assuming that at every point in time t at most one revision of an object is created in the system, it suffices to extend the object identifier with the corresponding timestamp. However, to keep track of variants and to enforce the underlying orthogonality of the two concepts, it is also worthwhile to include an indication in the object identifier to which variant a revision belongs. In Definition 6 we specify the syntax and the semantics of the extended object identifier used to reference objects in our system.

Definition 6 (Extended Object Identifier). The format of the extended object identifier that is used to reference versioned objects as a whole or in parts is given in Backus-Naur Form (BNF) below.

$$\texttt{"o"} \; oid \; [\; \texttt{"@"} \; rev \;] \; [\; \texttt{"["} \; var \; \texttt{"]"} \;]$$

The object itself is referenced by the oid part of the extended identifier, whereas its revisions and variants are identified by the two specifiers rev and var, respectively. An example of an extended object identifier would be o927@9[3] which references variant 3 in revision 9 of object 927.

As can be seen from the definition of the extended object identifier, the specification of both a revision and variant specifier are optional. This flexibility has been built into the object identifier to support both specific and generic references, as introduced in Chapter 3. In our model, a specific reference to an object is made using the full format of the object identifier, allowing a specific version of the object to be pinpointed. Generic references, however, are supported through partially specified identifiers that reference all versions, or a subset of the versions, of an object. At run-time, such partially specified identifiers are completed by the system to form a fully specified reference. To illustrate how generic references work in our model, it is necessary to first understand how identifiers are assigned to the versions of an object. An example of a versioned object is given in Figure 4.5.

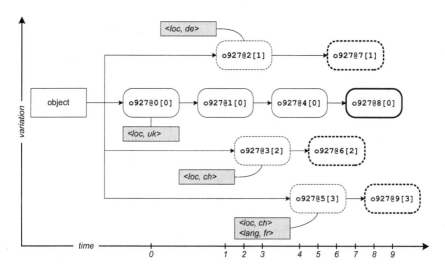

Figure 4.5: Example of a versioned object

The figure shows the evolution of object 927 along the time and variation axes. The object itself is symbolised by the rectangle shown at the left hand side of the figure. Its evolution in terms of revision and variants is represented by the tree rooted at the object. Each version of the object is shown as a rounded rectangle containing the fully specified object identifier of the corresponding revision or variant. At time $ts = 0$, the first version of the object is created. It is the default variant of the object and, as indicated by the context value $\langle loc, uk \rangle$, its content has been designed for the United Kingdom. Note that, in our version model, the first variant that is created for an object and all its successors are assumed to be the default variants. This is indicated in the figure by representing these versions with a rounded rectangle delineated by a solid line. The same fact, however, is also represented in the object identifier as all default variants have $var = 0$ as their variant specifier.

At time $ts = 1$, the default variant is updated and a new revision created. Note that the revision specifier of the new version is incremented to
$rev = 1$, while the variant specifier is left unchanged. Also, the properties associated with the original revision of a variant are not duplicated
to its successor as our model does not allow properties to be changed
over time. The creation of a variant of the object is shown in the figure
to occur at time $ts = 2$, when a variant for Germany is added to the
object. As mentioned before, to create a variant, a set of context values
has to be provided that is different from all existing variant properties.
As the set consisting of the context value $\langle loc, de \rangle$ is different from the
set specified by the default variant, the new variant is valid and can be
created. The variant specifier in the object identifier of the new version
is set to $var = 1$ to reflect the fact that this version is an alternative to
the existing versions of the object. This situation is captured graphically
in the figure by representing variants other than the default variant with
a rounded rectangle delineated by a dashed line.

Later, two additional variants are created at times $ts = 3$ and $ts = 5$
to reflect the requirements of Switzerland and the French speaking part of
Switzerland. Again, the rule that a new variant has to define properties
that do not match any of the previously defined sets has to be observed.
Note that the set $\{\langle loc, ch \rangle\}$ of variant 2 and the set $\{\langle loc, ch \rangle, \langle lang, fr \rangle\}$
of variant 3 are not in conflict as they are not considered to be the same,
due to the additional value in the properties of variant 3. The most
recent revisions of each variant are those furthest to the right and are
depicted as rounded rectangles delimited by a bold line. In contrast to
default variants, where it is possible to encode their special status in
the object identifier using variant specifier $var = 0$, distinguishing the
latest revision in such a way is not possible, as versions gain and lose
that status as the object evolves. Hence, this metadata about the object
is managed by a look-up table stored in the object itself that maps each
variant specifier to the revision specifier of the latest version.

In order to access the data represented by an object, it is necessary to
reference the required version of the object using a fully specified object
identifier. As previously stated, generic references are supported based on
partially specified identifiers and hence there has to be a way to complete
such partial identifiers. Having defined the notions of latest revisions
and default variants, our model can rely on these concepts to determine
which version is referenced by an incomplete object identifier. If the
object identifier does not contain a revision specifier, the corresponding
specifier of latest revision is inserted. Otherwise, our model uses the

variant specifier of the default variant if the object identifier omits this information. Finally, if an object identifier consists of the object specifier only, both the latest revision and the default variant are accessed. In this way, our version model is also capable of transparently interfacing with client applications that do not require the management of revisional or alternative data. Table 4.1 shows three examples of such completions of generic references.

Partial Identifier	Completed Identifier
o927[3]	o927@9[3]
o927@3	o927@1[0]
o927	o927@8[0]

Table 4.1: Completing generic references

The first line shows how an object identifier that omits the revision specifier is completed. The given references specifies that variant 3 of object 927 should be accessed. Coming back to the example given in Figure 4.5, this partial object identifier can be completed to include the revision specifier $rev = 9$, as this is the latest revision of the specified variant. The case presented in the second line of the table is more complex. As the object identifier does not reference a specific variant, the default variant has to be accessed. However, in order to do so, it is not sufficient to simply insert the variant specifier $var = 0$ pointing to the default variant. As can be seen from the figure, there is no version of the object that is identified by the resulting completed object identifier. Hence, it is necessary to also adapt the revision specifier to obtain a valid object identifier. The revision specifier in the scope of the default variant that corresponds to $ts = 3$ in the scope of the whole object can be found by traversing the revision chain of the default variant to find $max(T_{var=0}) \leq 3$. Doing so, the correct revision specifier $rev = 1$ is found, and the complete object identifier as shown in the table can be constructed. Finally, if both the revision and the variant specifier are omitted, the latest revision of the default variant are accessed. This completion process is again very straightforward, as the revision specifier $rev = 8$ and the variant specifier $var = 0$ can simply be inserted into the object identifier.

An important aspect of object-oriented systems is the fact that objects do not exist in isolation but are interconnected with other objects to form complex graph structures. To form such structures, the OM data model provides two concepts that allow an object to be associated with other objects. Simple references, as known from most object-oriented programming languages, can be expressed by defining an attribute that points to another object. Such simple references are managed within an object. They are uni-directional and do not provide referential integrity. When the referenced object is deleted, the problem of a dangling reference can arise if the value of the corresponding attribute of the referencing object is not updated accordingly. To address these issues, the OM data model provides the previously mentioned concept of associations that expresses relationships between objects both at the conceptual and the implementation level. Analogous to collections that contain object identifiers, associations are also represented by objects, but contain tuples of object identifiers. These object identifier tuples capture which object is connected to which other object. Hence, associations are managed outside the objects as first-order concepts. They can be navigated in both ways as they are completely symmetrical. Due to the fact that they express references among objects explicitly, associations can be directly addressed in the query language, based on their name. Finally, associations provide a natural point in the system to manage and enforce cardinality constraints as well as to prevent referential inconsistencies.

The question arises whether relationships between objects should be versioned together with the objects. We believe, that the information content of an object-oriented database consists of both the objects and the relationships. Therefore, the capability to version relationships is desirable and should be supported by our version model for context-aware data management. In the case of simple references, versioning is supported by the fact that these relationships are expressed as attribute values of an object. Using specific references, different versions of the referencing object can point to different versions of the referenced object. As a consequence of the versioning of the object containing the reference, the relationship itself appears to be versioned. Clearly, this solution suffers from the deficiency that the relationship cannot be versioned independently from the object. Again, associations provide an elegant solution to this shortcoming. As associations are themselves objects, they can have revisions and variants as with any other object in the system. Therefore associations can be used to capture any state of the relationships in an object-oriented system that is specified based on the OM data model. While the fact that both objects and relationships can be versioned using one set of concepts validates our approach, it also demonstrates the power of the OM data model at the same time.

4.3 Context-Aware Query Processing

Based on the presented version model that defines how the revisions and variants of an object are organised, a query processing mechanism has been defined. In contrast to traditional database management systems where the result of a query is entirely defined by the query itself, in our system the outcome of evaluating a query depends on additional factors. While the revision of an object that will be accessed during query processing depends on the current time, the retrieved variant can change according to the context in which the query is evaluated. However, similar to the definition of the extended object identifiers, care has to be taken to ensure that the augmented query processor is compatible with systems that do not require additional functionality. Thus, the query processor has to be able to also produce meaningful results in the absence of time and context specifications. Apart from query evaluation, compatibility with traditional applications also has an impact on the query language used by the system. While some changes have to be made, it is not desirable to define a whole new query language to profit from the additional features of the model. Rather, all modifications should be made in the form of optional extensions to the language that can be omitted if not required. In the remainder of this section, our approach to define such a query processor will be presented. While queries along both the time and the variation axis are possible, the discussion will focus on the context-aware aspects of the system in terms of selecting appropriate variants. The processing of queries involving time has been well researched in the field of temporal database systems and is thus not presented here.

4.3.1 Influencing the Context State

As mentioned before, all context factors that can affect the evaluation of a query are captured by the context values within the context state $C_\star(S)$. Influences other than these values will have no effect on context-aware query processing as proposed by our approach. Therefore it is important that client applications can configure the context state to reflect all relevant context information. To provide support for influencing the context state, two major issues have to be addressed. The first issue is to design interfaces that enable applications to communicate their present state to the system. The second issue is to determine the sphere of influence of these communicated context values on a conceptual level. While the range of interfaces supported by our system will be presented later in

Level	Description
global	The global level is the most general level and allows context values to be specified that apply to all queries evaluated by the system.
session	Context values specified at the session level influence all queries that are evaluated in the corresponding client session.
command	The finest level of granularity is the command level that allows context values to be specified that influence a certain set of commands only.

Table 4.2: Granularity levels of $C_\star(S)$

Section 4.4 describing the implementation of the version model, at the moment, we focus on the scope of the context state of an application. Depending on the application requirements, it makes sense to consider influencing $C_\star(S)$ at different levels of granularity. For example, certain context values, such as the preferred language or the location of a user, are valid within a single client session only, while other factors may be shared among several sessions or even the entire system. Finally, it is also imaginable that certain applications require the context to change within a single query, to perform inter-context computations combining data valid in separate contexts. Based on the application requirements presented in Chapter 2, we have decided to offer three levels at which $C_\star(S)$ can be influenced. An overview of these granularity levels is given in Table 4.2.

Introducing a hierarchy of granularity levels raises the question of precedence among the different levels. As it is possible to define context values with the same name and different values at several levels, the value that will be used by the system has to be defined. The most natural solution is to consider the values defined at the lowest level first. Therefore, a value defined at the command level takes precedence over values defined at the session level, while session level values are used before global values. This simple approach using inheritance and overriding is, however, not sufficient to cover all application requirements, and further refinements are necessary. When a client application influences a subset of the context state at the session level, context values defined at the global level only could interfere with the requirements of the application. Assume for example, that the global context state contains the value

Mode	Description
inherit	The inherit mode is the default mode and uses values from a higher level if they are not specified by the level that is currently used to define the context.
replace	Context values that are not specified by the defining level are assumed to be undefined, as the replace mode blocks inheritance.
combine	In the combine mode, values from the level used to define the context and all the above levels are integrated.

Table 4.3: Precedence modes

$\langle lang,\ fr \rangle$ and the application sets the value $\langle loc,\ ch \rangle$ at the session level. As the language context is not set by the application, it will be inherited from the global level and thus all subsequent queries are evaluated in the context of the French speaking part of Switzerland. Depending on the application scenario, this result could be unintended and hence it should be possible to block the inheritance of context values in some cases. In addition to the three granularity levels, a context-aware query processor therefore also needs to give control over the precedence among those levels to the application. Table 4.3 details three modes that can be used in conjunction with the granularity levels to obtain better configurability. As an example of how the combined mode is used, assume that the session level defines the context value $\langle lang,\ de \rangle$ while the context value $\langle lang,\ en \rangle$ is defined at the global level. The resulting context state $C_\star(S)$ will then reflect that both English and German language variants are valid.

4.3.2 Context Matching

Context matching determines which variant of an object is accessed during query evaluation. It uses a scoring function f_s that compares the context state $C_\star(S)$ to the variant context $C_v(S)$ of each variant v of an object o. In this comparison, f_s assigns a score value to every object variant, which is then used to select the highest scoring variant. For a variant to be selected, however, its score has to be higher than a certain threshold that can be configured in the system. If no variant scores higher than this threshold or if two or more variants are assigned the highest score, the default variant is used instead. The notion of thresholds controlling variant selection has been introduced to prevent unintended results in situations where, due to unexpected context values, all variants are assigned a low score or multiple variants obtain the highest score. The solution of returning the default variant in these cases has been chosen to ensure deterministic behaviour under any circumstances that would not be guaranteed if a variant were to be selected at random.

As f_s ranks the different variants in terms of their suitability in the current context, context matching uses a best match rather than an exact match algorithm. This approach is motivated by the special characteristics of context-aware query processing. True to the nature of context-aware computing as described in Chapter 2, the context state of the system does not represent an integral part of the query, but rather optional information that is used by the system to augment or enhance the query evaluation process. Apart from the fact that the system also has to produce meaningful results when no context information is available, another consequence of this understanding of the notion of context is that it should not be regarded as a specification that has to be followed exactly. However, in order to support this notion of context, it has to be possible for the query processor to use the default variant of an object instead of another variant at any time during query evaluation. This assumption that the default variant is always a valid choice to represent an object is a strong premise as it will have a noticeable impact on how variants of an application object have to be designed in order to obtain the desired context-aware behaviour of the whole application.

Based on these considerations, the matching algorithm that is expressed in Figure 4.6 in terms of the operations of the algebraic query language has been defined. Given the object o that needs to be accessed by the query processor and the context state $C_\star(S)$, the algorithm returns the best matching variant. If a best matching variant according to the conditions described earlier is not found, the default variant is returned. As specified by the algebraic expression on line 1, the algorithm begins by retrieving the set of all variants V_0 of the given object o. In the next step on line 2, the algorithm uses the map operation ($\propto$) to generate a set V_1 that contains tuples relating each variant to its set of property values. The map operation takes as arguments a set and a function. It then returns the set that results from applying the given function to each member element in the given set. Here, the function $x \rightarrow (x \times rng(\text{HasProperty } dr(\{x\})))$ is mapped to the set V_0, causing every element $x \in V_0$ to be represented by a corresponding tuple in

V_1 specified by the function using the tuple constructor ($\times$). To illustrate the functioning of the map operation, assume a possible member of V_1 could be the tuple $\langle v_1, \{\langle lang, en \rangle, \langle loc, uk \rangle \} \rangle$. The map operation is used once again in the following processing step, when the function $x \rightarrow (dom(x) \times f_s(rng(x), C_\star(S)))$ is mapped to the set V_1 on line 3. In the resulting set V_2, each element of V_1 is represented by a tuple relating the variant to its score value computed by f_s according to the context state $C_\star(S)$. Without making any assumption about the definition of f_s, the member of V_2 corresponding to the example tuple given above might take the form $\langle v_1, 0.75 \rangle$. Note the use of the *dom* and *rng* operation to access the left-hand or right-hand side of a tuple, respectively.

$\text{MATCH}(o, C_\star(S))$
1 $V_0 \leftarrow rng(\textit{HasVariants } dr(\{o\}))$
2 $V_1 \leftarrow V_0 \propto (x \rightarrow (x \times rng(\textit{HasProperty } dr(\{x\}))))$
3 $V_2 \leftarrow V_1 \propto (x \rightarrow (dom(x) \times f_s(C_\star(S), rng(x))))$
4 $s_{max} \leftarrow max(rng(V_2))$
5 $V_3 \leftarrow V_2 \% (x \rightarrow rng(x) = s_{max})$
6 **if** $|V_3| = 1 \wedge s_{max} \geq s_{min}$
7   **then** $v \leftarrow V_3 \, nth \, 1$
8   **else** $v \leftarrow rng(\textit{DefaultVariant } dr(\{o\})) \, nth \, 1$
9 **return** v

Figure 4.6: Matching algorithm

Based on V_2, the maximum score value s_{max} over all variants of the object o is computed on line 4. On line 5, this maximum score is then used to select the variants that reach this value. In order to do so, the matching algorithm uses the selection operation (%) that applies a Boolean function to each element of a set. If the Boolean function returns *true*, the corresponding element will be included in the result set and omitted otherwise. To only include variants with the maximum score in V_3, the algorithm uses the predicate function $x \rightarrow rng(x) = s_{max}$. Finally, lines 6–8 check if only a single variant has obtained the maximum score and whether this score is higher than the system threshold s_{min}. If both of these conditions are fulfilled, the algoritm uses the *nth* operation to extract the first element of V_3 and assigns it to v. Otherwise, the default variant is retrieved and assigned to v. In the last step, the algorithm returns v which now contains the best possible representation of o under context state $C_\star(S)$.

The functioning of the matching algorithm itself is generic, as it only defines the process of how a variant of an object is selected. The decision as to which variant will be selected is encapsulated in the scoring function f_s. It is therefore the scoring function rather than the algorithm that influences the result of the matching process. This separation of concerns between the algorithm and the scoring function is the basis of matching behaviour that is specific to a particular application scenario. Although the selection process is always the same and built into the system, the matching can be configured by using different scoring functions for different requirements. The major advantage of this approach is that it supports a certain degree of flexibility without abandoning control over context-aware behaviour completely. This trade-off accommodates both the needs of applications and the requirement of data management systems having to operate within well-defined boundaries. While there can be no universal scoring function that will produce satisfactory results for all applications, we have developed a scoring function general enough to cope with most analysed scenarios. We now present how this function is defined and illustrate its operation.

At the core of every scoring function f_s lies the method which is used to match the context values in $C_\star(S)$ to the properties of a variant context $C_v(S)$. The definition of any such function has to specify the conditions under which a context value matches a property value. Although we have presented an equality for two context values, using this equality as the basis for a matching condition would lead to a rather limited system. Assume for example that an object variant represents content for both Switzerland and Liechtenstein. To characterise this variant, we associate the tuples $\langle loc, ch \rangle$ and $\langle loc, li \rangle$ with the variant. While this is a possible solution to solve this particular problem, it has some disadvantages. One problem is that this solution does not scale when more than just a few context values are represented by the same variant. Imagine, for instance, that a variant is valid during a certain time period only. Clearly, it would not be feasible to link a property value capturing each day of this validity period to the variant. Further, this solution is in direct violation of the definition of a context as Definition 3 states that no context can contain more than one value with the same *name* field. Of course, the definition could be changed accordingly to solve this particular problem. However, we believe that this solution would lead to a cumbersome representation of context that is hard to process by the data management system. As we will see in the following, there are also additional challenges that cannot be addressed by loosening the definition of a context.

For the reasons given above, we have decided to introduce a less restrictive condition to determine if two context values match. The first step towards such a matching condition is the definition of additional given sets that partition the VALUES given set as shown in Table 4.4. Based on these new given sets, the *value* field of a context value can be used to specify more than one value. The original behaviour resulting from using identity to define equality can still be obtained by using atomic values from given set ATOM. In addition to that, collections of atomic values can be expressed using a value from the SET given set. For example, the situation discussed above can now be resolved elegantly by assigning the property value ⟨*loc, ch:li*⟩ to the variant in question. To address problems such as validity periods, values defined by given set RANGE allow intervals to be defined based on a lower and upper bound. Finally, if a variant is an appropriate representation for all possible values of a context dimension, the wildcard value from given set STAR can be used. Providing a wildcard in this setting might seem paradoxical at first, as one might argue that the corresponding context value could simply be omitted. Its right to exist will be motivated later, when we present how the scoring function f_s computes the score value, based on value matching.

Set	Syntax	Description	Examples
ATOM	x	Atomic value	en, 27
SET	$x_1\{: x_i\}$	Set of atomic values $S = \{x_1, \ldots, x_n\}$	at:ch:de, red:blue
RANGE	$x_{min}..x_{max}$	Range of atomic values $I = [x_{min}, x_{max}]$	5.5..7.0, a..f
STAR	$*$	Wildcard	$*$

Table 4.4: Extended value syntax

Defining in which cases two context values specified using the extended value syntax match is the next step in establishing a less restrictive matching condition. As context values describe both the context space of the system and the variants of an object, it has to be possible to compare any combination of these four given sets. For each of the resulting sixteen cases, Table 4.5 defines the matching of extended values represented as ≅ by listing the conditions that govern when two values match.

x	y	Matching Condition
ATOM	ATOM	$x = y$
ATOM	SET	$x \in y$
ATOM	RANGE	$y_{min} \leq x \leq y_{max}$
ATOM	STAR	$\top$
SET	ATOM	$y \in x$
SET	SET	$x \cap y \neq \emptyset$
SET	RANGE	$\exists\, k \in x : y_{min} \leq k \leq y_{max}$
SET	STAR	$\top$
RANGE	ATOM	$x_{min} \leq y \leq x_{max}$
RANGE	SET	$\exists\, k \in y : x_{min} \leq k \leq x_{max}$
RANGE	RANGE	$max(x_{min}, y_{min}) < min(x_{max}, y_{max})$
RANGE	STAR	$\top$
STAR	ATOM	$\top$
STAR	SET	$\top$
STAR	RANGE	$\top$
STAR	STAR	$\top$

Table 4.5: Matching of extended values

The condition specified on the first line represents equality based on identity, as given in Definition 2. In contrast, the subsequent lines provide support for a more flexible description of the matching. The first group of equality conditions, for example, specifies when a context value containing an ATOM value matches one with a value represented by given set SET, RANGE or STAR. The definitions are straightforward as an atom matches a set or a range if it is contained within it. The symbol $\top$ is used in those lines of the table where at least one of the two context values contains a wildcard from STAR to indicate that these values always match any other value. Context values containing a SET value are compared to those of the four other types in the second group of conditions. While the first line simply reverses the condition given above, the second line states that two values contained in SET match if their intersection is not the empty set $\emptyset$. In order for a value of the SET given set to match a value of given set RANGE, there has to be at least one element that is within the interval boundaries. The third group of conditions relates context values containing a RANGE value to all other kinds of values. Again, the first two conditions are defined based on a previously discussed condition, with the roles of x and y interchanged. Two RANGE values match if the corresponding intervals overlap.

Finally, based on the extended value syntax and the extended definition of equality, a scoring function f_s can be specified. As can be seen from the matching algorithm presented in Figure 4.6, the scoring function takes as arguments two contexts and returns a real number indicating the score of the match. Even though this is not strictly required by the matching algorithm to function correctly, we assume that the score values returned by f_s are normalised and that $0 \leq f_s \leq 1.0$ holds. Generally, the value returned by a scoring function should quantify the similarity of the given contexts, where 0 indicates no correspondence and 1 represents a complete match. The scoring function given in Definition 7 exhibits these characteristics, as the returned score increases with the number of context dimensions that match.

Definition 7 (Simple Scoring Function $f_{s'}$). The *simple scoring function* $f_{s'}$ takes two contexts C_1 and C_2 as arguments and returns a scoring value representing the number of matching context dimensions of the two contexts normalised by $|N_1|$. It is defined as

$$f_{s'}(C_1, C_2) = \frac{1}{|N_1|} \sum_{n \in N_1} f_i(n, C_1, C_2)$$

where N_1 denotes the set of all names of context values specified by C_1 and the *indicator function* f_i is given by

$$f_i(n, C_1, C_2) = \begin{cases} 1 & \exists\, c_1 \in C_1, c_2 \in C_2 : \\ & \quad name_1 = name_2 = n \wedge value_1 \cong value_2 \\ 0 & \text{otherwise.} \end{cases}$$

Figure 4.7 shows a versioned object with three alternative representations for different contexts. Starting from this example, we will illustrate the functioning of a matching algorithm that uses the simple scoring function introduced above. Assume the context state of the system is defined as $C_\star(S) = \{\langle format, html\rangle, \langle lang, en\rangle\}$. Based on $C_\star(S)$, the scoring function $f_{s'}$ will assign a score of 1.0, 0.5 and 0.0 to the variants o927@0[0], o927@1[1] and o927@2[2], respectively. The first variant defines a variant context $C_v(S)$ that matches all context dimensions contained in context state $C_\star(S)$ and thus receives the maximum score. As the variant context of the second variant contains one matching value only, it gets a lesser score. Finally the score of 0.0 of the last variant is explained by the fact that none of the context values in its variant context match a value in $C_\star(S)$. Therefore, the matching algorithm would return the first variant which, incidentally, is also the default variant of the object.

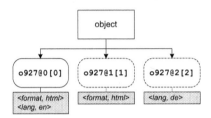

Figure 4.7: Example object

Unfortunately, this simple matching function does not always produce satisfactory results when used in conjunction with the presented matching algorithm. To improve the practical value of the proposed query processing mechanism, there are two major problems that still need to be solved. For example, ambiguous situations where multiple variants of an object obtain the highest score have to be avoided whenever possible. As the algorithm simply returns the default variant in this case, the potential of our approach in general is limited needlessly. And while it is neither possible nor reasonable to give complete control over the matching process to the application developer, the developer has to be in as much control as required to prevent undesired or unintended query outcomes.

Figure 4.8(a) shows another example of a versioned object that is very similar to the one presented in Figure 4.7. The only difference between the two objects is the fact that, in contrast to the previous object, variant o927@1[1] is additionally described by the context value $\langle loc,\ uk\rangle$. Assume that the object is involved in a query processed under the context state $C_\star(S) = \{\langle format,\ html\rangle,\ \langle lang,\ en\rangle,\ \langle loc,\ uk\rangle\}$. In that case, both variants o927@0[0] and o927@1[1] are assigned a score of $0.\overline{6}$ which is also the highest score, as the remaining variant o927@2[2] does not match at all and is consequently assigned score 0.0. In this case, the default variant, indicated by a solid line in the figure, is returned. Although the default variant is, by definition, always a valid representation of the object, the fact that this choice actually favours context dimension *lang* over dimension *loc* is somewhat unsatisfactory. Instead of weighting context dimensions implicitly, based on which variant they describe, the application developer should be given the means to specify these relationships among context dimensions explicitly.

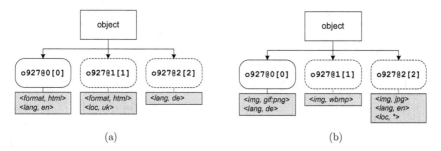

(a)   (b)

Figure 4.8: Example objects

An example of a situation where the matching algorithm returns an inadequate result is illustrated using the versioned object shown in Figure 4.8(b). The depicted object constitutes an image that has three alternative representations in terms of the image format. While the variant on the left-hand side is appropriate if the context state requests an image in the GIF or PNG format, the one on the right-hand side stores the image data in the JPEG format. Finally, the variant in the middle contains data in WBMP, a format required by older generations of mobile phones. Assume such a client querying for the object has set the context state to $C_\star(S) = \{\langle img, wbmp\rangle, \langle lang, en\rangle, \langle loc, uk\rangle\}$. By applying the scoring function to all three variants, the matching algorithm will obtain the values 0.0, $0.\overline{3}$ and $0.\overline{6}$ for the three variants from left to right, respectively. According to these scores, variant o927@2[2] will be used to represent the object in the context state $C_\star(S)$. This, however, will lead to problems, as the client that has set the context state will not be able to process the image data in this format. As motivated before, we see context information as an additional factor that is used to augment the functionality of our system. While we intend to stay true to this notion of context, we feel that it is necessary to give more control over the matching process to both the database developer and the client application. Therefore, in order to avoid situations such as the one just presented, we will describe how to raise the expressiveness of the syntax that is used to describe both the context state of the system and the variants of an object.

As mentioned before, ambiguous situations where more than one variant obtains the maximum score value can be reduced by explicitly weighting the context dimensions in relation to each other. Assume, for example, that in a given application scenario a match on the context dimension
format should be considered more important than a match on the *lang* dimension. This assumption is valid in many systems, as retrieving content
in the wrong language will at worst prevent the user from understanding
it, whereas content in the wrong format will not be displayed at all. In
order for our matching framework to support a mechanism that allows
the query evaluation to be influenced in this way, we define a function
that assigns a weight to every name of a context dimension relevant to an
application. The specification of this context dimension weight function
is presented in Definition 8.

Definition 8 (Context Dimension Weight Function). The *context dimension weight function* denoted by w returns a weight $w(n) \in \mathbb{R}^+$ for
every name $n \in N$, where N represents the set of the names of all context
dimensions.

The weight function $w(n)$ is inserted into the simple scoring function
as specified in Definition 7 as a factor which is multiplied with the indicator function f_i. It is therefore reasonable to assume that $w(n)$ returns
a value of 1.0 as the default weight. If a context dimension is considered
to be either half or twice as important as one with the default weight,
the weights 0.5 and 2.0 are used. Although weights are useful to prevent cases where the system needs to fall back to the default variant,
by reducing the probability of having multiple variants with the highest
score, they have to be specified globally and apply to all objects defined
in the system. This global nature renders the use of weights difficult in
situations where undesired query outcomes need to be prevented. Tuning
the weights to get the intended results in one case, may easily lead to
new situations where the system performs differently from the designer's
expectations. Depending on the complexity of the application, it can be
very hard to predict the impact of changing a weight. Since testing if
the system handles all context constellations correctly is not feasible in
an efficient manner, it is difficult to track down problematic situations.

To address the problem of unpredictable matching results at a local
level, we need to extend the syntax used for context values once again.
The goal of this additional extension is to empower the creator of a
variant to express required and illegal values of context dimensions. For
instance, in the example situation illustrated by means of Figure 4.8(b),

the client specifying the context state knows that it requires the image in the WBMP format but has no possibility to include this knowledge in the context state $C_\star(S)$. Therefore, we have introduced two prefixes $+$ and $-$ that can be used to indicate whether the prefixed context value is required or illegal respectively. Thus, in our example, the client could instead specify the context value $\langle img, +wbmp \rangle$ which would cause the scoring function to assign a value of 0.0 to all variants of an object that do not feature the value $\langle img, wbmp \rangle$ as part of their variant context $C_v(S)$. Consequently, the first two variants of the object now get a lower score which leads to the selection of the third variant, as intended by the client. In Table 4.6, we give the conditions under which two values x and y that are possibly prefixed are considered to match. Based on this table, we introduce the notation $x \cong_\pm y$ to specify that two values match according to their respective prefixes.

x	y	Match Condition
x	y	$x \cong y$
x	$+y$	$x \cong y$
x	$-y$	$\neg(x \cong y)$
$+x$	y	$x \cong y$
$-x$	y	$\neg(x \cong y)$
$+x$	$+y$	$x \cong y$
$+x$	$-y$	$\bot$
$-x$	$+y$	$\bot$
$-x$	$-y$	$x \cong y$

Table 4.6: Matching of prefixed values

Using the presented enhancements, it is now possible to define the general scoring function used as a default in our version model to support context-aware query processing. Definition 9 specifies this general scoring function f_s that incorporates the previously defined weighting function w as well as the notion of required and illegal context values. As mentioned previously, the weighting function is introduced as a factor multiplied with the indicator function f_s. Prefixed values are handled by a special function based on the matching condition $\cong_\pm$. Computing the product of all these comparisons and multiplying it with the score of the current variant will reset the value to 0.0 if a matching condition is violated and leave it unchanged otherwise.

Definition 9 (General Scoring Function f_s). The *general scoring function* f_s takes two contexts C_1 and C_2 as arguments and returns a scoring value representing the number of matching context dimensions of the two contexts normalised by $|N|$. It is defined as

$$f_s(C_1, C_2) = \frac{1}{|N|} \sum_{n \in N} (w(n) \times f_i(n, C_1, C_2)) \times \prod_{n \in N} f_{\pm}(n, C_1, C_2)$$

where N denotes the union $N_1 \cup N_2$ of the sets of all names of context values specified by C_1 or C_2. The indicator function f_i is used as given in Definition 7 and the weight function w as introduced in Definition 8. Finally, the matching function for prefixed values $f_{\pm}$ is defined as

$$f_{\pm}(n, C_1, C_2) = \begin{cases} 1 & \exists\, c_1 \in C_1, c_2 \in C_2 : \\ & \quad name_1 = name_2 = n \wedge value_1 \cong_{\pm} value_2 \\ 0 & \text{otherwise.} \end{cases}$$

Note that we use the union $N = N_1 \cup N_2$ of the sets of all names of context values specified either by C_1 or C_2 to normalise the scoring value returned by f_s. This change caters for the fact that either C_1 could specify more values than C_2 or vice versa. In this situation, taking the notion of these so-called under-specified and over-specified variants into consideration can be of additional help in preventing ambiguity. Normalising over all names of context values is one possible way of achieving this in a neutral manner. Depending on application requirements, however, it can be necessary to favour either under-specified or over-specified variants. To realise this behaviour, we would need to integrate an additional summand into the matching function that tips the scales into the desired direction.

4.4 Implementation

As a proof-of-concept and basis for experimentation, the version model for context-aware data management has been implemented in an existing database management system. The choice of database that was extended with the presented functionality is a consequence of the selection of the OM data model as the framework in which the version model has been specified. Therefore, the natural foundation for an implementation of context-aware data management has been a platform that already provides native support for the basic concepts of the OM data model, such as multiple instantiation, classification and inheritance, as well as bi-directional associations. In the past, several such implementations of the OM data model have been realised, leading to a family of Object Model Systems (OMS) that comprises platforms implemented in Prolog, Python and Java. Each of these platforms addresses specific requirements of the development process of a database application. Implemented in Prolog, *OMS Pro* [296] has focussed on rapid prototyping by providing tools that both facilitate the design of a database model and help with testing the model with sample data. A subset of the concepts defined by the version model for context-aware data management were implemented in an extended OMS Pro platform called *OMSwe* [202, 203, 204] as a first effort to support context-aware web engineering. The *eOMS* [182] platform was implemented in Python as an extension of the relational database management system PostgreSQL and addresses multi-user access to data and transactional query processing. Applications communicate with the eOMS server using OML in requests and get back XML as a response. Supporting the needs of object-oriented application programmers are *OMS Java* [167] and, more recently, *OMS Avon* that were implemented in Java, based on different solutions for object persistence. Both approaches feature a comprehensive application programming interface that supports data access and modification based on the concepts of an object-oriented language.

However, a seamless development process can only be achieved if it is possible to move freely from one system to another. Therefore, all implementations of the OM model share a common language for data definition, manipulation and querying. While the OM data model standardises the way data is represented, OML standardises how this data is processed. What is missing is an application programming interface shared by all platforms that defines how programs can work with an OMS database. To close this gap, a uniform Java interface providing access to heterogeneous OMS platforms was developed. This interface, called OMS[jp], offers a database concept to represent all aspects of an OMS implementation. Through this concept, the underlying platform can be configured and databases can be managed. OMS[jp] also provides functionality for querying the database as well as accessing data and metadata objects. As everything in OMS—even metadata and system objects—is modelled as objects, it makes sense to offer certain of these concepts in the interface. OMS[jp] therefore comprises objects that represent collections, associations, methods and types. The most important of these concepts is the representation of an object within the OMS database. As

the object model of OMS is very different from the object model that
is used in Java, it is, unfortunately, not possible to establish a direct
mapping between Java objects and OMS objects. Hence, the interface
simply offers one class that is used to represent all user defined object
types. It is through this class that data can be read from and written to
objects. Types are represented by special classes in the Java interface,
as they are used frequently and have special properties. As OMS differentiates between different kinds of types there are also classes for these
types in the interface. Also available as special classes are the fundamental concepts of object collections and associations. These objects offer
various operations of the collection algebra that is defined by the OM
data model. Hence, they can be used to implement complex queries on
the model, instead of sending a textual OML statement to the database.

In OMS, triggers can be defined that are fired when certain events
occur. As these events can be important to the client application, they
are also propagated to the programming environment. This allows an
application programmer to register code, by means of an event listener,
that will be executed when events occur. Finally, for reasons of performance, the application programming interface also incorporates a cache.
The cache is used to store query results and object data that have been
fetched previously. Retrieving data from OMS can be very expensive
and, since metadata in particular is very static, caching of results can
lead to significant improvements in system performance. The cache is
kept consistent using the previously discussed event listener mechanism.
Whenever the interface receives a notification that a certain object has
been changed or deleted, the corresponding cache entries are also in-
validated. The cache component has been designed with extensibility
in mind. A client can provide its own cache according to its needs and
memory limitations. By default, the system uses an unlimited cache that
grows corresponding to the number of objects in the underlying database,
and has no replacement strategy.

The architecture and properties of OMS^{jp} as discussed above make
it an ideal framework for experimentation with our version model for
context-aware data management. Therefore, in this section, we will start
by presenting the aspects of the architecture of OMS^{jp} that have formed
the basis for its extension. We then go on to discuss those extensions
and show how context-aware data management has been integrated into
OMS^{jp}. A high-level overview of the architecture of OMS^{jp} is shown
in Fig. 4.9. As shown in the figure, the framework consists of three
parts. Close to the *Database Application*, the *OMS^{jp} Interface* that

defines the way in which an application interacts with the framework is shown. The interface is then implemented by a platform-dependent *Driver* which translates the functionality offered by the interface into the concepts offered by the database server. As with Java Database Connectivity (JDBC), the driver is completely decoupled from the interface and thus the back-end database server can be exchanged at any point in time. Whereas this decoupling of interface and driver is the main advantage of OMS^{jp}, a disadvantage inherent in this approach is that the interface has to be defined as the intersection of the functionalities offered by each platform. Therefore, the potential strength of certain database servers cannot be leveraged when they are accessed through OMS^{jp}.

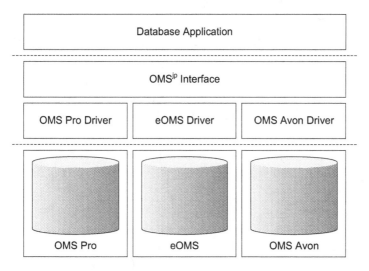

Figure 4.9: Overview

The functionality defined by the OMS^{jp} interface can be subdivided into three main areas. First, it provides support to manage the drivers required to communicate with the underlying OMS platform. When a client application initiates a connection to a database server through OMS^{jp}, it requests a suitable driver by specifying a URL that describes which platform, server and database are to be used. Based on a driver registry maintained by the interface, the corresponding driver is loaded, initialised and returned to the application. From this driver, the application can gain access to the specified database, which is the second area of functionality offered by the OMS^{jp} interface. As mentioned before, the database abstraction gives access to all functionality as well as to both data and metadata of the OMS system. Finally, the last part, the so-called value interface, defines how objects and values retrieved from the underlying OMS database are represented in Java and how Java values are converted to native values of the OMS platform.

While the first two parts of the OMS^{jp} interface are not relevant to the discussion of the implementation of our version model, the value interface is where the extension is most visible. An overview of the value interface as a UML diagram is given in Figure 4.10. At the top of the figure, interface **OMSValue** describes an interface that contains the methods common to all values that exist in the underlying OMS platform. At this level, the only method is **toNative()** that converts a Java value back to its native representation as defined by the database back-end. As can be seen from the specialisations of **OMSValue** shown in the figure, the interface defines several classes to represent different kinds of values. Interfaces **OMSObject** and **OMSInstance** probably define the most important kinds of values provided by the framework. They give access to the database objects and their instances. As mentioned above, it is not possible to express the concept of an object as defined by OM using a single Java class. Therefore, one OM object is represented as an instance of **OMSObject** and a set of instances of **OMSInstance**, each representing one of the object's types. The relationship between an object and its instances will be discussed in more detail later, as it is the focal point of the extension allowing objects to have versions.

Special predefined extensions of the **OMSInstance** interface represent concepts unique to the OM data model or system metadata. For example, interfaces **OMSCollection** and **OMSBinaryCollection** represent the concpets of unary and binary collections, as defined in the model, together with the corresponding algebraic operations. Associations between collections are captured by interface **OMSAssociation** and type metadata is accessible through **OMSType** and its extensions. Most OMS platforms offer three different kinds of value types, represented by interfaces **OMSObjectType**, **OMSStructuredType** and **OMSBaseType**. While instances of **OMSObjectType** describe what attributes and methods an object has, instances of **OMS-BaseType** provide metadata about the types of base or atomic values. Finally, some OMS platforms support the notion of structured values that enable the database designer to define data records without having to create an object type. The most common use of these structured values that are described by instances of **OMSStructuredType** is to represent members of n-ary collections, with $n > 1$.

On the right-hand side of Figure 4.10, three additional types of database values are shown. First, values described by interface **OMSBaseType**

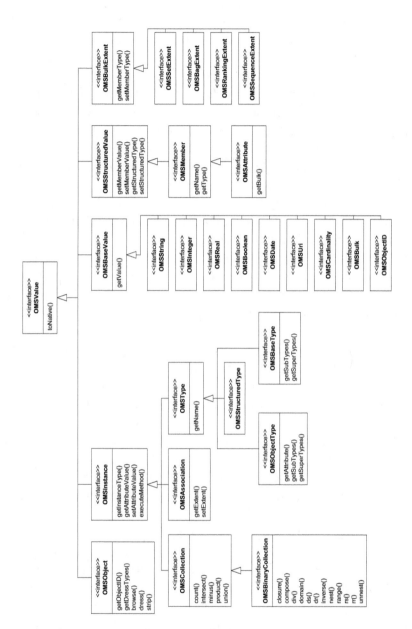

Figure 4.10: OMS^{jp} value interface

are represented in OMS^{jp} through interface **OMSBaseValue** and its specialisations. These values correspond to the basic data types defined in all OMS platforms, such as **string, integer, real** or **date**. Interface **OMSStructuredValue** represents database values that have been defined as records by an instance of **OMSStructuredType**. Two specialisations of this class are featured in the interface to facilitate access to metadata. Interfaces **OMSMember** and **OMSAttribute** provide access to the members and the attributes of a structured and an object type, respectively. The purpose of the third kind of values is to represent the collection extents. As introduced in the description of the OM data model, an extent value is either a set, a bag, a ranking or a sequence, depending on the type of collection. To cater for the different semantics and the different operations associated with these types of extent values, the OMS^{jp} interface defines four specialisations, **OMSSetExtent, OMSBagExtent, OMSRankingExtent** and **OMSSequenceExtent**, of interface **OMSBulkExtent**.

The OMS^{jp} interface has been implemented for several OMS platforms by providing a driver that maps the presented concepts to a database back-end. However, a comprehensive discussion of the platform-dependent details of such a driver implementation is out of the scope of this thesis. Nevertheless, it is important to examine the relationship between an object and its instances further by looking at the classes found in the abstract implementation which is the common basis of all platform drivers. It is this relationship that has to be modified in order to incorporate versioning into the implementation of OMS^{jp}. Figure 4.11 contains an excerpt of the original implementation of OMS^{jp} that shows the three most important classes involved in the relationship between an object and its instances. Represented in UML, these three classes are **OMSObjectImpl, OMSIntanceImpl** and **OMSObjectTypeImpl**, which implement the previously introduced interfaces **OMSObject, OMSIntance** and **OMSObjectType**, respectively.

As shown, class **OMSObjectImpl** stores all properties that are inherent to the concept of an object in the OM data model. The field **oid** stores a reference to the object's identifier represented as an instance of class **OMSObjectID** which is not shown in the figure. The object identifier can be obtained using method **getObjectID()** but it cannot be set. Object identifiers are assigned to an object when it is created by the underlying platform and are therefore read-only. As an OM object can have multiple types, class **OMSObjectImpl** manages a collection **types** with references to all types of the object represented by instances of class **OMSObjectTypeImpl**. This relationship between an object and its types is also represented

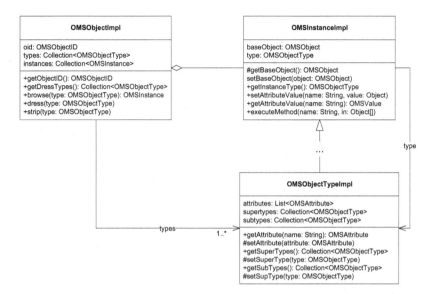

Figure 4.11: Excerpt of the OMS^{jp} implementation

in the figure by the aggregation between the corresponding UML classes. The types of an object can be retrieved using the **getDressTypes()** method that returns the set of types the object is currently dressed with. To modify this collection of types, methods **dress()** and **strip()** can be used to add or remove object types. While dressing an object with a given object type leads to the creation of a new instance of the object, stripping an object of a given type deletes the corresponding instance. The current set of instances of an object is maintained by the field **instances** that contains references to instances of class **OMSInstanceImpl**. This relationship between an object and its instances is again represented using an aggregation between the corresponding UML classes. Note, that members of the **instances** collection can not be added or removed directly, but rather through the use of methods **dress()** and **strip()** only.

A striking property of the **OMSObject** interface implemented by class **OMSObjectImpl** is the fact that it lacks any methods that would allow access to the object's data. In contrast to object-oriented systems such as Java that feature single instantiation, OM allows its objects to have instances from parallel or even unrelated inheritance hierarchies. As a consequence, the type of an object cannot be determined without additional information about the role in which the object is currently browsed. Including methods providing access to an object's data in the **OMSObject** interface would therefore potentially lead to ambiguous situations, as it would allow the object to be accessed without the required role information. As a solution to this situation, OMS[jp] offers the browse() method in the OMSObject interface together with the interface OMSInstance that provides the required methods to retrieve and update data on the object as well as executing its methods. As browse() expects an argument of type OMSObjectType, it sets the role in which the object is browsed and eliminates any ambiguities by returning the corresponding instance of OMSInstance. Class OMSInstanceImpl implements the OMSInstance interface and thus provides methods getAttributeValue() and setAttributeValue() to read and write the values of an object's attributes. To invoke a method, its name and the corresponding input parameters have to be given to the executeMethod() method which evaluates the method and returns any result values computed by the method. Also visible in the figure is the fact that class OMSInstanceImpl maintains a reference to its base object and to the type of which it is an instance. This information can be accessed using the getBaseObject() and setBaseObject() methods as well as method getInstanceType(). In contrast to the methods discussed so far, the method providing read-access to the base object is protected as this functionality should only be open to the subclasses of OMSInstanceImpl. Write-access to the base object of an instance is even more restricted, as the corresponding method has default access and thus is only open to other classes in the same package.

Class OMSObjectTypeImpl is a specialisation of class OMSInstanceImpl that represents an object instance that describes the attributes and methods of other objects. To do so, class OMSObjectTypeImpl maintains a list of OMSAttribute instances that describe which attributes an instance of this type will have. As the order of these attributes is important, they are managed as a list. The attributes defined by a type can be retrieved by name using the getAttribute() method. A new attribute can be appended to the type using setAttribute(). In addition to the metadata about a type's attributes, class OMSObjectTypeImpl also maintains information about the type's supertypes and subtypes. As the OM data model allows types to inherit from multiple supertypes, the references to both supertypes and subtypes are stored in a collection. As these collections cannot be accessed directly, the interface of class OMSObjectTypeImpl provides methods to retrieve and insert both supertypes and subtypes. Similar to class OMSInstanceImpl, methods providing read-only access are public and can be invoked by any other class. Methods that modify the metadata, however, have protected access to ensure that they are not called from the outside. To modify the database schema in OMS[jp], the previously discussed database concept offered by the interface has to be used. In contrast to the representations of metadata objects, the database concept also takes care of the required data evolution operations that have to be executed to ensure database consistency.

To accommodate versioned objects, as defined at the beginning of this chapter, the OMS^{jp} interface and its implementation has been extended with the necessary concepts. As point of extension we have chosen the driver that manages the database back-end of an OMS^{jp} interface implementation. In our extended implementation, the driver maps the versioned objects visible to the application programmer to the metamodel, shown in Figure 4.4, which is used to manage versioned objects at the storage level. Since the driver now takes on the management of revisions and variants as well as version-aware query processing, in addition to the mapping between OM concepts and Java concepts, it effectively becomes a part of the data management system itself. Apart from the back-end implementation, the OMS^{jp} interface itself has to be adapted as well. At the heart of this augmented interface is the extended model of an OM object shown in Figure 4.12 as a UML class diagram. For reasons of conciseness, we have decided not to discuss the interface and implementation of the extended object representation of OMS^{jp} in two separate figures. Although the concepts shown in the figure are labelled with the names of the interfaces introduced previously, they nevertheless represent classes materialising these interfaces where all methods that have public access are implementations of interface methods. Thus, the interface corresponding to any of the classes shown can be derived from the name of the class and the set of its public methods. Methods and fields that retain their meaning and functionality from the discussed basic OMS^{jp} object model are shown in grey, while extensions to the model are set in black.

Before presenting each of the adapted classes in some more detail, it is worthwhile discussing the general structure of the new object model first. The most visible change is the introduction of a new class **OMSObjectVersion** that has been included as an additional step of indirection between the object and its instances. The changes that have been made to the classes **OMSObject** and **OMSInstance** are mostly direct results of the new structure of the object model. In contrast to the storage layer that uses two distinct concepts for revisions and variants, the interface layer only uses the concept of a single version representation that represents both revisions and variants. The motivation for this deviating representation of a versioned object is rooted in the different requirements that

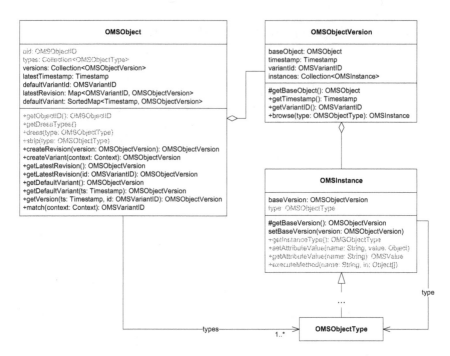

Figure 4.12: Extended object model in OMS^{jp}

need to be addressed at different levels of the implementation. At the storage level, the representation of a versioned object has been designed to favour the evaluation of certain kinds of queries. The needs of database application developers are the primary influence that has shaped the structure of the extended OMS^{jp} interface. At this level it is important the keep the number of concepts small in order to provide an elegant and minimal interface. Therefore, we have decided that the differentiation between revisions and variants should not be visible in terms of interface classes but rather in the functionality offered by these classes.

As shown in the figure, class **OMSObject** continues to be the principal Java representation of an object as defined by the OM data model. Apart from the instances field and the browse() method that are no longer a part of this class, all other methods and fields continue to have the same purpose as discussed above. In particular, all methods that affect the object's set of types remain at the level of the object itself to ensure that all versions of the object have the same set of types at any point in time as required by our definition of the version model. In addition to these class members, the extended representation of an OM object defines a set of fields and methods that manage revisions and variants.

For example, the versions field maintains a collection of references to all versions of the object represented as instances of class OMSObjectVersion. The relationship between an object and its versions is also explicitly shown in the figure as an aggregation of two UML classes. The class interface does not provide direct access to the collection of versions but allows new revisions and variants to be created using the methods createRevision() and createVariant(). As an object can have multiple variants, the application developer needs to specify the version of the object for which they would like to create a new revision. However, the creation of a new revision is only successful if the given version is one of the latest revisions of the object. Otherwise, the call to createRevision() fails and an exception is raised. Our definition of the version model requires all variants of an object to specify a set of context values that is different from the properties of all other variants. Therefore, whenever a variant is created, the application developer needs to state the context in which the variant will be suitable. Method createVariant() then checks if the given set of context values fulfils this constraint prior to creating the variant in the storage layer and raises an exception if a variant for the same context already exists.

To provide efficient access to both the latest revision and the default variant, class OMSObject further maintains the two look-up tables latestRevision and defaultVariant. The interface method getLatestRevision() accesses the first of these look-up tables to retrieve the latest revision of the object. While the latest revision of the default variant can be obtained by using getLatestRevision() without parameters, the latest revision of a specific variant is retrieved by the implementation that takes the corresponding argument. If no variant identifier is specified, the latest revision is computed based on the value stored in field defaultVariantId. The default variant is accessed analogously by using the method getDefaultVariant() of the interface of OMSObject. If no parameter is given, the latest revision of the default variant is returned, based on the value captured by the field latestTimestamp. However, if the application designer specifies a certain point in time as an argument to the method, the latest version smaller or equal to the given value is retrieved. To facilitate this computation, defaultVariant is implemented as a sorted map that maintains an ordering over the sequence of recorded timestamps and therefore supports range queries. To access an arbitrary version of the object, the interface of class OMSObject provides the getVersion() method that allows both the specification of a time-stamp and a variant identifier. The matching algorithm presented in the previous section is invoked by calling method match() and passing the current context as an argument. The method matches the given set of context values to the properties of the available variants and returns the identifier of the best matching alternative. This identifier can then be used to access the variant version itself, by using the methods we outlined earlier. Although the interface of the object class provides methods to create new revisions and variants, there are no counterpart methods that would allow these versions to be removed. The simple reason for this omission is the fact that the semantics of such an operation are not defined by our version model.

As mentioned before, the inclusion of class **OMSObjectVersion** presents the only structural change distinguishing the extended from the original value interface. An instance of this class represents a version of the base object it is associated with. It therefore maintains a reference to the base object in the **baseObject** field. The base object is accessible to descendants of the class and other classes in the same package through method **getBaseObject()** that has protected access. A version of an object is identified by the values stored in fields **timestamp** and **variantId**. Similar to the object identifier in class **OMSObject**, both fields can be accessed by methods **getTimestamp()** and **getVariantID()**. Also, as the identifier of the object, these values cannot be updated as they have to remain constant throughout a version's existence. The **browse()** method that was part of the original interface of **OMSObject**, as shown in Figure 4.10, has been moved to the class representing a version of an object. The reason for this refactoring is that the object in the extended model is no longer directly connected to its instances. Therefore, this functionality is now offered as part of the interface of class **OMSObjectVersion** that also maintains a set of references to the object's instances in field **instances**. Finally, the only changes made to class **OMSInstance** reflect the fact that it is associated with an instance of class **OMSObjectVersion** in the extended model, instead of an instance of class **OMSObject** as in the original object model. Consequently, field **baseVersion** replaces the previously defined field **baseObject** and the two access methods to this field have been renamed accordingly.

4.5 Discussion

As a response to the requirements of context-aware applications, we have presented a version model that provides support for the management of alternative versions of data objects while at the same time supporting the system development process with the provision of revisional versions. The model has been defined formally within the framework of the OM data model, an extended E/R model for object-oriented data management. Based on a comparison of the original metamodel of an object as defined by OM to the extended model that introduces a set of new concepts and constraints, we have shown how our model accommodates revisional and alternative versions. An important characteristic of this extended model is how objects are identified and referenced. To allow both generic and specific references, the concepts of a latest revision and a default variant have been presented. Based on these types of references, we have demonstrated how relationships between objects can be versioned using the same concepts as for the objects themselves.

At the heart of our context-aware data management stands an algorithm that matches the current context of an application to the variants of the objects involved in a query. For each variant, the matching algorithm computes a score and then selects the one with the highest score as the representation of the object according to the context. In our version model, context is seen as information that can be used to augment the result of a query rather than a specification that has to be followed strictly. Hence, instead of computing an exact match between the context and the set of object variants, the algorithm uses a best match approach, with the default variant as fall-back option, if no variant scores above a predefined threshold. As system developers have to be given as much control as possible, our matching algorithm further supports the notion of required and illegal values for context dimensions.

Many of the ideas and concepts presented in this chapter have their origin in solutions proposed for temporal and engineering databases as well as software configuration systems. Although all of these systems are capable of either supporting revisional, alternative or even both kinds of versions, none of them has been developed for the management of context-aware data. We argue that this difference in the area of application of a version model gives rise to new requirements that need to be addressed by adapting and extending concepts introduced earlier. As mentioned before, the main difference between existing solutions and our approach is the interpretation of information that exists in addition to the query. As this information is seen as a part of the query in temporal and engineering databases as well as in software configuration systems, these systems are not at liberty to deliver a result representing a best effort. If an object has no version that matches this additional specification exactly, the query processing needs to be aborted and an error reported. For example, if a software configuration system is used to build a system for a certain platform and one module is not available for this platform, it generally cannot be substituted by a version intended for a different platform.

As our model assumes that this additional context information is orthogonal to the query, there are several important implications that distinguish our system from existing solutions. Although most existing version models feature the concept of a latest version and a default variant, their purpose is completely different. In those systems, these two concepts exist only to cope with queries that do not use or are not aware of versions. While this purpose persists in our model, the default variant is also used as a fall-back representation of the object which avoids exceptions during query processing. Such a use of this concept would never be possible in the example of a software configuration system, as it would inevitably lead to faulty results, and therefore exceptions are vital information to the users of such systems. In contrast, having a fall-back variant that is always possible is the enabling factor for a best match algorithm instead of an exact match algorithm. The importance of this approach becomes clear when we go back once again and compare the nature of the additional information in both existing solutions and our version model. Apart from its interpretation, another key difference is where this information originates. In the case of an engineering database or a software configuration system, for example, both the type and the values of this information are defined by the same developers that define the alternative versions. In a context-aware application, however, the developer of the database and the client specifying the context are two different actors. Therefore, our model for context-aware data management has to cope with context configurations that have not been envisioned at design-time. In this setting, using an exact match approach is not possible for two reasons. On the one hand, even small changes in the context values could lead to situations where our system would not be able to deliver satisfactory or even any results. On the other hand, using an exact match would require a variant to be defined for each context configuration. Clearly, such an approach is not feasible, due to reasons of scalability.

The different application of the version models is also manifested in the operational model defined for each solution. In temporal databases, versions are normally created automatically when data is modified based on the current time-stamp, even though systems exist that also provide explicit operations for this purpose. Engineering databases and software configuration systems do not create revisions and variants by default but define a set of commands that allow the version graph of an object to be manipulated. In this respect, our version model is more like these latter systems, as we have not defined a mechanism for automatic version generation, such as a high-level operational model or policies that control when versions are created by the system. In contrast to many of those systems that use the library model of operations where objects are checked out, modified, and later checked in, our system uses an operational model based on the interface presented in the previous section. Both engineering databases and software configuration systems support a merge operation that is used to combine two alternative branches of revisions. As, in practice, this operation will almost always involve some kind of user interaction to resolve conflicts between the variants involved, it is virtually impossible to offer an automatic merge operation. Also, in the setting of context-aware data management, the semantics of merging two variants are not defined and therefore we believe that it is not very likely that this operation will be required. Hence, we have abstained from including a default implementation of this operation in our version model and leave its implementation, if required, to the application developer.

Query processing, or building a configuration, as it is called in software configuration systems, is another area where our system distinguishes itself from existing solutions. If information that is provided in addition to the query is considered to be a form of specification, the query processor has to ensure that the returned result is consistent with the specification in its entirety. Software configuration systems, for example, have proposed a technique where the specification is becoming more and more complete with every object that is included. To do so, the values of parameters that have not given to the query are inserted into the specification, based on unused values obtained from the descriptions of the selected variants. This approach results in a stable and consistent configuration but its outcome highly depends on the order in which objects are accessed. Other solutions have proposed building the entire query tree first and then computing a matching over all objects. While this algorithm leads to a deterministic and consistent result, it is not usable in on-line systems such as our own, for reasons of performance. Our notion of context allows the matching of context to be effected at the time each object is accessed by the query processor. The task of augmenting an existing query evaluator with support for our notion of context-awareness is therefore not a complex one.

Much of the power of the OM data model lies in the fact that the model is completely specified by a metamodel that is also expressed in

OM. As a consequence, most of the OMS platforms that provide native support for databases designed with OM use objects to store both data and metadata. In other words, concepts such as collections, associations, methods or types are all represented and stored as OM objects. Therefore, traditional OMS platforms provide an elegant way of managing, accessing and querying data and metadata in a uniform way. With our extended object model, however, the question has to be raised whether to apply its additional functionality to metadata objects as well. The two extreme solutions—disallowing or allowing all metadata to have versions—do not promise to be very useful. Whereas the first approach imposes an unnecessary restriction that prevents a concept from being used in places where it could be wise to do so, the second solution will undoubtedly lead to a system that would be hard to understand, maintain and control. Hence, we believe, that a selected number of metadata concepts should be allowed to have versions while others continue to exist without them. Ideal candidates among the different types of metadata objects are concepts that are already hard to classify as either data or metadata such as, for example, collections and associations. As previously discussed, versioned associations in particular constitute a powerful concept to track the evolution of entire object systems, as they capture the relationships between objects. Another metadata concept that benefits from the additional functionality of our version model are method objects. Whereas revisional versions are an ideal solution to keep track of the development of a method, alternative versions of a method object can be used to provide context-aware behaviour that goes beyond the presented query processing algorithm.

We firmly believe that the presented version model for context-aware data management has the potential to address the requirements of context-aware applications and to facilitate their development. Nevertheless, in its current form, the version model also has a few limitations that will have to be addressed in the future. In the following, we discuss a few of these shortcomings and provide some thoughts as to how they could be overcome. A drawback of our model is the assumption that an object is either entirely context-dependent or it is not. However, in reality, this is seldom the case as often only parts of an object change depending on the current context. Imagine, for example, an object used to represent a person. Some attributes, such as text containing the biography or a short curriculum vitae, can vary according to context dimensions such as the language in which the object is accessed. Then again, other attributes, such as the name of the person or their phone number, remain the same in all contexts. In a way, this issue relates back to the question that arose in temporal databases, whether the entire tuple or individual attributes should be versioned. Our decision to apply versioning at the level of objects is comparable to the notion of tuple-versioning introduced in these systems. Therefore our model is not able to distinguish between context-dependent and context-independent information within an object, which could lead to data being replicated in all variants. Clearly, storing redundant information requires great care when updating these values, and can lead to consistency anomalies. Fortunately, there are solutions to this shortcoming in our system. Context-independent values could be represented by a special null value in all variants except the default variant. This special value would cause the system to access the default variant whenever this attribute is read in a version that has no data defined for it. If this additional level of indirection implicates a performance penalty that outweighs the benefits of having consistent data, the metamodel of a versioned object would need to be revised and manage context-dependent and context-independent data separately. This second solution relates back to version models that provide the concept of a generic object that represents the properties that are common to all object versions.

While we have presented several techniques to improve the quality of results computed by the matching algorithm, there are still many cases where the outcome is ambiguous. The fact that the matching algorithm needs to resort to the default version in this case is highly unsatisfactory as it prevents our system from tapping its full potential. Therefore, we believe that further refinements of the matching function are necessary. One possible starting point is the different classes of matches that were introduced in Table 4.4. As of now, matches from all classes are considered to be equally good and thus weighted the same. However, it is reasonable to assume that, for example, a variant that is matched with a wildcard is of lower importance than one that specifies the exact value. As a further improvement of the matching algorithm, the presented weighting function could be extended to assign different weights to matches, depending on the class that has been used to specify the context value. Related to this issue is the drawback that our value syntax does not support the definition of priority lists or rankings. Instead of being limited to simply specifying a set of acceptable values for a context dimension, a context should be able to express preferences for these values. For example, if a system considers language as a contextual factor, then it should be possible to declare that English takes precedence over

German. As a consequence, a variant designed for the German context would be assigned a lower matching value than the one for the English context. This behaviour could easily be implemented by extending the scoring function to deal with an additional given set that represents such rankings. However, the integration of a given set RANKING would render the whole system more complex. The need for such a class of values has, therefore, to be underpinned by additional application scenarios.

Finally, another deficiency of our approach pertains to the implementation of versions on the storage level. As presented in Section 4.4, our version model has been realised as part of a database library providing access to different OMS platforms. As our implementation is not integrated into the database system itself, it has to work with the concepts offered by these platforms, instead of being able to access their internal structures. As an example, it would be desirable to use deltas to minimise the space required for storing versions. Instead, every version has to be represented as an object in the underlying database. Apart from space consumption, this approach suffers from additional undesirable characteristics. As our layered approach operates at a relatively high level, it has only limited control over how data is managed. Hence, it is difficult to provide index structures that would allow objects and their versions to be accessed efficiently. As a consequence, the performance of query evaluation in our system does not compare well to a traditional database system. While additional versioning functionality will always be coupled to a performance penalty, we believe that this shortcoming is best addressed by truly integrating the concepts presented in this chapter into the core of a database management system.

5
Web Content Management

As an application of the version model for context-aware data management presented in the previous chapter, an implementation platform for context-aware web engineering has been developed. Web engineering is a particularly interesting domain for our version model as it is concerned with many aspects of context-awareness, such as multi-channel and multi-format delivery, personalisation and internationalisation. A vast number of solutions have been developed to address these challenges, based on differing technologies and coming from a variety of backgrounds. By abstracting from the details distinguishing these approaches, most of them can, however, be classified as belonging to one of two groups of solutions. The first category consists of model-driven approaches such as HDM, OOHDM, WebML, UWE and Hera which have already been discussed in Chapter 2. While most of these solutions come from an academic background, there is a second group of systems consisting of content management systems that have a more technological focus. Examples of such content management systems include Vignette [282], OpenText Livelink [209], Zope [298] or Typo3 [278]. Since model-based approaches address the design and specification of a web site and content management systems provide support for the implementation of web applications, both approaches are complementary. As we will see, support for context-aware web engineering has not yet been fully realised by currently available implementation platforms, even though most model-based approaches have already addressed these requirements.

In this chapter, we present an implementation platform that supports the realisation and operation of context-aware web sites, as specified by various model-based approaches. Apart from support for context-awareness, the platform also addresses the requirements that are common to existing content management systems. In contrast to most existing solutions that have been developed incrementally and often lack conceptual underpinning, our system is built on a general model [260, 169, 120] that defines the information concepts central to such platforms. This model has been based on a detailed analysis of requirements of all actors involved in designing, implementing and operating a web site. At the core of the model, there are information concepts essential to all web engineering systems separating content, structure, view and presentation. Beside these semantics, the model also incorporates concepts for user management and for business workflows. Based on the model, a web content management system has been developed that consists of a server and a client component. Each of these components will be discussed in a later section of this chapter.

5.1 Requirements

Together with the web's evolution towards an important and widely-used information platform, new requirements for creating, publishing and managing content have arisen. Web sites have dramatically grown not only in number, but also in complexity. Hence the job of managing a site is no longer the task of one single web master but rather of a team of professionals with varying technical backgrounds. User roles include content providers, editors and web designers that collaborate together to create, maintain and deliver up-to-date and correct information. To manage and organise the work of such teams, many web site owners have established complex workflow and revision processes to ensure quality of content at all times. In this section, we will describe the most important requirements that an implementation platform for web engineering should address. As these requirements often depend on different kinds of user roles, such as content editor, web designer, web officer, web site manager and web developer, they will be discussed accordingly.

Content Editor   Authoring the information provided by a web site is the line of work of content providers or editors. Their task is to create and maintain content. Neither do they decide how their content is to be presented nor do they design how it is accessed or navigated. This separation of concerns leads to a set of basic requirements every web engineering platform should meet. The first of these requirements is the well-known separation of content and presentation. By separating these two concepts, the implementation platform is able to support a number of content authors while ensuring that all content abides by the defined presentation guidelines, such as corporate design or corporate identity.

Looking at the content itself, the requirement of content in multiple formats becomes apparent. As the Internet is a global institution and can be accessed from virtually anywhere, many modern web sites are available in different languages. A great number of these sites are already capable of adapting to the language preferred by the requesting user-agent. Language however is only one dimension where so-called multi-format content is useful. With an ever-increasing set of web browser technologies and support for a wide range of platforms, such as mobile phones, media phones and PDAs, content has to be adapted to many different characteristics. Among these are file format, resolution and size of images or version and level of detail for text.

Another important requirement is the notion of users, user roles and permissions. When a potentially large number of authors are working on one web site, it is paramount to track the origin of all changes and to control who should be allowed to perform these changes. Hence, in addition to revisional versioning, a web engineering system must offer the possibility of creating and authenticating users. To manage and classify these users in hierarchical groups, the concept of user groups or user roles has to be present in the system. But users and user groups themselves are not sufficient. Customisable and extensible permissions and user rights must also be managed and enforced by the system at all times. A joint model of users, groups and permissions that allows the manager of a web site to implement the required user scheme is therefore clearly needed.

Web Designer   The web's evolution into a platform where global players and large companies present themselves leads to different challenges in terms of the design of web pages. Companies have extended their corporate identity and corporate design guidelines to include their web site. Graphical designers and artists are employed to develop the look of the individual pages. Clearly, a web engineering platform has to be aware of this situation and present concepts to solve any problems that might arise. Again, separation of content and presentation emerges as a central requirement to enable such a mode of web site development.

As a matter of fact, the presentation and design of a web site should address the needs of the client requesting the page. Web clients vary greatly in terms of capabilities. Personal computers with browsers capable of displaying HTML are certainly the most commonly used clients. However, other devices that have entered the picture provide limited or no support for HTML and are very heterogeneous in terms of display size, colour depth and rendering facilities. Therefore even if such a client supports HTML, it clearly needs a different variant than a desktop browser to cater for the different screen dimensions. The possibility of defining multiple designs uncoupled from the content is the next requirement that a web engineering system must meet.

Web Officer   Up to now, we have concerned ourselves with content and presentation, but there are other key dimensions in designing a web engineering platform that tend to be forgotten. These further requirements that surpass the simple separation of content and presentation are introduced by the emergence of web officers. Web officers have only come into existence since the rise of large-scale corporate web sites. A web officer's job involves determining the overall structure of a web site, designing its navigation and deciding upon personalisation options.

To be able to design the navigation and content structure of a web page independently from the content and presentation, it is necessary not only to distinguish between these two concepts, but also to enforce a clear separation of content, presentation and structure. This requirement is particularly needed when creating web sites for multiple presentation channels. If structure is mingled with either content or presentation, it has to be recreated or even duplicated for every presentation channel. Of course, separating structure from presentation does not mean that it cannot vary across such channels if necessary.

Designing and creating a personalisation scheme for a web site is a further task of a web officer. Specification and implementation of such personalisation schemes is, therefore, another general requirement of a web engineering system. Such a scheme determines which parts of a site can be personalised and what options are available. For instance, it could be possible for a user of a web site to create his own version of certain content. A more restrictive option would be that the common user may only annotate or comment the content of the web site. We will call this user-centric personalisation explicit personalisation, because the user decides how the web site should behave. Another form of personalisation is implicit personalisation. Here the client context influences how the platform for web engineering delivers the pages to the user.

Web Site Manager Every major company uses a set of business processes and predefined workflows that describe how a content object has to evolve until it is published on the corporate web site. Using such processes, a manager can guarantee that no incorrect or out-of-date content is ever shown on a page. Since all personnel supervised by the web site manager develop the web site via the implementation platform, these workflows have to be integrated and enforced by the system. A graphical representation of a simple example for a publishing workflow is given in Figure 5.1.

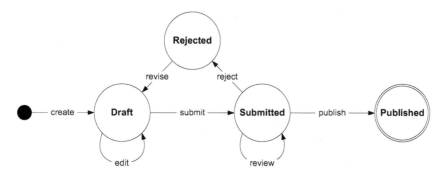

Figure 5.1: Example workflow

Initially, a content author creates a content object. While they are editing the object, it is in the state of *Draft* and cannot be accessed or viewed by anyone else. As soon as the editing is finished and the content should be published, the state of the object is changed to *Submitted*. Submitted objects are reviewed by the supervisor. If the object is found to be ready for publication, it is published and enters the *Published* state. Objects that have been approved become visible for everybody visiting the web site. If, however, the object cannot be published in its current state, the supervisor rejects it and it assumes the *Rejected* state. The corresponding content author is informed and they may choose to revise the object which then enters the *Draft* state once again.

This simple workflow consists of four states. However, a platform for web engineering should be capable of supporting arbitrary processes, as these tend to vary between companies and application domains. Of course, it must also keep track of changes using revisional versioning. The system should further be able to notify the corresponding persons whenever state transitions occur.

Web Developer The last group of personnel involved in creating a web site are the web developers. Many web pages today are not only presenting information to a user, but are also highly interactive applications such as e-learning systems or e-banking solutions. Web developers are responsible for these active elements of a web site, which may involve programming to implement a certain application logic.

A web engineering platform must provide web developers with a coherent and open application development platform that offers basic web functionality, such as user tracking and shopping carts as optional software modules. A system that meets this requirement prevents developers from implementing the same components over and over again for every solution they are building, and introduces the principles of good software design into the realm of web site programming.

5.2 Approach

Most existing implementation platforms have been developed to suit a specific need or to address a given problem and are therefore heterogeneous in nature. A common design principle shared by many of these systems is the concept of separation of content, structure and presentation. As previously stated in the requirements section, this concept alone is not sufficient to address all challenges posed by today's web sites. To address this situation, we have created a consistent and sufficient model for implementing web sites that require both context-aware functionality as well as traditional features of content management, such as user access control and workflow management. However, before discussing our model in detail, we first present a classification of existing implementation platforms that will help to relate our work to previous approaches.

The first methodology of designing a web engineering platform has evolved in the database community. We therefore call it the database-based approach. With the growing importance of the Internet, the need for web access to databases and publishing the contents of a database on the web has arisen. Many different solutions have been developed that allow databases to be browsed over the web and some of them have gone as far as integrating the concepts of content management into their solutions. The possibility of bringing any existing database to the web clearly is the main advantage of this approach. But there are also other more subtle concepts that can be considered very useful. As the database community has developed a great number of data models that can be used to represent content in a semantically rich way, these models can now be employed to design the data underlying a web site, thereby enabling the content editor to work with richer data concepts than just texts and images. Alongside these benefits and advantages, there are also a number of serious disadvantages and limitations to this approach. The most severe is, of course, the lack of support for context-aware data management that would allow content in different variants and formats. Another drawback that can be observed in most of these systems is their limited support for dynamic content modification, as too many models and layers mediate between the actual data and its final presentation.

The second approach is orthogonal to the first and has emerged in the publishing community. As this approach focuses around mapping documents to a database rather than bringing a database to the web, we shall call it the document-based approach. Instead of using an arbitrary database with a freely definable schema to store the data of a web site, systems belonging to this category employ a specialised database with a schema tailored to the data types occurring in documents. Such a schema commonly will include concepts such as texts, images, URLs or links. Clearly, it is very easy to design a schema like this to separate the concept of an object and its actual content, thus enabling content objects in multiple formats and variants. Another advantage of such systems is their great flexibility. As there is no complex application model involved, it is very easy to perform small changes to a web site without defining new types of objects. However, with great flexibility always comes loss of control. As there is no possibility to define user-types belonging to the application domain of a web site, there is also no semantic information that a set of texts, images and links actually represents such a user-defined object. Upon modification of the data, the system is not able to check whether the changes are valid or if they violate an implicitly assumed concept in the application domain. But there are also other more aggravating consequences to the lack of object-orientation that come with the lack of support for user-defined types. Data reuse becomes tedious or even infeasible. Imagine, for example, a person object consisting of text representing a person's name, an image and a link capturing the person's homepage. A document-based system can only manage these three pieces of data independently, as it offers no notion to group them into a person object. If this person appears on multiple pages of a web site, the content editor must repeatedly re-establish the person concept by hand. Such a procedure is painful at best, but it is also very likely to be error-prone.

Both the database-based and document-based approaches have their advantages and disadvantages. The first approach is very strong on conceptual data modelling, supporting both high-level object concepts and semantic information about the application domain. The latter has strong concepts for representing data types typical to the web. As a logical consequence, our implementation platform for web engineering focuses on combining the powerful aspects of these orthogonal approaches into one consistent model. In the remainder of this section we present the important parts of this model and show how these information concepts can be used to satisfy the proposed requirements. But before going into the details of the model, we first introduce some key ideas and concepts that enable database-like application modelling to be integrated with traditional content management.

At the heart of our model is the key concept of separation of content, structure, view and presentation. To adequately meet all proposed requirements, we found that separation of content, structure and presentation is not sufficient. Many model-based approaches feature a concept that defines which aspects of a content object are displayed to the user. Further, most of them also allow content to be aggregated by leveraging the relationships defined in the underlying data model. In an adaptive web information system, views are an important aspect of tailoring information to the current context. Implementation platforms, such as content management systems, do not provide adequate support for this concept. Therefore, an important construct that we have introduced in our model is the view concept. Relational databases already feature the notion of a view on a data table. Although this concept is similar to the one introduced by our model, it cannot be used to implement the desired behaviour in a straightforward way. To allow the implementation platform to manage views it is important to make them a first order concept and store all related metadata in the system.

Figure 5.2 gives an overview of the entire information model used in our platform for web engineering. The model is specified using the graphical notation of the OM data model, as introduced in Section 4.2.1, and is organised as follows. In the centre, a collection hierarchy with the root collection **Elements** represents the information concepts, content, structure, view and presentation, as used in our implementation platform. To its right another collection hierarchy below the **Users** collection manages users and user groups as well as the access rights granted to them. Finally, in the upper left corner of the model, concepts for modelling business processes in terms of workflows are shown. In order to graphically represent concepts that can have revisional and alternative versions, as defined in the previous chapter, we have introduced an extension to the graphical notation of OM. In the figure, collections that are shown having a member type with a double shadow will have context-aware and revisional behaviour.

Content   The **Contents** collection of type **content** contains all the objects representing information that has been created for a given web application. The nature of the actual content objects is highly application dependent and can therefore not be shown in the figure. For example, if our platform were to be used to implement a web site design specified by one of the model-based approaches, all concepts defined in their information model would be realised as suptypes and subcollections of **content** and **Contents** respectively. Otherwise, if the platform were to be extended to offer functionality common to a document-based content management system, subtypes representing document objects such as text, image, table or link would need to be defined. Clearly, it is also possible to intertwine both approaches by defining both application and document types at the same time. Moreover, since all types are defined within one system, application types can be defined to have attributes referencing document objects and vice versa. Therefore, based on extensibility and inheritance, type **content** is the concept provided by our model that allows the document-based approach to be integrated with the database-based approach. As indicated by the double shadow of the member type of the **Contents** collection, content objects have revisional and alternative versions. In this way, our platform can both keep track of the evolution of a content object and offer context-dependent behaviour at run-time.

Structure   To embed content objects into a possibly complex structure, our model uses the composite pattern [116] which is a well-known solution in software engineering used to build hierarchical tree structures. The composite pattern builds structures based on the notions of components and containers where components are the leaf nodes and containers are inner nodes. Since a container is also a component, arbitrarily complex

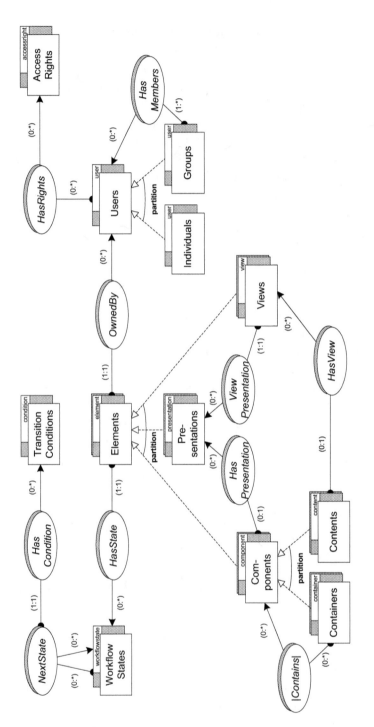

Figure 5.2: Data model of the implementation platform

structures can be represented using recursion. In our data model, the composite pattern is represented by collections **Components** and **Containers** as well as by the association |*Contains*|. The association captures which components are contained in a container. As order is important, it has been modelled as a ranking collection. In contrast to the pure composite pattern where leaf nodes are represented as components, we have chosen to introduce collection **Contents** to represent those nodes for the reasons stated above. The **partition** classification constraint over the two subcollection constraints ensures that every object of **component** contained in the **Components** collection is either of type **container** or **content**.

Due to its simplicity, this approach of representing structure in a web engineering platform is very general. In the case of realising a traditional content management system, containers take the roles of directories, subdirectories and files, whereas contents are used to represent pieces of text or images. However, if our system were to be used as an implementation platform for a WebML hypertext, containers would take on the functionality of site views, pages and page areas, while the various units are mapped to content objects. Since structure objects are also represented as versioned objects, our implementation platform can offer additional functionality that has not yet been considered in the existing approaches. For example, all container objects may have context-dependent variants that provide support for adapted content structure on different devices. Clearly, a mobile device such as a PDA or a media phone requires a different structure and navigation than a traditional web browser. Based on the object referencing mechanism introduced in the previous chapter, different variants of a structure node can contain different sets of component objects. This behaviour is achieved by associating the fully specified object identifiers of a container object with the partially specified identifier of the component object in the |*Contains*| association. If, instead, only a partial identifier is used to reference the container, all its variants contain the same components.

View   As motivated before, views are an important concept for personalisation and therefore have been incorporated as a core construct in the information model for content management. They are represented by collection **Views** with member type **view**. Each view can be linked to a content object through the *HasView* association. This association captures which view the system will use to render the content. Basically, a view object consists of two attribute values. First, it specifies a query that expresses which parts of the content object are used or which content is aggregated, based on the underlying database schema. Second, it states for which type of content objects the view object is applicable. The latter attribute is recorded mainly for type safety to ensure that the object type expected by the view matches the one of the content object. Again, versioned objects are used to represent views in our model. Therefore, content objects may be represented differently in different contexts. If the context information includes data about the current user, views can be used to personalise the content of a web site.

Presentation   The presentation objects contained in collection Presentations transform the content objects into a format that can be displayed by the client. Type presentation specifies that every presentation object must contain a rendering template that can be used to transform the content, as described. As with views, each presentation object also states for which type of content object it is intended, to make sure that the content and the template match. Through the use of variants, a presentation object may specify several versions of the template that are selected according to the current context. For example, a presentation object for the application type person could contain a variant for an XHTML browser, a Wireless Mark-up Language (WML) browser on a mobile phone, and a VoiceXML client. A presentation object is either linked to a component using the *HasPresentation* association or to a view by association *ViewPresentation*. If a content object is not rendered using a view, the template of the presentation object linked to it by *HasPresentation* will be used. However, if a view is applied to a content object, the type and shape of this object may change, as attributes may be omitted and others may be aggregated from related objects. Therefore, each view object has to be associated with a presentation object that is capable of handling the dynamic type created by the view. This is expressed by the (1:1) cardinality at the source of *ViewPresentation*. However, this constraint is not sufficient, as the different variants of a view object may produce different dynamic output types. Actually, each variant of a view object has to be linked to a presentation object, but at the moment there is no way to specify such a constraint graphically.

Workflow   The workflow model used to meet the requirements of a team of web site authors with various user roles is shown in the upper left corner of our data model. A collection Elements has been introduced to contain all information concepts introduced so far. The **partition** constraint ensures that every member of the Elements collection is either a component, presentation or view object. Each element object in our system is linked to a member of collection Workflow States. Type workflowstate provides the necessary means for a web site manager to define how an object evolves during its life-cycle. We have chosen to represent workflows as directed graphs with labelled edges. The nodes of the graph are represented by the members of collection Workflow States, while the edges connecting them are captured by the *NextState* association. Each workflow state can have any number of successor states. If a state has no successor, it is called an accepting state indicating that the corresponding workflow has terminated. Each edge is associated through the *HasCondition* association with a member of collection Transition Conditions. Transition conditions control whether it is possible for an element object with a given workflow state to pass into one of the successor states. As workflow states are linked to element objects, the evolution of all information concepts can be controlled by a predefined business process.

User Management   The last part of our information model is the user management part of the model shown on the right-hand side of Figure 5.2. The Users collection contains the objects representing all users of our system. To keep track of who is responsible for an element object, each one of them is associated with exactly one of these users through the *OwnedBy* association.   Our system knows two different kinds of users represented by the collections Individuals and Groups. A user group can contain other users linked to it by the *HasMembers* association. Again, the previously discussed composite pattern is used to allow fine-grained hierarchies of users and user groups to be modelled. User rights are represented by members of collection Access Rights which are used to build Access Control Lists (ACL) by linking the corresponding rights to an individual user or a user group through the *HasRights* association. Profiting from the hierarchical organisation of users, our system provides support for inheritable rights by checking the rights, not only at user-level, but also by traversing the user-tree to its root and checking the rights at every node encountered on this path.

5.3   Implementation

Based on the information model and the concepts it defines, a web content management system has been implemented that constitutes a suitable platform for context-aware web engineering. The system consists of two main components, a content server and a management client application. The server component handles requests from a variety of clients and returns appropriate responses, whereas the client application is used to create and manage the web site. Figure 5.3 gives a high-level overview of the components involved in our content management system.

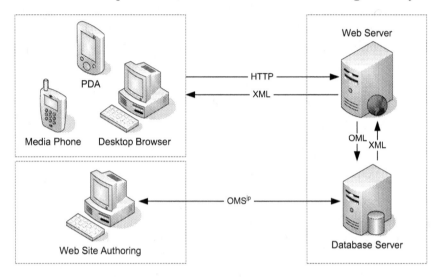

Figure 5.3: System architecture overview

On the left-hand side, the possible clients that are supported by the content management system are depicted. At the top, a non-exhaustive set of possible client browsers, such as media phones, PDAs and desktop browsers is shown. These clients access the server component using the HTTP and, as a response, get back an XML document format such as XHTML, WML or VoiceXML. Below these browsing clients, the management client is shown. In our system, web sites are authored using client software that guides the development process along the concepts discussed above. In contrast to client browsers that communicate with the server through standard Internet protocols, the authoring client uses the OMS[jp] library presented in the previous chapter to access the content management database on the server side.

The content server of our web content management is shown on the right-hand side of the figure. The content server consists of two components. First, the database server manages all data and metadata of the web site according to the information model. Second, the web server, is responsible for handling client requests by retrieving the information from the database server and transforming it into the appropriate representation. The web server uses the OML to send queries to the database. The query results are then returned in an XML format that represents OM objects. In the remainder of this section, both the content server and the management client will be discussed in more detail. Together they form a web content management system which, due to its flexibility, we have called *Extensible Content Management System (XCM)*.

5.3.1 Content Server

The content server [119, 252] handles requests coming from browsing clients and the management client. Since the management client communicates with the database server directly, there is no additional logic on the server side to handle such requests. Consequently, this interface will not be discussed in further detail as it has already been presented in detail in the previous chapter. Here, we focus on how the content server handles requests from browsing clients and how it publishes content across multiple delivery channels. Browsing clients contact the content server using HTTP. To handle such requests, the web server component of our system is implemented as a Java Servlet, as this technology provides a simple but powerful way of implementing custom server components. The servlet consists of several modules that take care of different tasks during request handling.

The context gathering component analyses the request sent by the client and extracts all context information. Context information can be transmitted from the client to the content server in two different ways. On the one hand, implicit context information can be extracted from the header of the HTTP protocol. For example, the browser string can be analysed to determine the capabilities of the client in terms of the desired mark-up and device properties. Context can, on the other hand, also be given explicitly to the content server. When this option is used, context information is encoded in the query string of the HTTP request or in terms of client profiles such as Composite Capabilities/Preference Profiles (CC/PP) [163]. Context information is then used to set the current context state on the database server. As each request handled by the content management system has its own connection to the database server, we use the session level to set the context state. Doing so, each request can be handled according to the context it has specified.

After the context has been determined, the component object requested by the client has to be identified. Clients can request the delivery

of either a container object or a content object. As there is no point in
serving presentation or view objects to the client, this option is not available in the system. To improve usability, all component objects can be
identified using a human-readable name instead of the object identifiers
used by the system. This name is also transmitted to the content server
as part of the query string contained in the client request. After it has
been extracted, it is forwarded to the content publisher component that is
responsible for creating a suitable presentation of the requested content.
The publishing process used by this component is shown in Figure 5.4

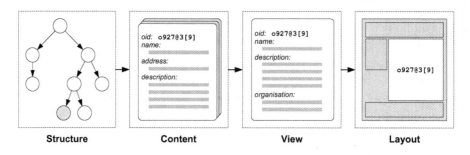

| Structure | Content | View | Layout |

Figure 5.4: Publishing process

The first step undertaken by the content publisher depends on whether a container or a content object has been requested. If the client
requested a container object, the publishing process described below has
to be applied recursively to all components contained within the container. If, however, a content object is requested, the publishing process
is executed only once. Assume that the grey circle in the figure represents the component object requested by the client. Since it is one of the
leaf nodes of the structure tree, it represents a content object and can be
directly retrieved from the database. As shown in the figure, the content
object could represent a person object with attributes *name*, *address* and
description. When retrieving the object, the underlying database system
automatically selects the object variant that is most appropriate to the
current context. In the figure this is suggested by representing the object
as a stack of versions where the top version with identifier o927@3[9] is
the one with the highest score value. The content publisher then retrieves the view object associated with this content object and applies
it. In our example, the application of the view object results in the
disappearance of attribute *address* and in the appearance of aggregated
information about the *organisation* this person works for. Finally, the
publishing component retrieves the presentation objects for the object

it is currently rendering. By applying the template to the object, the final presentation of the content is generated and returned to the servlet which sends it back to the client.

During the publishing process, our system exploits the fact that all query results obtained from the database server are represented in XML. Therefore, while rendering a component object, the content publisher assembles an XML document that either contains a single content object, as described above, or a tree of content objects representing a container object. The hierarchical nature of XML makes it an ideal representation format for the notion of structure as defined by our approach. Note that the exact structure of the created document is entirely based on the metadata stored in our system. Figure 5.5 shows how the person object introduced in the above example is represented in XML. Each component object is mapped to a <**webobject**> element. As shown in the figure, the element has at least the three attributes **stamp**, **oid** and **type**. The first of these attributes is a unique identifier added to the element by the publishing component. In contrast to the second attribute that represents the identifier of the object within the database, the **stamp** is required as the same object can be included more than once in one content delivery. In this case it should still be possible to render the different occurrences of the content object using different templates. To define which template is intended for which occurrence of the content object, each of them has to have a unique identifier different from the database object identifier. The third attribute included contains the type of the object. This information is included for two reasons. First, it can be useful for developers if they need to trace the system's operation. Second, the value of this attribute can be used to create type-safe templates that are only applicable to the types of objects they have been designed for. In the given example, the value `view:pers-org` indicates that the content object is not of a type defined in the database schema but rather has been produced by applying a view called `pers-org`. The attributes of the content object are represented by <**property**> elements with an attribute **name**. Attribute values are captured in XML by an element named after the database type of the attribute. In the figure, all attributes of the content object are of type string and are represented by <**string**> elements. Note that the first <**property**> element is not an attribute defined by the user but a human-readable identifier of the component object as discussed above.

When the XML document is created, an XSLT stylesheet is dynamically generated by assembling all templates stored in the presentation

```
<webobject stamp="we0" oid="o927@3[9]" type="view:pers-org">
  <property name="sys:name">
    <string>...</string>
  </property>
  <property name="name">
    <string>...</string>
  </property>
  <property name="description">
    <string>...</string>
  </property>
  <property name="organisation">
    <string>...</string>
  </property>
</webobject>
```

Figure 5.5: XML representation of a person object

objects. Since our system already uses XML to represent the content of a web page during the rendering process, the choice of XSLT as the language for the presentation templates is only natural. In a final step, the XML document is transformed into the appropriate mark-up using this generated XSLT stylesheet. Since all pages in our system are generated dynamically from the database, another important factor that has great influence on the performance of the system is the caching strategy used on the server side. In our system caches can be used at various levels of granularity. Not only is it possible to cache objects or queries at the database level, the system can also manage caches for partial or complete XML and XSLT documents and even fully generated pages that are known to change rarely.

5.3.2 Management Client

Defining a web site in terms of the information concepts defined by the presented data model is a challenging task, as the model is very complex and fine-grained to allow maximum flexibility of dynamically composing web sites. When considering the differing backgrounds of all the personnel in charge of creating and maintaining a web site, working at the level of database query and data manipulation statements is hardly an option. Therefore, a graphical management client, the *XCM SiteManager* [299, 45, 121], has been developed to work with the database that implements our information model. Apart from making working with the content management system more user-friendly, XCM SiteManager also serves another important purpose in that it breaks down the design process into well-defined steps. These steps relate to the different user roles of the personnel that work with the system.

The first phase consists of defining the data model of the content that is presented on the web site. Data modelling is followed by the content authoring step which creates all required content objects. In the next phase, structure definition, content objects are placed in containers and structured hierarchically. Finally, the last phase defines the presentation in terms of layout templates. Currently, XCM SiteManager does not allow views for objects to be defined graphically and thus there is no design step to support this task. In the following, we will present each of these four phases of creating a web site and discuss how they are supported by XCM SiteManager. The presentation is based on the example of a web site for an academic research group. Apart from a welcome page, the web site will include areas that provide information about the group's research, the teaching and the people that work in the research group. Within the research area, information about projects and publications will be made available, whereas the teaching section contains details about lectures, seminars and student projects. Finally, in the people section of the web site, each group member is represented by a personal web page with their address and a short curriculum vitae.

Model   As mentioned before, the first task in creating a web site with XCM SiteManager is to model the underlying application domain. This is the task of a data management expert who decides which types of content objects should be available on the web site and how they are defined in terms of attributes. In the example of a web site for a research group described above, types to represent persons, lectures, seminars, student works, publications and projects have to be defined. This task is supported by the model panel of the XCM SiteManager, shown in Figure 5.6. The model panel is divided into two areas. On the left-hand side, all types currently defined in the system are shown as a hierarchy representing the inheritance relationships between them. XCM features a set of built-in document types that are always available to the web site developer. The names of these types are prefixed with cm. Built-in types can neither be modified nor deleted by the user. The user can, however, browse the definitions of built-in types and create user-defined types by specialisation of system-defined types.

These built-in document types are either a specialisation of type cmcontainer or of type cmcontent and correspond to the types container

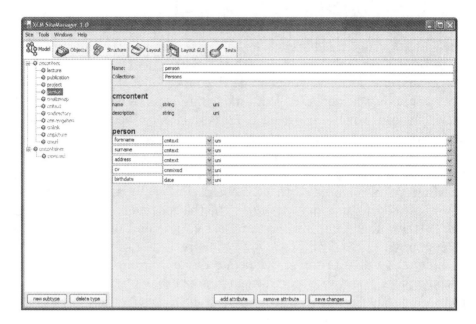

Figure 5.6: Model panel

and content in our information model. On the one hand, document types representing common content formats such as texts, pictures, URLs and links are provided. On the other hand, XCM offers document types that can be used to create dynamic content objects, such as navigations and site-maps. Using the buttons at the bottom of the type hierarchy, user-defined types can be created as subtypes of already existing types. Similarly, previously created types can be deleted if they are no longer required. In contrast to system-defined types, user-defined types can be edited and updated at any time.

To browse or modify a type, the type has to be selected in the type hierarchy on the left-hand side. This action will display the properties of the selected type on the right-hand side of the model panel. Figure 5.6 shows the type editor that is displayed when the application type person is selected. This type represents the members of the research group. At the top of the type editor, the name of the type and the default collection for objects of this type can be set. Below that, the attributes of type cmcontent are shown. Since cmcontent is a system-defined type, these attributes cannot be changed. Next are the attributes that have been defined by the data management expert to represent a member of the research group. Each person has a forename, surname, address, curriculum vitae and a date of birth. Note that apart from the database type **date** that is used to represent the date of birth, all other attributes are defined based on the document types provided by XCM. Attributes of user-defined types can be added and removed using the corresponding buttons at the bottom of the type editor.

Content Based on the application types defined by the data model, content providers author the required data in terms of content objects. While the definition of the application model of the web site is clearly the first design step, data can also be added at any point in time, even when the subsequent phases of the design process are also already under way. The user interface that XCM SiteManager offers for content providers is shown in Figure 5.7. In contrast to the model panel, the object panel is divided into three zones. At the left of the panel, two lists provide access to all objects currently defined in the system. The list of object types provides a filter for the list of objects that then displays all objects of the selected type. In the example given in the figure, type **cmtext** is selected and thus all three text objects available on the web site are displayed. At the bottom of the list of all objects of a given type, two buttons are available to create a new object or to delete one.

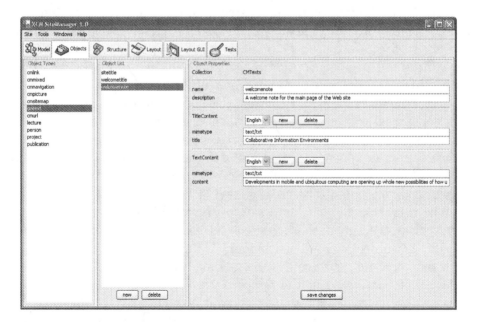

Figure 5.7: Objects panel

On the right-hand side of the object panel, the object editor for the selected object is shown. At the top of the object editor the attributes *name* and *description* that are common to all content objects can be defined. Below these attributes, the content specific to an object of type cmtext can be authored. Type cmtext defines two attributes that represent the title and the body of the text content object. At the start of each attribute section, a drop-down list allows the context state to be set in which the entered content is appropriate. Whereas the XCM system itself does not predefine any notion of context, the graphical interface of XCM SiteManager is currently only capable of providing authoring support for content adaptation based on the language context. Therefore, the list of possible context states includes the names of the languages in which the web site will be accessible. XCM SiteManager does however support the definition of additional languages for the web site through a special dialogue accessible from the main menu. Alternative versions of the objects are managed using the buttons next to the list of context state that allow new variants to be created or old ones to be deleted.

Structure   The next phase of creating a web site with XCM SiteManager involves the web officer who decides how the authored content is to be structured. Based on the previously discussed composite pattern, a web officer defines a hierarchical structure that makes the content accessible to the browsing clients. To ease this task, three special kinds of container objects are used to build a structure in a more user-friendly way. Inspired by the concept of folders and files, XCM SiteManager provides directory and web page container objects. While directories can be nested hierarchically and contain a set of pages, pages can only contain content objects. An exception to this rule are collections, the third kind of container objects that support the reuse of frequently occurring groups of content objects, such as found in the header or the footer of web pages. The structure panel that is used to create and edit a hierarchical organisation of content objects is shown in Figure 5.8.

The region on the left-hand side of the structure panel displays the hierarchical structure of the web site as a tree consisting of the three types of container objects mentioned before. The tree is rooted at a directory with the name *root* that cannot be modified by the user. The container object that is selected in the figure bears the name *index.html* and is of type web page. It represents the main or home page of the web site that is currently being created with XCM SiteManager. As can be seen from the figure, the home page contains one further container object.

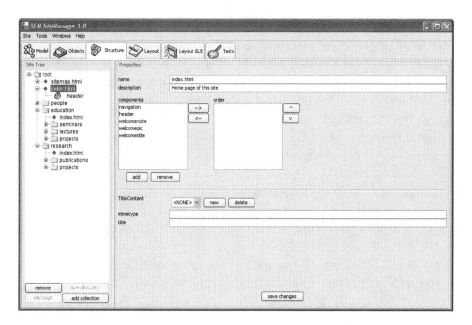

Figure 5.8: Structure panel

It represents the header of the main page and is a collection container object. At the bottom of the web site structure tree, a set of buttons is provided that allow directories, pages and collections to be created or deleted. On the right-hand side of the structure panel, the structure object editor is shown. It displays the properties of the currently selected object in the tree view of the site structure. Two attributes, *name* and *description*, that are common to all structure objects can be edited at the top of the editor. Below them, the editor displays a list of all components that have been placed in the container. In contrast to the structure tree that only displays structure objects, this list contains both structure and content objects. Using the buttons below the list, existing component objects can be added or removed. As the association linking a container to its child components has been defined as a ranking collection, XCM SiteManager allows a partial order to be defined over the components objects. This is achieved by moving all components for which order is important into the second list to the right of the first. Using the two buttons on the right, the order of the components can be defined by moving the selected component up or down. Finally, at the bottom of the editor, a title for the structure object can be defined by creating a variant for the desired language context state.

Presentation   The last step of defining a web site with the management client application is the task of the web designer to design what
the pages are going to look like for all available presentation channels.
XCM SiteManager offers two possible ways to define the look and feel.
The low-level option is implementing all required layout templates manually and associating them with the corresponding component objects.
For this approach, XCM SiteManager offers a layout panel that allows
each component of a web site to be selected and an appropriate XSLT
template to be created. To ease this process, a preview of the selected
component as it will be rendered in XML is displayed. Clearly, creating the presentation of an entire web site is neither feasible nor suitable
for graphical designers that are accustomed to work graphically. Therefore, this functionality of XCM SiteManager will not be discussed in
further detail. Instead, the graphical layout editor that provides an intuitive and easy-to-use way of creating the required XSLT templates is
presented. Generally speaking, it has to be noted that specifying the
presentation of web pages both at the conceptual level during web site
modelling and at the implementation level is a research area that has not
yet yielded satisfactory solutions. While many web site models shy away
from offering a suitable model for presentation specification, very few
graphical template editors have been proposed that can leverage the full
potential of a language such as XSLT [121]. The graphical layout editor
of XCM SiteManager shown in Figure 5.9 is capable of designing a web
site graphically, while at the same time supporting multiple presentation
channels.

   As shown in the figure, the user interface is divided into two regions.
On the left hand side, the structure of the content of the current web
page is displayed. The designer can place content by drag-and-drop onto
the preview of the web page shown on the right hand side. When placing
content, the editor calculates the minimum space required to display the
selected item and displays a shaded box of the appropriate size. Conflicts
resulting from overlap or lack of space are detected automatically and
shown to the user by changing the colour of the placeholder to red. In
addition to content objects of the basic document types presented above,
the graphical layout editor also provides support for the basic concepts of
component and container, as well as content objects that are generated
by the server at run-time, such as navigation and site-map components.
Since the type model of XCM can be extended by the user, the graphical
layout editor also provides fall-back support to cope with these unknown
data types. It is, however, possible to also extend the editor in order

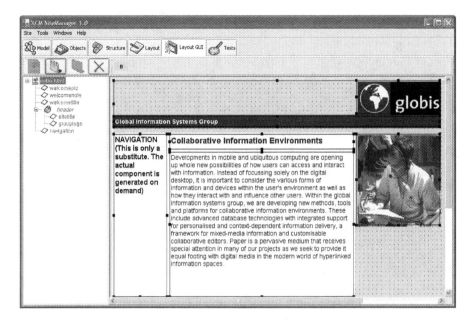

Figure 5.9: Graphical layout panel

to work with user-defined data types. The application further provides support to set attributes governing the appearance of the content such as text style, size and colour or image width and height. It is, for example, possible to define a background colour for a container to visually group all of the components contained within that container. When doing so, the user can also choose to propagate settings from one level of the hierarchy down to the levels below.

After the web designer has completed the layout of a page, the work is saved as presentation metadata in the content management system. Naturally, previously defined layouts can also be loaded into the editor and changed as seen fit at a later point in time. As discussed before, presentation metadata is managed as database objects storing layout templates. Therefore, saving the layout of a page corresponds to creating these templates and presentation objects as well as associating them with the component objects to which they apply. To generate the presentation templates, the graphical layout editor uses a process based on the so-called metatemplates. The name metatemplate comes from the fact that in contrast to presentation templates that render content to be displayed on the client, metatemplates are templates that generate templates. An overview of the four main steps of this process is shown in Figure 5.10. Before explaining each of these steps in detail, we briefly give an overview of the process. At the beginning is the generic specification of the layout which is expressed in XML. The metatemplates then transform the layout into a set of templates. Multiple metatemplates can be applied to achieve multi-channel presentations. The generation of templates is done at design-time and therefore has no negative impact on the overall system performance. In the third step at run-time, the templates generated in the second step are used to render the final representation. Finally, in the fourth step, this representation is sent back to the browser and displayed to the user. In the following we will explain the entire process step-by-step in more detail.

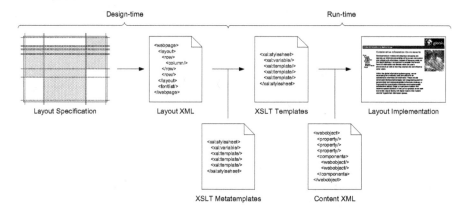

Figure 5.10: Metatemplate process

To allow designers to generate layouts that work for multiple presentation channels, it is important to represent the features they have in common in a standard way. It should, however, still be possible to extend this representation with features that are special to one presentation channel only or requirements that are yet to emerge. We have designed an XML-based mark-up language to express such generic layouts. All visual layouts partition a two-dimensional space into non-overlapping regions where content is placed. Hence, we have chosen the notion of a grid to model the basic content of a layout. A grid can contain an arbitrary number of columns and rows. The exact number of these two dimensions is determined by the concrete layout in question. Cells are used to store content and can be located at any point (x, y) where x denotes the column and y denotes the row in the grid. Although it is also possible for cells to span multiple columns or rows, it is not allowed for any two cells to overlap. To profit from full flexibility, cells can also contain other layout grids to allow previously defined layouts to be reused. This approach of modelling the layout is very similar to the one used in most toolkits which implement graphical user interfaces. For instance, in the Abstract Window Toolkit (AWT) within the Java Platform, there are layout classes such as `GridLayout` or `GridBagLayout` that are used to display graphical components on a two-dimensional plane.

To determine which types of content should be provided as standard visual controls for all presentation channels, we determined the set of document elements that can be found in all of these channels. As a result, we decided to offer text, image, uri and link. It is important to distinguish here between a Universal Resource Identifier (URI) and a link. The URI is merely a pointer to a resource on the World Wide Web, whereas the link is the combination of such a pointer with a resource, for example, a text or image. Also, the set of attributes that are supported on all presentation channels, and thus should be editable in these standard types, had to be determined. As presentation channels vary greatly in this respect, the set of common editable attributes is small. It comprises properties such as font size, style and colour for text, or width and height for images. An excerpt of the Document Type Definition (DTD) of our layout mark-up language, illustrating a link component, is shown in Figure 5.11.

```
<!ELEMENT link (component|text|picture)>
<!ATTLIST link
    name        CDATA    #REQUIRED
    id          CDATA    #REQUIRED
    parent      CDATA    #REQUIRED
    background  CDATA    #REQUIRED
    width       CDATA    #REQUIRED
    height      CDATA    #REQUIRED
    x           CDATA    #REQUIRED
    y           CDATA    #REQUIRED
>
```

Figure 5.11: Excerpt of the layout DTD

Clearly, restricting the capabilities to these common features will lead to very limited support for the needs of today's web designers. Hence, additional concepts have been built into the layout specification to ease customisation to the needs of a specific layout. One of these concepts is extensibility, the key to provide additional, more complex types than the ones mentioned before. Imagine again the web site for an academic research group. As discussed before, the data model of such a web site will contain high-level application objects such as lectures, publications, projects and persons. As it is not advisable to break these objects down into basic types, the metatemplate approach supports the definition of new additional types that mirror the extensibility of the database schema.

The next step in the generation process is the application of the metatemplates to the XML representation of the layout specification. Metatemplates are an additional step of indirection, necessary to generate more than one set of templates from the described layout representation. Clearly, this could also be done using software modules to generate the various stylesheets. This approach, however, is far too static and has very poor support for extensibility. In contrast, using metatemplates to generate the sets of templates is very flexible and additional channels or variants are added easily. Figure 5.12 shows a metatemplate for a link. This simple version merely creates an HTML anchor tag and sets the <**href**> tag accordingly. Note how the template delegates the rendering of the resource contained in this link to another template by invoking <**xsl:apply-templates**>. Although the template shown in the figure seems to be quite long and complicated at first sight, it is important to bear in mind that these templates are implemented by expert programmers and do not have to be updated or replaced often. Metatemplates are not affected by changes of the web site layout as they do not encode the layout itself. The only point in time that calls for new metatemplates is when a new presentation channel or additional features of an existing one are to be supported.

Working with metatemplates is more challenging than implementing transformations to a desired mark-up directly in XSLT. A metatemplate combines three levels of mark-up. At the lowest level is the mark-up that will appear in the final document, e.g. the <**a**> tag in our example. One level above are the tags that will make up the template generated by the metatemplate. It is important to understand that since, in metatemplates, XSLT is used to generate XSLT, the tags to be generated cannot simply be included in the metatemplate. The XSLT transformer would not be able to decide which directives to execute in order to generate the template and which to include in the output. Our first attempt to solve this problem involved using different namespaces, a core concept of XML. However, some of the transformers that we are using were unable to cope with such stylesheets and we found that XSLT itself provides a concept to output such nodes. The directive <**xsl:element**> can be used to generate nodes that otherwise would be misinterpreted by the transformer. Together with the element <**xsl:attribute**>, XSLT provides everything

```
<xsl:template match="link">
<xsl:comment>
    Template rule matching a CMLink
</xsl:comment>
<xsl:element name="xsl:template">
  <xsl:attribute name="match">
   <xsl:text>//webobject[@oid='</xsl:text>
   <xsl:value-of select="@parent_id"/>
   <xsl:text>']//webobject[@oid='</xsl:text>
   <xsl:value-of select="@oid"/>
   <xsl:text>']</xsl:text>
  </xsl:attribute>
  <a>
   <xsl:element name="xsl:attribute">
    <xsl:attribute name="name">href</xsl:attribute>
    <xsl:element name="xsl:value-of">
     <xsl:attribute name="select">
      <xsl:text>
         property[@name='target']/webobject/
         property[@name='reference']/string
      </xsl:text>
     </xsl:attribute>
    </xsl:element>
   </xsl:element>
   <xsl:variable name="resource_id">
    <xsl:value-of select="child::*/attribute::oid"/>
   </xsl:variable>
   <xsl:element name="xsl:apply-templates">
    <xsl:attribute name="select">
     <xsl:text>
        //components/webobject[@oid='
     </xsl:text>
     <xsl:value-of select="@oid"/>
     <xsl:text>
        ']/property[@name='resource']/webobject[@oid='
     <xsl:text>
     <xsl:value-of select="$resource_id"/>
     <xsl:text>']</xsl:text>
    </xsl:attribute>
   </xsl:element>
  </a>
</xsl:element>
</xsl:template>
```

Figure 5.12: Metatemplate for a link

needed to generate XSLT. Note how these two concepts have been applied in the example given in Figure 5.12. The last and top-most level of mark-up is the XSLT that is executed by the transformer.

The next and final step of the proposed generation process is the application of the generated templates to the content to generate the final mark-up. Figure 5.13 gives the template that is generated by the metatemplate given above. Looking at the template, one can see that all XPath queries, i.e. specifications of which elements match this template or are selected by the <**xsl:apply-templates**> directive, have been generated automatically by the metatemplate. Clearly, selection based on object ids as done in the example is very restrictive and leads to poor template reusability. This behaviour, however, can be changed very easily by using a slightly more sophisticated metatemplate that would produce more general match and select clauses. Hence, it is more a demonstration of the flexibility of the metatemplate approach, than a disadvantage. Further, as XCM manages the metadata specifying which template is used to render which object, it edits the match clause as generated by the editor at run-time to select the value of the previously introduced **stamp** attribute of the corresponding <**webobject**>.

```
<xsl:template match="//webobject[@oid='...']//webobject[@oid='...']">
   <a>
      <xsl:attribute name="href">
         <xsl:value-of select="property[@name='target']
               /webobject/property[@name='reference']/string"/>
      </xsl:attribute>
      <xsl:apply-templates select="//components/webobject[@oid='...']
               /property[@name='resource']/webobject[@oid='...']"/>
   </a>
</xsl:template>
```

Figure 5.13: Template for a link

It is important to note that the metatemplates are not hard-coded into the application. Rather, there exists a directory hierarchy where all metatemplates can be placed according to the kinds of templates they will produce. This plug-in mechanism to handle metatemplates ensures flexibility and extensibility. Applying the metatemplates will generate a set of templates for the components used in the web page. These templates are then stored in the content management system and metadata associations are established between the content and the generated templates. When XCM Server now receives a request for this web page on a specific presentation channel, it will retrieve the appropriate generated templates to render the page. Hence the page will be delivered to the browser as envisioned and designed by the web designer.

5.4 Discussion

We have presented a web content management system that can serve as an implementation platform for web engineering applications. To support the adaptation requirements of modern web sites, the platform takes advantage of the version model for context-aware data management introduced in Chapter 4. As a motivation for such a content management system, we have gathered a series of requirements according to the user roles that are involved in creating and maintaining a web site. We believe that many existing solutions that addressed these requirements in the past lack clear information concepts and a uniform underlying model. In contrast, we have developed information concepts that should be used to address these challenges and introduced a model suited to building a content management system. Central to this model is a clear separation between content, structure, view and presentation. These four concepts represent the elements of web content management and are used in our model to uniformly realise context-aware behaviour, user management and workflows.

The model forms the core of our web content management system which consists of a server component and a management client. The implementation of both system parts has been discussed in detail, highlighting the capabilities and functioning of the platform. The server component uses the metadata stored in our context-aware data management system to publish adapted content in a process closely related to the presented information concepts. The management client uses the same concepts to structure the design process of a web site into well-defined steps that mirror the tasks of the different user roles. Apart from providing support for designing the application data model as well as authoring and structuring its content, the management client uses an innovative and flexible solution, based on metatemplates, to generate the site presentation. This solution has been developed to close the gap between the technical requirements of the system and the graphical demands made by web designers. Based on an example, both the functioning of the process and its ability to create multi-channel presentations from an intuitively specified layout have been demonstrated.

Many model-based approaches define the hypertext of a web site in terms of the structure of each element and by the links that interconnect these different elements. However, the data model underlying our implementation platform does not incorporate information concepts to manage links as a first order element. While this might seem to be a limitation of our approach, there are several reasons that have led to the decision of excluding links from the information model. One of these reasons is that our system is intended to be used as an implementation platform and therefore does not aspire to be a modelling tool. On the implementation level, links have less semantic meaning and can thus be represented by a simple type of document object that contains an anchor and a target object. An example of this approach of implementing links has been given in the discussion of metatemplates in this chapter. Another reason is that general and powerful linking frameworks have already been proposed in the past. For example, Signer [259] describes a cross-media information server that is capable of managing links between different multimedia resources. This *iServer* platform can be extended through a plug-in mechanism that allows new resources to be described and registered with the server. If the demand for links as a first order concept in our platform arises, we believe that their integration should be effected by leveraging the functionality of such a platform rather than by extending our model with a proprietary representation of links. In this way, our system would remain open, extensible and able to interlink with resources that have already been defined within the iServer platform.

6

A Mobile Personal Information System

Nowadays, multi-channel information systems are often built based on standard web engineering technologies, as they provide basic support for delivering information across channels. In mobile applications, however, accessing information with one of the many different web browsers available for mobile phones, media phones or PDAs is often unsatisfactory. Due to the small screens of portable devices, the information bandwidth is very limited and devices with larger screens often require the use of both hands. Therefore, new web channels such as voice or even paper-based interaction have recently emerged. These new modes of interaction are fundamentally different from the traditional paradigm of accessing information with a web browser. While on the move, a user's environment can change, giving rise to multi-modal interaction patterns. Multi-modal interaction allows different clients and delivery channels to be combined freely, where requests made using one client can trigger responses that are potentially delivered across another channel that is currently more suitable. Hence, the area of mobile and multi-channel information systems provides a challenging application area for context-aware data and content management.

In this chapter we present how the XCM content management system discussed in the previous chapter was used as an implementation platform for a mobile tourist information system. The system was developed to provide information about the Edinburgh festivals to visitors while they explore the city. In this setting, we will discuss how the decision to build our context management system on top of the version model for context-aware data management has aided the development of such an information system. We start by describing the environment into which the application was deployed, and present the essential characteristics of the Edinburgh art festivals. After establishing the background, we go on to present an overview of the architecture and the functionality of our mobile tourist information system. We then discuss in detail how data management and content delivery were implemented using XCM. Finally, we highlight some of the advantages of our approach and point out a few limitations that still need to be addressed.

6.1   The Edinburgh Festivals

Every year, the city of Edinburgh in Scotland is home to a variety of international arts festivals that take place during the month of August. Apart from the world-renowned military tattoo, book, film and music festivals, the Edinburgh Festival Fringe is the world's largest art festival. Over a period of four weeks, the stages of the Fringe festival see around 1,800 events performed. This large number of different shows is supported by an infrastructure of more than 340 venues distributed throughout the city. The venues of the Fringe festival range from spacious theatres and music halls to pubs and tiny cellar rooms as well as impromptu outdoor assemblies. Many shows take place daily or at different venues, leading to a total of about 27,000 performances. The Edinburgh Festivals attract countless tourists each year that visit the city, participate in the festival events and explore Edinburgh's sights and history. Even without international festivals taking place, staying in an unknown city can easily lead to disorientation if the relevant information is not available to the tourist. In this setting, traditional tourist guides that help with the orientation within the city and provide information about its cultural heritage are of limited use. While the historical and geographical content made available by tourist guides is static, information about the festival is highly dynamic as it is frequently subject to change.

The different characteristics of the information that has to be made available to tourists that are in town for the festivals gives rise to a number of delivery channels that are offered in parallel. Purely static information such as content about the history, the sights and the geography of the city itself is published as guide books and maps that are only revised every few years. During August, each festival releases a brochure containing descriptions of all events and schedules indicating when each event will be performed. In addition, most of these festival brochures also provide information about the venues where the events will take place and instructions how to get there. While this information can hardly be considered to be dynamic, it should be noted, nevertheless, that its life-cycle of four weeks a year is drastically shorter than that of traditional tourism information. National newspapers print up-to-date daily listings. In contrast to the festival brochures, these listings can compensate at short notice for changes such as a show being cancelled or relocated to another venue or time. Finally, the delivery channel most suited to dynamic information is the web where current content is always accessible from the web sites of the various festivals. To help visitors, many venues and ticket offices provide kiosk terminals where the latest information about festival events can be accessed on-line.

Each of the delivery channels available to the festival visitors is appropriate in a certain situation or task. However, it would be desirable to have a delivery channel that is capable of supporting all requirements of tourists attending the festivals. For example, the brochure of the Festival Fringe orders the events in alphabetical listings that are grouped together according to event categories such as comedy, music or theatre. This organisation is very useful to get an overview of all events at the festival and is therefore the appropriate information source during the planning phase of the visit. It does, however, not provide the desired information while on the move, as such a festival brochure is not capable of answering queries to find the events that are on nearby or will start in the next half an hour. This information can be obtained from the daily schedule published as a newspaper supplement, as it structures the events based on the time that they start. Although these listings help with establishing which events are about to take place, it is easy to lose oneself in the information, as they combine events from all categories and all festivals. Further, they cannot help with determining what is going on at a certain venue. While larger venues publish a programme of the shows that are performed there, the only way to access such information for smaller venues is often to physically go there and look at the billboards. The only medium that is currently capable of supporting a variety of different access modes to festival information is the web. Here, a visitor to the Edinburgh festivals can browse for events by category, artist, venue or time. While this solution is vastly superior in terms of the dynamics in which information can be updated and accessed, it lacks support for mobility. Current mobile devices suffer from technical limitations such as small screens, poor contrast in outside environments, limited battery life and lack of support for collaboration. It is therefore important to build a system that is capable of delivering content to all possible channels while at the same time allowing the channels to be combined freely.

6.2   A Mobile Multi-Channel Information System

To address the need for multi-channel information access, a tourist information system has been developed that offers the functionality required by visitors of the Edinburgh festivals on a number of very different channels. In this system, called *EdFest* [261, 207], XCM was used as the server component responsible for content management and delivery. The tourist information system can therefore be seen as the first end-user application of the version model for context-aware data management. Based on the requirements of tourists travelling to Edinburgh for the festivals, a set of information services that the information system will support together with a range of possible access channels has been defined. As discussed above, there exist already a number of specialised channels in which information is delivered to festival visitors. In contrast to other tourist information systems that attempt to replace these existing delivery channels with one device that integrates all functionalities, our system aims at recognising the reasons why these channels have been established. Our approach is therefore rather based on augmenting and consolidating existing means of conveying information to tourists than replacing them with new delivery channels.

Following this reasoning, the EdFest tourist information system uses two major delivery channels to publish content about the city of Edinburgh and the festivals. The first channel it uses continues to provide information through festival web sites that can be accessed over the web and through kiosk computers that are located at fixed locations throughout the city. The second channel included in EdFest is a mobile information browser that is implemented based on the interactive paper technology described by Signer [259]. While the festival web sites and the kiosk systems present comparatively traditional requirements to a content management systems such as XCM, the presence of a paper-based browser introduces additional challenges that have not been addressed by previous systems. To support interactive paper, a content management system actually needs to provide two separate delivery channels. First it has to be capable of publishing the content in a format that is suitable to the creation and printing of the actual paper documents. Later, when the documents are being used, the content management system needs to deliver the responses that are triggered when tourists interact with the paper. Currently, digital paper technologies capable of dynamically displaying information on paper are not readily available. Therefore, the result of a user interaction can generally not be displayed on paper but has instead to be delivered through another channel. In the scope of the EdFest project, we have experimented with a number of output channels for interactive paper, such as head-mounted displays, SMS and voice-based content delivery.

The information services that have been defined and implemented for the EdFest tourist information system can be classified into several different categories. As providing information to festival visitors is a primary goal of the system, a large number of services fall into the category of information browsing. The EdFest system provides means to obtain additional information about events and venues. For events, this may include background information about the artists performing the event and indications whether the event contains abusive language or nudity. For venues, browsing services have been defined that provide information about bars and restaurants at a venue as well as how to get there by public transport and whether it is accessible to people with disabilities. Also in this category falls a query interface allowing users to search for events, based on several criteria such as date, time or venue as well as the user's interest or current location. The second category of information services provides a set of functions that implement a simple item recommending system [81]. For any event, a visitor may record a rating on a scale from one to five. These ratings are managed centrally and, upon request, the average rating is calculated and returned to the tourist. In addition to ratings, the EdFest system allows written comments to be recorded that can later be used to select an event based on the recommendations of other people. Finally, to customise the behaviour of the previously discussed search functionality, preferences can be recorded. A festival visitor can configure the system with the categories of events that they are interested in or a list of shows that they would like to see. The process of locating places in a foreign city is a category of information services that is not specific to a festival guide such as EdFest, but common to most available tourist guides. Our system offers services to pinpoint the position of festival venues or the location of the tourist on a map. To locate positions on a map, an interactive process turns the visitor's attention towards the target using an iteration through a series of stepwise refinements of direction specifications. The EdFest system further provides support for checking the availability of tickets for a given performance. Together with a ticket reservation system, this functionality falls into the category of ticket booking services. For any show that is not sold out, a visitor can book up to eight tickets using the reservation system. Finally, the last group of functionality contains services for reminding the tourist about events. If a visitor has expressed interest in a certain event and chosen to set a reminder for it, the system will proactively inform them in time before the show starts.

An overview of the architecture of the EdFest system is given in Figure 6.1. The server component of the tourist information system is shown on the right-hand side of the figure, whereas the range of currently supported clients is shown on the left. The server module consists of three major components. The role and functioning of the web server and the database server managing the data of the XCM system have already been discussed in detail in the previous chapter. In the example of the web site of an academic research group given in that chapter, both content and publishing metadata were managed directly within the database of the XCM system. Within the EdFest system, however, only publishing metadata is managed by XCM, while the actual content is stored on a dedicated application data server shown on the far right-hand side of the figure. This architecture has been chosen for two reasons. First, the content provided by the festival organisers does not require a database that is capable of storing revisional and alternative versions. Keeping the content accessible to applications that do not need content management functionality, such as the management tools of the festival administration is the second motivation for this design. In order for XCM to access the data stored in the application database, we have defined a special type of content objects that act as bi-directional wrappers between the two databases. Given an object identifier and an object type, these wrappers are capable of accessing the data stored in the application database in an almost transparent way.

On the left-hand side of the figure, the clients for which the system currently provides support are listed. The *Kiosk Client* shown at the top represents the traditional access channel of browsing tourist information using an HTML browser on a stationary computer. Kiosk functionality

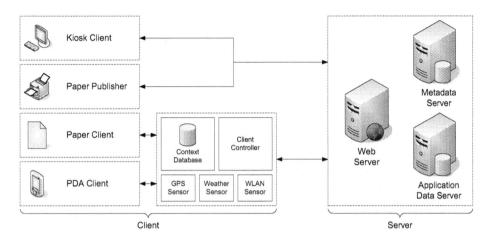

Figure 6.1: Overview of the EdFest architecture

is either accessed at home before visiting the city or in one of ticket offices or larger venues of the festival. Through the kiosk web site, all functionality of the EdFest system as discussed before can be accessed. In addition, visitors can create and print personalised event schedules that only list the events that they are interested in a given period.

Below the kiosk client, the two output channels for the interactive paper client are listed. The *Paper Publisher* client is responsible for creating and printing interactive paper documents based on a specific XML format. In contrast to the other delivery channels, the transformation of the content into a mark-up that can be displayed by the client is not handled by XCM. In the case of the paper publisher, XCM exports the structured content without presentation information. The rendering is then done by the paper publisher when it generates a printable document. This slightly different process is necessary, as the paper publisher needs to keep track of linking metadata during the rendering process. This metadata is then exported and stored in a cross-media information server [259] that links information concepts represented on paper to additional digital information. More detailed information about the publishing process of interactive paper as used in the EdFest system can be found in Norrie et al. [206, 205]. Within our tourist information system, the paper publisher is used both to create a booklet containing all festival events and personalised programmes that visitors print at the kiosk information points.

At run-time, the *Paper Client* uses this cross-media information server to access the digital content managed by XCM whenever tourists interact

with the augmented paper using their digital pen. By decoding an almost invisible dot pattern printed on the paper, the digital pen is capable
of computing the coordinates on the page to which the tourist pointed.
Based on a semantic document model, this (x, y) position is mapped
to a selector that has either been authored manually by the application
designer or generated by the paper publisher. A selector can be an anchor of any number of links that associate it with resources. It is out
of the scope of this thesis to discuss this cross-media information server
and the interactive paper technology in more detail. A complete description of the design and implementation as well as an overview of realised
applications is available in Signer [259].

In the EdFest system, most resources are content management components within the XCM system. Thus, a tourist pointing to a particular
area on the paper triggers the retrieval of content from the server. As
mentioned before, it is currently not possible to display the response of
such a request on paper. The EdFest system, therefore, uses voice output to deliver information to the tourist. This decision was based on the
hypothesis that audio feedback is less intrusive than visual information
delivery through a head-mounted display. Further, as many historic sites
already use personal audio guides to inform visitors, it is relatively safe
to assume that this delivery channel will be well received. As a consequence of unsatisfactory results of experiments with an earlier version
of the EdFest system where voice was used as an input channel as well,
the latest version separates paper and voice into non-overlapping input
and output channels. It should be noted, however, that this decision was
not influenced by the architecture of the system. Technically it would
be perfectly feasible to implement interactive speech dialogues and the
absence of this functionality is entirely due to usability considerations.

The paper client is composed from three different documents shown
in Figure 6.2 that each gives access to information services provided by
XCM. The main document is a brochure that mirrors the information
contained in the programmes published by each of the festivals. Figure 6.2(a) contains one page of the EdFest brochure listing information
about four events. Apart from the static content provided by XCM
using the paper publisher delivery channel, the booklet, when used together with the digital pen, gives access to additional information that is
not found on the pages. For example, a tourist can request information
about ticket availability or set a reminder for a given show. The second
document shown in Figure 6.2(b) is a bookmark appropriately sized to
be used together with the brochure. As can be seen in the figure, the

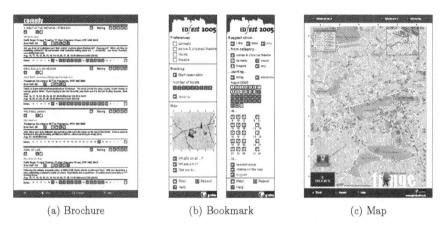

(a) Brochure   (b) Bookmark   (c) Map

Figure 6.2: Documents of the EdFest paper client

bookmark has two sides. The front side depicted on the left of the figure allows preferences to be set and tickets to be booked. Shown on the right of the figure, the back side of the bookmark provides a query interface that can be used to retrieve an event based on a set of specified criteria. Finally, the third document is a map of the city of Edinburgh showing the location of all festival venues. Through the icons seen at the top of Figure 6.2(c), the map provides information about what is going on at a venue, helps the tourist to locate their own position and navigates them to other places. As the navigation service coexists in parallel to the information services offered by XCM, it will not be discussed in more detail in this thesis. A detailed description of functionality and implementation of the interactive paper map used for EdFest can be found in Grossniklaus et al. [122].

As an alternative to the interactive paper client, a mobile *PDA Client* can be used in the scope of the EdFest project. As most PDAs are capable of rendering content formatted with HTML, the required delivery channel is very similar to the one used for the kiosk computers. To account for the reduced screen size of these devices, minor adaptations in terms of how information is presented are however necessary. As shown in Figure 6.1, both the PDA client as well as the paper client connect to the content management system through a proxy that runs on each client device. Since context gathering, augmentation and processing have been explicitly excluded from our version model for context-aware data management, this functionality has to be provided by another component of the EdFest system. In the present architecture, this function is fulfilled by a proxy server that appends context information to every request which passes through. For the management of context on this server, a dedicated context database [21, 22, 23, 25] is used. This so-called context engine allows sensor and context types to be defined in a database. It then accesses the physical sensors which are represented as instances of the defined sensor types. The data gathered from the sensors is processed and stored as high-level context information based on the context types specified by the application. For EdFest, three sensors—a location sensor based on a GPS receiver, a weather sensor that downloads up-to-date meteorological data from the Internet and a network sensor that accesses the WLAN interface of the client device—have been defined. Apart from this context information that is gathered from these physical sensors, the context engine also manages logical context information about the client. For example, it also records which user is currently interacting with the system and what delivery channel is currently being used.

Apart from managing the context, the client proxy also serves as the basis for asynchronous communication between the mobile client and the content management system. While in traditional web-based applications, communication between the client and the server is always synchronous, context-aware applications require asynchronous communication enabling the server to contact the client whenever the context changes. This proactive behaviour of the content server can be implemented in several different ways. For example, the solution discussed in Ceri et al. [60] uses a client-side module that is downloaded to the mobile device as a response to the first request. When running on the client, the module computes a digest value of the current context and compares it to the corresponding value obtained from the server. If the two values do not match, the context on the server has changed and the page is refreshed by the client-side module. In contrast to this approach using polling, our client proxy contains a server process, the so-called client controller, that listens for requests from the server on a specific port. Although the polling solution is more secure, as the client does not need to open network ports, we believe that the advantages of our approach outweigh this concern. Depending on how the communication between the server and the mobile client is realised, polling can lead to unnecessary costs, as the client may be charged for the volume of data transferred rather than for the duration of the network connection. Also, by building the server process on the client on top of standard protocols, such as secure HTTP, the risk of exposing the client to security risks can be vitally reduced. In the EdFest system, the client controller is primarily used to provide the reminder functionality. When a tourist registers a reminder for a specific event, this information is sent to the content management system and an acknowledgement is sent back to the client. Later, when the tourist has to be notified that the event is about to begin, the content management system connects to the client controller and triggers the corresponding message. The point in time when the reminder is delivered can, of course, be influenced by contextual factors, such as where the tourist is currently located in the city.

6.3 Implementation

The information services of the EdFest tourist information system pre-sented in the previous section have all been implemented in terms of the XCM content management system discussed in Chapter 5. In this section we discuss how XCM has been extended to handle the requests from different clients. The process of developing the content compo-nent for the EdFest system has been slightly different than the develop-ment of the example web site presented in the previous chapter. Nev-ertheless, the presentation in this chapter will broadly follow the same course. In contrast to the example given before, the application model of the tourist information system was not developed as an extension of the types defined by XCM. As mentioned before, the festival content is rather managed by a dedicated database than inside the database stor-ing the XCM system metadata. The data model of XCM has therefore primarily been extended with two additional wrapper types that allow data from other databases to be accessed from inside XCM. The first of these types, type cmxcontent, wraps simple content objects into a content component, while the second, type cmxstructure is capable of representing external data structures in term of a structure component. Another ad-dition to the component types of XCM has been necessary to allow the database to be updated. In order to provide this functionality, a content type cmoperation has been defined that executes an operation such as a database macro and returns its result as a component object.

The data model that has been designed to store the content of the EdFest system is shown in Figure 6.3. In the design of this data model, several requirements had to be met. First of all, it had to be possible to import and store the data that was provided by the organisers of the Edinburgh Festival Fringe as a collection of XML and CSV documents. In addition to this requirement, information concepts had to be added that support the desired system functionality. At the centre of the model stands the classification hierarchy with root collection InfoItems. Objects of type infoitem are primarily characterised by their name, a description and a web address. They represent the main items about which the tourist information system provides content. As shown, these information items are either events, venues or festivals represented by the three subcollections of InfoItems, Events, Venues and Festivals respectively. The first two collections hold the information about events and venues that was provided by the festival organisers. The third collection, Festivals, captures the different festivals that are taking place at the same time. However, since we have only obtained data from the Edinburgh Festival Fringe, the collection Festivals does not serve a concrete purpose in the current system and will thus not be discussed any further. Event objects can be classified as festival highlights by placing them in the Highlights subcollection of Events. Every event is linked through the *BelongsTo* association to a category stored in the Category collection and performed by an artist represented by a member of collection Artists and associated with the event through *PerformedBy*. In contrast to events and venues, providing information about artists is not a primary function of our information systems. As this data is considered to be additional information about an event, it has not been modelled as a subtype of infoitem. To capture the fact that an event can be performed on a number of different days or more than once on a single day, performances have been introduced into the model to represent the actual instances of an event. Each object of type performance is a member of the Performances collection and linked to the corresponding event using the *PerformanceOf* association.

Apart from events, venues represented by type venue are the main focus of the EdFest tourist information system. Venues are organised hierarchically, i.e. each venue can be a collection of subvenues, such as multiple theatres in a single cinema. The hierarchical relationships between venues are captured by the *includes* association which links a venue object to another. Similar to events, venues can belong to categories that express what kind of place a certain venue is. Examples of categories are bars, restaurants or theatres which can be managed in a hierarchy represented by the *SubCategoryOf* association. To capture where a venue is located, each element of the Venues collection is associated with exactly one GPS coordinate stored in collection GPSPositions through the *LocatedAt* association. The type gpsposition defines three attributes for objects, representing positions as longitude, latitude and altitude, according to the GPS standard. The geographic information about venues was not

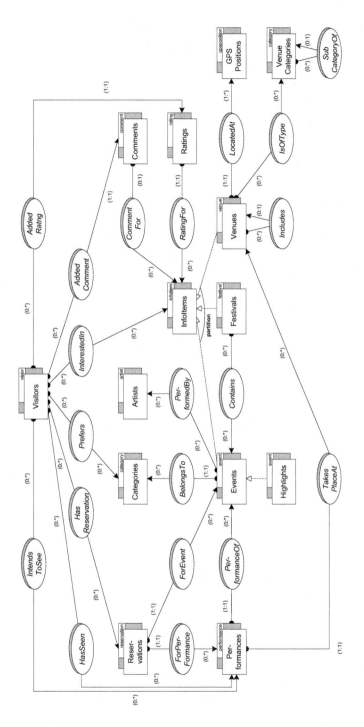

Figure 6.3: EdFest data model

provided by the festival organisers and had to be gathered manually, which has led to a few issues of data quality in the running system. Note that the position of a venue could also have been expressed by adding additional attributes to the **venue** type. However, since location information is an important context dimension in our tourist information system, we decided to represent positions as a proper concept.

Apart from information items and related concepts, another important concern is representing the tourists and related information. Each tourist is represented by an object of type **visitor** in the **Visitors** collection. Type **visitor** defines attributes to record the login, password name, e-mail address and mobile phone number of a tourist. The mobile phone number of the user is required as a fall-back option in the implementation of the reminder functionality when the server is unable to contact the client controller. Visitors can interact with the EdFest system in a number of ways. To provide feedback to other visitors, tourists can write comments and store them in the database collection **Comments** where comment authorship is captured by the *AddedComment* association. Comments can either be of a general nature or they can refer to a specific information item which is expressed by the *CommentFor* association. Numeric ratings stored in the **Ratings** collection can also be of help to other tourists who are interested in a certain information item. In contrast to comments, however, each rating has to be linked to an information item, as required by the (1:1) cardinality constraint of the domain side of association *RatingFor*. To facilitate the future integration of a recommender system into EdFest it is important to keep track of which user recorded a specific rating. This information is recorded in the *AddedRating* association which allows user profiles to be established. Such profiles could then be used to infer the visitor taste and to serve as the basis for the recommendation of related items.

The EdFest system provides several options for tourists to record their interests and preferences. This information could later also be used to influence the recommendations calculated by the system. For example, using the *InterestedIn* association, visitors can express their interest in certain information items. Similar to that, the association *Prefers* allows a set of preferred event categories to be specified by the tourist. Events of these categories are then weighted higher in the list of results when the user accesses the search functionality of the system. Further, the system keeps track of which events a user intends to see and has seen, by recording the corresponding information using associations *IntendsToSee* and *HasSeen*. Finally, tourists can book tickets through the EdFest system which uses the **Reservations** collection to store their reservations. A reservation has a reference to a certain event and an actual performance of this event captured by the associations *ForPerformance* and *ForEvent*. In addition to this information, the type reservation defines an attribute storing a reservation number which the visitor can use to buy the tickets at the box office.

To access content data stored in the application database, a number of components have been defined to retrieve external data from within XCM. These components use the two types cmxcontent and cmxstructure introduced at the beginning of this section. As mentioned before, the EdFest tourist information system mainly provides information about events and venues. Therefore it has only been necessary to create two XCM components to access external data, one for objects of type event and one for type venue. However, since objects of both types are delivered to the client in quite a few different views, we decided to create a content component for every view that is required by EdFest. As an alternative to this approach, it would also have been possible to only define one very general content component for each of the two types and associate these with a view object that has a number of variants. While this solution would demonstrate another use case for context-dependent variants, it also suffers from a conceptual shortcoming. In this solution, the type of a content component effectively becomes context-dependent through the application of a view variant. Although context-dependent views are an intended feature of the XCM system, it has not yet been defined how this functionality can be combined with the type system of XCM. For the time being, we have thus chosen a solution that represents the type of the delivered object based on the content component rather than based on the applied view. Table 6.1 shows a listing of all the components that were created to access external content and describes their purpose. In the upper part of the table components that retrieve information about events are shown, while components retrieving content related to venues are shown in the lower part.

Some information services of the EdFest tourist information system do not directly correspond to a single object in the application database. Also, some functionality requires that the application database is updated as a result of a client request, which cannot be handled by the existing XCM concepts. Therefore a mechanism is needed to handle operations that are more complex than what is possible with the queries represented by the XCM view concept. As mentioned before, the newly introduced type cmxoperation allows arbitrary operations in an external

Component	Description
getEventComment	Retrieves a comment about an event that has been recorded previously.
getEventInfo	Delivers extensive information about an event including the provenance of the artist and possible disclaimers.
getEventRating	Computes the current numeric score of an event based on the stored ratings.
getAccessibilityInfo	Provides information about the accessibility of a venue for the disabled.
getBarInfo	Returns the opening hours of the bar that is colocated at a given venue.
getFoodInfo	Retrieves the opening hours and the menu of the restaurant at a given venue.
getPublicTransport	Delivers information about how to get to a venue by public transport.
getVenueInfo	Returns copious information about a venue, including a detailed description.

Table 6.1: Components for external objects of types event and venue

database to be executed. In the scope of the family of OMS platforms, operations can either be object methods or database macros. Both methods and macros can return values that are then represented in XCM as a component. Within EdFest, several components have been implemented based on this new type. Table 6.2 gives an overview of the names and a description of each component. Operations that are used to provide complex information services are shown in the upper part of the table, and the lower part lists those components that update the application database as a request side-effect.

Based on these components, the structure of the EdFest application has been defined. The structure designed for the kiosk and PDA client follows the traditional approach of building a hierarchy based on directories and pages as discussed in the previous chapter. Using directories, the web site is organised into different areas that provide different access methods to the festival content. For example, events and venues can either be browsed based on their name or according to the category they belong to. Whereas multiple access strategies can coexist in parallel in

Component	Description
getMapPosition	Depending on the scale of the map used, computes and returns the distance between two points on paper.
getSuggestion	Suggests an event based on specified criteria such as time, date or preferences.
getTicketsInfo	Provides information about ticket availability for a performance.
setEventBookmark	Records the tourist's interest in a given event.
setEventComment	Stores a comment about an event in the application database.
setPreference	Marks an event category as preferred for the current user.
setReminder	Sets a reminder for the given event.
setReservation	Guides the tourist through a series of steps to book tickets for an event.

Table 6.2: Anchors for database operations

these delivery channels, an interactive paper document can only support one access structure at a time. All content intended for delivery to paper is structured and printed at design-time. At run-time, it is thus not possible to dynamically change the way in which content is accessed, as such changes would require the printing of a new set of documents. An interesting feature of the interactive paper channel is the fact that it is actually split into two delivery channels. Static design-time delivery is addressed by the paper publisher channel, whereas dynamic run-time interaction is supported by the paper client. The role of structure elements in these two delivery channels differs significantly. The content delivery for the paper publisher heavily relies on structure elements to integrate almost all data of the application database into one content hierarchy. In contrast, information delivered to the paper client hardly uses any structure elements, as individual components are accessed from paper. To bridge the gap between these static and dynamic parts of the interactive paper channel, a print functionality allowing personalised documents to be created was implemented for the festival kiosks.

The next step of the XCM design process is the creation of view objects that define which attribute values are retrieved from the database and whether related objects are delivered to the client. As it is not possible to discuss all view objects that were developed for the EdFest application in the scope of this thesis, we limit the discussion to the example of the `getEventInfo` component. The content delivery represented by this component combines information from an object of type event with the corresponding object of type artist. To retrieve the artist object depending on the current event object, a view is required that gathers this information. In XCM each view object stores a parametrised database query that is instantiated and evaluated when the object associated with the view is rendered by the server component. Below, the view query that retrieves the performer and returns a tuple containing the event and the artist is given in algebraic form.

$$(\textit{PerformedBy } dr(\{o\})) \; nth \; 1$$

In the EdFest application database, the association *PerformedBy* stores a collection of tuples relating events to the artists performing them. Before evaluating the query, XCM replaces all occurrences of the o placeholder with the event object it is currently rendering. Thus, using the dr operation, the domain of the *PerformedBy* association is restricted to the event in question. Finally, the nth operation is applied to extract the first tuple of objects in the resulting set.

The tuple returned by the view query is then transformed by the XCM server into an XML document conforming to the format introduced in Chapter 5. Figure 6.4 shows a simplified version of the XML representation created by XCM for the request of information about the festival event "Pool of Life". As can be seen from this example document, the generated <**webobject**> element has the name `getEventInfo` and the type `view:getEventInfo` as denoted by the <**property**> child element and the **type** attribute, respectively. Since the `getEventInfo` information service combines two database objects, it is represented by XCM as a structure component. In the XML format representing XCM components, a structure component has a <**components**> child element that contains all subcomponents of the structural container. In the example, the <**components**> element has two child <**webobject**> elements. The first with attribute value event for the **type** attribute represents the event "Pool of Life" from the EdFest application database. The second represents the artist performing the event, as indicated by the **artist**

value of attribute **type**. Note that attributes for which the corresponding database object provides no value are shown as empty <**property**>
elements.

Defining the layout of the application in terms of presentation templates is the final step of the XCM design process. As detailed earlier,
presentation templates in XCM are expressed using XSL transformations. Each component is associated with exactly one template that
governs how the XCM representation of the component will be transformed. Continuing the example of the `getEventInfo` component, we
will now discuss the presentation template that was defined to render
it. For reasons of conciseness, however, we will only present the variant of this template that was created to represent the component in the
context $C_v(S) := \{\langle format,\ vxml\rangle, \langle lang,\ en\rangle\}$. Hence, the template
given in the abbreviated listing shown in Figure 6.5 produces output
for the VoiceXML channel in English. The template contains a single
<**xsl:template**> element that represents a transformation rule that will
be applied to all elements of the source document that fulfil the condition
specified by the **match** attribute. As shown, the template does not specify such a condition. Writing match conditions can often be a challenging
task in a large system since the set of components that are associated
with a template can change over time. Clearly, it would be error-prone to
maintain the match conditions manually whenever the content of a web
site evolves. XCM therefore generates these conditions at run-time and
updates the corresponding attribute. In the given example, the value
of the **match** attribute will be changed to `webobject[@stamp='we21']`
during the publishing process.

The body of the template shown in the figure generates a VoiceXML
document with element <**vxml**> as root element containing a single
<**form**> element. Similar to HTML, VoiceXML allows forms to be de-
fined that consist of a series of blocks. Each block can contain prompts
that will be read to the user and can optionally be used to gather feedback from the user, based on speech recognition. As mentioned before,
voice is used in EdFest purely as an output channel and not for interaction. Hence the given template simply generates a <**prompt**> element
for output and no <**field**> elements that would be required to input
data. Inside the <**prompt**> element, a series of <**xsl:if**> elements are
used to determine which information is available and should be read to
the tourist. If an artist has been associated with the current event in the
application database, the template will first include this information in
the generated output. Then it checks whether the event is the premiere

```
<webobject stamp="we21" oid="o5107" type="view:getEventInfo">
   <property name="sys:name">
      <string>getEventInfo</string>
   </property>
   <!-- subsequent property elements omitted -->
   <components>
      <webobject stamp="we22" oid="o2451" type="event">
         <property name="name">
            <string>Pool of Life</string>
         </property>
         <property name="description">
            <text>Following his critically successful show of
               2003, [...]</text>
         </property>
         <property name="webaddress"/>
         <property name="author"/>
         <property name="premiere">
            <string>World premiere</string>
         </property>
         <property name="warnings"/>
         <property name="capacity">
            <integer>72</integer>
         </property>
         <property name="twoforone">
            <boolean>true</boolean>
         </property>
         <property name="cancelled">
            <boolean>false</boolean>
         </property>
      </webobject>
      <webobject stamp="we23" oid="o12429" type="artist">
         <property name="name">
            <string>Big Value Comedy</string>
         </property>
         <property name="webaddress"/>
         <property name="type">
            <string>Professional</string>
         </property>
         <property bulk="uni" name="origin"/>
         <property bulk="uni" name="members">
            <string>1</string>
         </property>
      </webobject>
   </components>
</webobject>
```

Figure 6.4: XML document of getEventInfo

```xml
<xsl:template match="">
    <!-- variable declarations omitted -->
    <vxml version="2.0" xmlns="http://www.w3.org/2001/vxml">
        <form id="xcmprompt">
            <block>
                <prompt>
                    <xsl:if test="string-length($artist) &gt; 0">
                        <xsl:text>The event: </xsl:text>
                        <xsl:value-of select="$name"/>
                        <xsl:text>is performed by </xsl:text>
                        <xsl:value-of select="$artist"/>
                        <xsl:if test="string-length($origin) &gt; 0">
                            <xsl:text>from </xsl:text>
                            <xsl:value-of select="$origin"/>
                        </xsl:if>
                        <xsl:text>. </xsl:text>
                    </xsl:if>
                    <xsl:if test="string-length($premiere) &gt; 0">
                        <xsl:text>It is the </xsl:text>
                        <xsl:value-of select="$premiere"/>
                        <xsl:text>of this show. </xsl:text>
                    </xsl:if>
                    <xsl:if test="string-length($general) &gt; 0">
                        <xsl:text>The producers wish to inform you
                            about the following: </xsl:text>
                        <xsl:value-of select="$general"/>
                        <xsl:text>. </xsl:text>
                    </xsl:if>
                    <xsl:if test="string-length($explicit) &gt; 0">
                        <xsl:text>Be aware of the subsequent warning:
                        </xsl:text>
                        <xsl:value-of select="$explicit"/>
                        <xsl:text>. </xsl:text>
                    </xsl:if>
                    <xsl:if test="string-length($agerange) &gt; 0">
                        <xsl:text>Suitable for the age range:
                        </xsl:text>
                        <xsl:value-of select="$agerange"/>
                        <xsl:text>.</xsl:text>
                    </xsl:if>
                </prompt>
            </block>
        </form>
    </vxml>
</xsl:template>
```

Figure 6.5: XSL template for getEventInfo

of the show and generates the appropriate notification for the tourist. Finally, any existing remarks of either a general nature or concerning the language, as well as the suggested age range, are added to the response. The content delivery that results from applying this template to the XML representation of the event "Pool of Life" is shown in Figure 6.6.

```
<?xml version="1.0" encoding="utf-8"?>
<vxml xmlns="http://www.w3.org/2001/vxml" version="2.0">
    <form id="xcmprompt">
        <block>
            <prompt>The event: Pool of Life is performed by
                Big Value Comedy. It is the World premiere of
                this show.</prompt>
        </block>
    </form>
</vxml>
```

Figure 6.6: XCM response of `getEventInfo`

Having presented the broad implementation of the EdFest tourist information system based on XCM, it is worthwhile to discuss some aspects of the system in more detail. In order for XCM to adapt its response to the current context, the required information has to be transmitted from the client to the server. To do so, the client controller proxy that manages context information using the context engine intercepts requests originating from a mobile client. Before sending the intercepted request to the server, the client controller augments the request with the necessary context information. For instance, to access the `getEventInfo` information service presented in the above example, the paper client would send the following request to the client controller proxy.

```
http://.../xcm?anchor=getEventInfo&event=o2451
```

After intercepting and augmenting the request, the extended URI given below will be issued to the XCM server by the proxy.

```
http://.../xcm?anchor=getEventInfo&event=o2451&format=vxml&
            lang=en&user=guest
```

By inserting these additional parameters into the query string of the request, the client provides information about the format it is capable of handling, the preferred language, and the user that is currently logged into the system.

To conclude this section which discusses the implementation of the EdFest functionality, we take a look at the reservation process, as it demonstrates some of the challenges of mobile multi-channel information systems. In the following, we compare the implementation of the reservation functionality for the kiosk channel and the interactive paper channel. So far, existing multi-channel information systems that support clients, such as web browsers, mobile phones, media phones or PDAs have addressed the requirement of making all aspects of the content delivery context-dependent. Although these traditional delivery channels differ substantially in their capabilities, the way in which users interact with them is rather similar. All of these devices display information graphically, use links for navigation and forms for data acquisition. Interactions such as a user registration or an ordering process are often composed from several steps. In this case, the responses that are delivered to the different clients can take a variety of shapes, whereas the steps of the process and hence the business logic on the server side stay the same.

The addition of interactive paper to the set of delivery channels invalidates this property of multi-channel information systems. In the case of interactive paper, the communication patterns between client and server, as well as the application logic required to process the interaction on the server, diverge considerably from traditional delivery channels. To substantiate this argument, Figure 6.7 shows a side-to-side comparison of the user interface of the EdFest reservation process on the kiosk client and the corresponding extract of the bookmark document. A tourist accessing this functionality through the stationary kiosk client will be presented the HTML form shown in Figure 6.7(a). To reserve tickets, the tourists enter the event, the date and the number of tickets they require into the corresponding form fields. By clicking the *Reserve* button at the end of the form all parameters are transmitted to the server in a single request and processed there. Note that the reservation form is part of the prototype implementation of the HTML delivery channel and does not represent an end-user interface in terms of usability. The interaction process in the case of the paper-based user interface shown in Figure 6.7(b) is quite different. The reservation process is started when a tourist points with the digital pen to the icon labelled *Start reservation*, triggering a voice response from the server asking them to select the event. Events can be selected in the booklet document by touching the icon below the event title with the pen which sends another request to the server. The corresponding response prompts the tourists to specify the date of the performance that they would like to book tickets for.

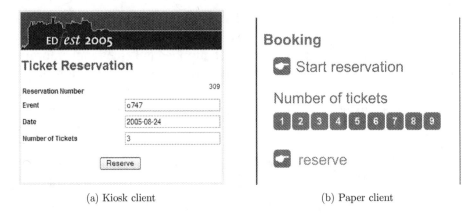

(a) Kiosk client   (b) Paper client

Figure 6.7: User interfaces of the reservation process

The date is also selected in the brochure by pointing into the timeline at the bottom of the corresponding event description. Again, a request is sent to the server transmitting the new information and resulting in a response asking the tourists to select the number of tickets on the bookmark. After they have done so, a summary of their reservation is read to them, which they can acknowledge by clicking on the *reserve* icon on the bookmark. This last request to the server will trigger the booking to be processed and a voice confirmation to be sent to the client.

The differences that are visible at the level of the user interface can also be witnessed by examining the communication pattern between each of the two clients and the server. The communication patterns resulting from the user interaction scenarios discussed above are shown in Figure 6.8. The sequence of requests and responses that is generated by a tourist interacting with the server through the kiosk client is depicted in Figure 6.8(a) whereas the communication pattern of the same interaction through the paper client is given in Figure 6.8(b). As can be seen in the figure, accessing the reservation process from the kiosk client results in two request and response pairs where the first retrieves the empty form and the second uploads all values to the server for processing. The picture in the case of the paper client is quite different, as each data value required to process the reservation request is sent to the server encoded in an individual request. Additionally, the selected values have to be managed in a session on the client and retransmitted with every request. In the kiosk interface, users are able to find out what they can do, and control their actions by looking at what is currently displayed on the screen. Tourists interacting through the paper interface, however, have

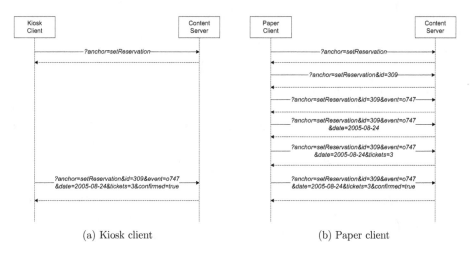

(a) Kiosk client   (b) Paper client

Figure 6.8: Communications patterns of the reservation process

to be given immediate responses after completing each step, to confirm their actions to them and to guide them through the process.

Implementing the server-side application logic that handles the reservation process across multiple channels is a difficult task if the interaction patterns of the different channels are as heterogeneous as in the example. In the EdFest system, our solution to that problem was inspired by the method dispatching strategies found in object-oriented programming languages. Many object-oriented languages allow methods to be overloaded, i.e. support the definition of multiple versions of the same method with different sets of arguments. At run-time, they select the so-called most specific method from the set of applicable methods, based on the number and type of arguments given by the caller of the method. In its basic nature, virtual method dispatching is not unlike selecting the best matching variant of an object. All that has to be done to simulate method dispatching based on the version model for context-aware data management is to define an object type that represents operations, and treat the parameters specified by the client as context values. Since all OMS platforms already provide the notion of operation, and most of them use an object type as part of their metamodel to describe these operations, the first prerequisite is already fulfilled. Further, both method arguments and context values are sent by the client to the server as parameters in the request query string. Hence, the second requirement is simply met by treating all transmitted parameters equally and including them in the current context state used to evaluate the request.

Figure 6.9 gives a graphical representation of the versioned object that handles the `setReservation` process. As shown, for each context state that occurs in the process shown in Figure 6.8(b), an alternative version of the object has been defined. As the context values that will be sent by the client cannot be known beforehand, the context states describing the variants use the value $+*$ which indicates that a value for the corresponding context dimension has to be set but the actual value is not important. The default variant is responsible for starting the reservation process by generating a reservation number and initiating a session on the client. All other variants of the object extract the provided context data, update the application database accordingly and send back a response that guides the visitor to the next step, except for variant `o369@5[5]` that informs the tourists that they have completed the reservation process successfully.

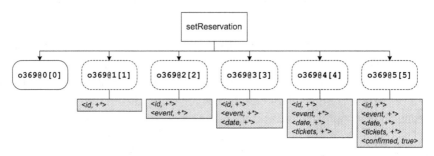

Figure 6.9: The `setReservation` object

The kiosk reservation process only needs to access the default variant and the variant shown on the far right in the figure. In the case of the paper client, however, the reservation process runs through all variants of the objects before completing. An interesting aspect of implementing such processes is the way in which errors made by the user are handled. While interacting with the paper client, it is impossible to cause an error by entering incorrect values into the reservation process, as all data is chosen from the preauthored paper. The tourist can, however, deviate from the process by prematurely selecting parameters that will only be gathered in a later step. In this case, the value will nevertheless be stored in the client's session but the response will be the same as before, asking the tourist to select the value corresponding to the current step. When this value is finally selected by the user, all steps that have been executed out of order are skipped automatically as those values have already been stored in the session on the client. Preliminary feedback from test users at the Edinburgh Festivals in 2005 has shown that this rather resilient way of handling the stepping through a process can be a feasible and comprehensible form of interaction.

While a tourist cannot deviate from the defined process in the web interface, it is possible to enter arbitrary values or to leave out certain parameters altogether. Hence, the system has to be able to additionally cope with these errors. The logic to check whether the form has been completed correctly by the user could be implemented on the client-side using embedded scripts. However, this solution is not generally possible on all required delivery channels, as scripting capabilities, if present at all, vary substantially. Our approach to implementing process functionality based on an object with multiple variants is already able to handle cases where the tourist has failed to specify a required value. Even if they are not required in situations where the tourist fills in the form correctly, in the case of an error, the additional variants defined for the interactive paper process can be used for error handling in the kiosk interface. A missing parameter will lead to the selection of one of these intermediate variants which will be rendered for the client as a form where the parameter is highlighted. Although context matching can provide a solution to missing values, it is not capable of addressing the problem of handling errors caused by incorrect data. To also implement this functionality, traditional parsing and error handling techniques have to be applied.

6.4 Discussion

In this chapter we have presented how XCM was used to implement the content back-end of a mobile multi-channel information system. Apart from rather traditional delivery channels, such as desktop web browsers and PDAs, the presented EdFest guide for festival visitors also supports a novel access channel based on interactive paper. Compared to existing web channels, interactive paper introduces a set of new requirements that have to be addressed by the content server. The implementation of the EdFest server component has been discussed in terms of the XCM development process that is defined around the concepts of content, structure, view and presentation. In doing so, we have shown how the version model for context-aware data management can be used to meet the challenges put forward by new modes of accessing information. Using the ticket reservation process available in the EdFest system as an example, we have argued that interactive paper not only affects the way in which content is accessed and delivered but also the nature of information interaction. In EdFest, this problem was solved by extending XCM with context-aware operations that have been realised using the versioning concepts put forward in this thesis.

XCM was developed initially to implement and support traditional browser-based web applications. To use it in the setting of the EdFest mobile tourist information system, new functionality had to be integrated into the system. For reasons given above, the festival data of the EdFest application is managed by a dedicated database and not the XCM database. This set-up required techniques to bridge the gap between the two databases in a seamless and transparent way. Furthermore, XCM has never been extended with features that would allow content to be updated at run-time using the web channel. In XCM, the content of a web site is defined using the XCM SiteManager application presented in the previous chapter. In order for tourists to submit comments, rate events, specify preferences and book tickets, the application has to handle updates resulting from user interaction. The foundation for the solution to both problems has been provided by the concept of extensibility that stands at the core of XCM. Building on this mechanism, three additional component types were defined to address these new requirements as extensions of already existing types. Two of these new types allow wrapper objects to be created in XCM that represent external content as either content or structure components. Objects of the third type enable XCM to execute arbitrary database operations to perform complex queries or to update the database. We believe that the realisation of the EdFest system has demonstrated the need for extensibility as a key feature in any implementation platform for web engineering applications.

Apart from the aspects already discussed in this chapter, the interaction processes implemented for the interactive paper client have additional interesting characteristics. Looking back at the communication pattern between client and server given in Figure 6.8(b), a similarity to modern web applications that transmit data values to the server as soon as the user has entered them can be observed. In order to prevent page reloads and provide immediate feedback to the user, these web sites use a technique called Asynchronous JavaScript and XML (AJAX). As indicated by its name, AJAX is a combination of existing technologies that are used together to provide more interactive web pages. In AJAX, a web page uses client-side scripting to connect to a server and to transmit values without reloading the whole page. At the time of opening the connection, a response handler is registered that will be invoked as soon as the request has been processed. Using JavaScript, the response handler can then update the web page asynchronously by accessing the Document Object Model (DOM) of the mark-up used to render the current page. Web applications based on AJAX communicate with the server at a finer level of granularity that is not unlike the interaction processes encountered on the paper client. The solution presented in this chapter that was implemented within the EdFest application to handle such processes could therefore form the basis to integrate delivery channels that support AJAX with those that do not.

7
Conclusion

In this thesis we have established the need for context-aware data management based on a survey of approaches to context-aware computing that have recently emerged in a number of application domains. In response to this requirement we have enunciated our hypothesis that context-aware data management should be addressed in terms of a version model to be implemented as part of a database management system. Supported by a comprehensive analysis of existing versioning systems, we have presented a version model that offers alternative versions, so-called variants, to support context-aware data management. Further, we have shown how these variants can be integrated with revisional versions to record the development process of a system. The implementation of our version model has served as the basis for a content management system that has been designed as a platform for current web engineering applications. In turn, the presented content management system has been used as component in a mobile tourist information system that features context-awareness in terms of multi-channel and multi-modal content delivery as well as location-dependent services.

To conclude this thesis, we critically evaluate our version model and its applications based on the hypothesis that we formulated. However, having already provided detailed points of discussion at the end of each chapter concerning our approach and its implementation, we will refrain from repeating these arguments. In this chapter we rather provide a summary of the most important aspects and show how the requirements we have established have been addressed. The goal of this evaluation is to uncover the areas of our version model that still provide room for additional improvement. These shortcomings together with suggestions on how to address them will be presented in the final section of this thesis. There we also provide an outlook on possible future research and applications stimulated by the concepts introduced in this thesis.

7.1 Discussion

From the diversity of context-aware applications that have recently been developed, we have derived universality as an important requirement for a context-aware data management system. Our version model embraces this challenge by refraining from imposing a predefined notion of context on a client application. Rather than specifying semantics, the context representation introduced in Chapter 4 establishes a common syntax for context that is shared between the application and the data management system. Due to this generic approach, the designer of an application can define which information is considered to be context. The version model itself extends the scope in which contextual information can be used to adapt the functionality of an application. Most existing systems limit adaptation to triggering information based on context rather than providing support to also adapt the information itself. This requirement has been addressed by our approach through the management of context-dependent variants of data objects that are used to represent information in different situations. Supported by research in the fields of computer-aided design, software configuration and web engineering as well as the requirements of current web content management systems, we have stipulated the importance of managing the evolution of a development process. This challenge is met by our work through the integration of revisions that keep track of previous versions of an object. For the scope of this thesis, however, we have decided to focus on context-aware variants rather than on revisions as we believe that this is the main contribution of our work.

Although some of the previous approaches that we have discussed also feature the notion of variants, it is important to point out that the intended use of our variants is completely different from the use of variants in existing systems. Our variants are exclusively targeted at context-aware data management, rather than supporting product engineering of software configuration management. As a consequence, this difference in how variants are used gives rise to a notion of context that distinguishes our system from previous solutions. As discussed in Chapter 3, contextual information in software engineering is regarded as a specification that needs to be followed exactly. In contrast, context is seen by most context-aware computing applications as optional information that can be used to augment the operation and functionality of the system. We have claimed that this character of context has an impact on several aspects of the proposed version model. The way in which versions are organised in our model is one such area where these effects are visible. Whereas most existing systems use a directed acyclic graph to structure the version history of an object, it is sufficient in our approach to use a tree. This decision is supported by the fact that variants expressing different representations of an object do not need to be combined. Therefore, it is not necessary to support an operation to merge two branches of a tree that would lead to the creation of a graph structure. Additionally, the notion of context supported by our model has motivated the decision to favour variants over revisions in term of access structures at the level of the internal representation of a versioned object. Incidentally, this approach is very similar to the version organisation proposed by most existing solutions. Interestingly, some of these systems also opt for the inverse solution of structurally favouring revisions over variants. This fact is evidence that the organisation of versions in existing approaches is less determined by the notion of context but rather dependent on other factors.

Another part of our model where the role of contextual information is directly apparent is the design of the matching algorithm used to evaluate queries. Unlike software configuration systems, for example, that use an exact match to compute a specific configuration specified by context values, our algorithm is based on a best match strategy. Whereas an exact match will fail when the requirements given by the context are not satisfied, our best match algorithm always returns a result. The situation that falling back to a default representation of the object is always possible in our version model is another impact of the understanding of context as found in mobile, ubiquitous and pervasive computing as well as web engineering. As contextual information is seen as optional in these systems, falling back to the default variant corresponds to the way the application would operate in the absence of context. Therefore, our approach meets another important requirement of recognising the application logic represented by a query and the adaptation based on context as two orthogonal system dimensions. At the end of Chapter 2 we have also postulated that a data management system designed to support context-aware applications needs to be configurable to allow for different modes of operation. Although the matching algorithm that realises context-aware behaviour is built into our system, we have addressed this requirement by providing support for influencing its behaviour. A central step of the matching algorithm is the scoring function that assigns a value expressing the correspondence between the properties of a variant and the values of the current context state. If an application should require to do so, the default scoring function presented in this thesis can be substituted with a function that reflects the requirements of a specific domain.

An additional feature that distinguishes our version model from most of the existing systems is the fact that it is defined in the setting of an object-oriented data model. Whereas the version organisation mentioned above determines how an individual object is versioned, we have also presented how a network of objects that are connected through relationships is versioned. As in previous approaches, the proposed mechanism is realised based on the well established notion of specific and generic references that are directly supported by the extended object identifiers used in our model. An extended object identifier is composed of a field identifying the whole object as well as two optional fields referencing a specific revision and variant of the object, respectively. Whereas a specific reference to an object is expressed by an identifier where all three fields are set, generic references to the same object can be specified with an identifier that omits either or both of the two optional fields. To resolve generic references, the concepts of the latest revision and default variant have been introduced for any field that is not specified in a partial object identifier. Although specific and generic references provide support for version-aware references, they suffer from several limitations. As such relationships are maintained as an internal part of the versioned object, they are both uni-directional in nature and cannot be versioned independently of the object. Fortunately, the OM data model on which our approach is based features a bi-directional association concept that is external to the objects. Further, as associations are themselves represented as objects they can be versioned using the same concepts as data objects and are thus free from the limitations of simple references.

In Chapter 5, we have shown how the version model for context-aware data management has been used to implement a content management system. The content management system is intended to serve as an implementation platform for web engineering applications and has therefore taken the requirements model-based design methodologies into account. The resulting system is based on the separation of the concepts of content, structure, view and presentation. All data and metadata that is represented in terms of these four concepts is managed by the content management system based on the presented version model for context-aware data management. Therefore, the corresponding objects are capable of both capturing the development process of a web site at design-time and exhibiting context-dependent behaviour at run-time. As a consequence, our context management system is capable of adapting the content of a web site as well as its structure and presentation to context, as defined by the application at hand. Existing content management systems have been shown to fall in either of two categories. First of all, there are systems that publish the content of existing application databases on the web. These so-called database-based content management systems are very strong in terms of supporting model-based development, as user data types can be directly represented. However, these systems lack support for data types that are specific to the web. Document-based content management systems, in contrast, address this requirement by providing a set of document types such as text, image or link. A major goal of our content management system was to close the gap between these two approaches. The solution we have presented is based on the object-oriented nature of the underlying data model that allows a set of core document types to be extended with application-specific types using inheritance. The development and implementation of web sites with our content management system is supported by a client application and a server component.

Another application of the version model presented in this thesis has been discussed in Chapter 6. As the enabling technology behind our content management system, the version model has served as part of a mobile personal information system supporting tourists that visit the Edinburgh festivals. The presented tourist information system is capable of delivering information about the events and venues of the Edinburgh festivals as well as about the city itself over multiple delivery channels. Apart from delivery channels based on traditional desktop and PDA clients, the mobile information system also features an interactive paper channel as input and speech as output. This novel web channel has given rise to a series of new requirements that have not been present in previous delivery channels. One such requirement is that the interactive paper client actually comprises two delivery channels that have to be supported by the content management component. Whereas one of these delivery channels is used to generate the interactive paper documents at design-time, the other is responsible for delivering additional information based on the tourist's interaction at run-time. In comparison to browser-based interaction, another new requirement is that paper-based interaction is non-linear, as users have the complete user interface at their disposal and can thus point with the digital pen to anything they like. This inability of the paper client to control the user interface in terms of what is displayed to users and thus guide them through a series of well-defined steps also has an impact on the content server. When processing a complex trans-action such as the presented reservation process, the content server has to notify the tourists after every step to prevent them from getting lost. Addressing this requirement results in a communication pattern between client and server that is fundamentally different from the browser-based pattern. Our content management system addresses context-dependent interaction processes by extending the notion of context to also include the current state of a transaction. As operations such as object meth-ods or database macros are also represented as objects in our system, they too can have context-dependent variants and thus can be matched against this interaction context. In our opinion, having been able to do so is further evidence that our version model satisfies the requirement of supporting an open concept of context that can be tailored to the demands of an application. Moreover, we believe that the application of our approach in a content management system and thus as a part of a mobile tourist information system has validated our hypothesis of providing context-aware data management based on a version model in general.

7.2 Outlook

Having explained why the proposed version model satisfies the require-ments of context-aware data management, we discuss some issues that we regard as shortcomings of our approach and a vision about new directions of research. Two such limitations of our model have already been men-tioned in Chapter 4. The first of these shortcomings is the fact that our version model has currently no support to distinguish between generic and version-specific attributes. As a consequence, data that is common to all versions of an object has to be replicated over the entire version graph. A second drawback stems from the proposed query evaluation process that matches context to each participating object individually.

Potentially this could lead to inconsistent results as context dimensions that are not specified in the current context state could be handled differently for different objects. Possible solutions that could help to address these deficiencies have also been discussed in the corresponding chapter.

Another point where our model needs further improvement emerges from the lack of a clearly defined operational model that governs how clients interact with the version model. As discussed in the section detailing the implementation, the basic operations to create and retrieve both revisions and variants have been defined in our approach. What is missing is a transactional model that builds on top of these primitives to determine the evolution of the version graph and to provide controlled concurrent access. Taking the lessons learned from engineering databases and software configuration management systems into consideration, such a transactional model could be based on client workspaces that support long-running transactions through check-out and check-in operations. Coupled to the missing transactional model is the lack of possibilities to define policies that govern the evolution of the version graph in terms of which modifications require the creation of a new version. With respect to context-aware data management, the system should also support the specification of constraints that check whether the variants defined for an object are consistent. Whereas, at the moment, it is only possible to check that no two variants of an object define the same set of properties, it is possible that future context-aware applications will have more sophisticated requirements. Finally, it has to be noted that the matching of a context state to the variants of an object, as currently implemented, has not been optimised in any way. Clearly, the processing of context-aware queries would benefit from index structures over the properties of the variants that provide efficient access to the desired variant. Index structures have been proposed for both temporal and engineering databases as well as software configuration management systems. As of now, however, their applicability in the setting of context-aware data management remains open to investigation. In order to address these open questions, we are planning to integrate the concepts put forward in this thesis in OMS Avon, the latest member in the family of systems that provide support for the OM data model.

In spite of these issues that need further work, we believe that systems based on the version model presented will constitute valuable components in future context-aware applications. An example of such an application domain are reactive information environments which we see as a further step in the evolution of information systems. Whereas the presented tourist guide for the Edinburgh festivals has demonstrated the immediate future of information systems in the setting of mobile computing, information environments will lead the way towards pervasive information systems. In contrast to mobile and personal information systems that are mostly based on traditional synchronous user interaction, information environments are embedded in the environment and provide ambient information asynchronously. Therefore, the use of context in information environments is different than in mobile personal information systems. As information environments do not provide a user interface in the traditional sense, the system has to rely almost entirely on context information to decide which piece of information should be published in a given situation. Similarly to mobile applications, contextual information, at the same time, is the basis for determining where information is displayed and how it is presented. Hence the use of context in information environments can be seen as an extension of the use of context in mobile information systems that goes further beyond what we have presented in this thesis. The *Social Philanthropic Information Environment (SOPHIE)* [24] is an example of such an information environment that builds on an extended architecture for web information systems. In this setting, the content management system presented in this thesis has been proposed as a component to handle the context-dependent publishing of ambient information to various devices.

Another area where our context-aware content management system could unleash its potential is document management. Today, most documents are managed as files, which leads to a number of disadvantages. On the one hand, files represent documents at a relatively coarse level of granularity, as their internal structure is non-transparent and is maintained by a dedicated application. On the other hand, files often include data by value, meaning that the same content cannot be part of multiple files. Whereas the first of these two concerns has been partially addressed with the advent of application independent file formats that are based on XML, the second point is still an open issue. To demonstrate the benefits of managing application documents with a content management system based on our version model we will use the example of a slide show presentation as created by an application such as Microsoft PowerPoint. Seen through the eyes of content management, a presentation document is a container component that consists of a sequence of slides. In turn, each slide is also a container for other objects such as texts, tables or graphics. Attached to the presentation are templates that govern how the final show looks when presented or as a handout. At the level of slides, additional presentation templates define the layout of each slide. Although this separation of content, structure and presentation is easily mapped to a content management system such as the one presented in this thesis, current file systems are not capable of supporting such fine grained structures. Therefore, the functionality offered by content management such as presentations that behave and look differently depending on the audience of a talk remains unrealised.

Furthermore, our experience has shown that people who are regularly involved in giving talks and lectures build a repository of slides that they then reuse in different presentations. The limitations of current document management technologies make it necessary that the reuse of a slide can only be achieved through copying the slide from one file to another. Instead, our content management system includes components in a container by reference and thus does not suffer from the problems and pitfalls that arise when managing redundant data such as keeping all copies consistent when an error is found and corrected in one presentation. Also, the version model underlying our content management system would help to track the evolution and the provenance of a slide in case it should be required to adapt the content in the future. The proposition of using a database instead of a hierarchical file system has been made numerous times. To mention only one example, Rivera [228] proposes a database replacement for the file system of the Oberon operating system that is based on the same object-oriented data model as used in this thesis. While this relationship to our approach is one reason why we mention this work, another is the fact that an augmented slide show system has been implemented on top of it. An interesting development that coincides with the release of Microsoft Office 2007 is the introduction of the *Office Open XML* [227] file format. This new file format for Microsoft's office applications is based on a file archive containing a hierarchy of folders that organise a number of XML files. While this file format does not solve the problems associated with redundant data, we believe that it is one step towards a more fine grained structuring of document content. Also, due to the fact that it is based on open standards is becomes possible to consider this file format as an additional output channel for a content management system such as ours to realise the features discussed above.

At the end of Chapter 6 we discussed the implementation of the reservation process within the EdFest tourist guides. In order to address the situation that the paper client requires a different communication pattern than traditional browser-based clients, we have created

context-dependent interaction processes. Technically, these interaction
processes were realised through different implementation variants of the
database macro implementing the corresponding application logic. In
this setting, context has been used to dispatch the request made by the
client to the desired implementation, similarly to object-oriented programming languages that dispatch a call to an overloaded method based
on the parameters provided by the caller. The use of context in this
implementation raises an interesting question. Throughout this thesis
we have discussed how object variants are used to realise context aware
data management and querying. Now, we must ask ourselves whether it
is sensible to apply the same mechanisms not only to data but also to
programs. We have conducted preliminary research into this direction
with the implementation of a prototype language that supports multi-
variant programming [253]. The language is an extension of Prolog that
allows predicate implementations to be defined for a given context state.
The current context state of the system is managed by library predicates
that allow context values to be set and removed. Before a context-aware
Prolog program can be executed, it needs to be loaded by a special parser
that replaces all predicate calls in the program with a call to a dispatching
predicate that takes context into consideration. Experiences gained from
a set of example programs have shown that the approach has its merits
even though writing context-aware programs can be quite challenging,
especially if context-dependent predicates are allowed to modify the context state. Naturally, our prototype implementation suffers from a few
limitations and problems such as poor performance. Also, it is still un-
clear how to combine context-dependent predicate invocation with the
backtracking mechanism of Prolog. Nevertheless, we believe that the
potential benefits of this approach outweigh these challenges and will
therefore continue to investigate the application of our version model to
programming languages.

Bibliography

[1] G. D. Abowd. Classroom 2000: An Experiment with the Instrumentation of a Living Educational Environment. *IBM Systems Journal*, 38(4):508–530, 1999.

[2] G. D. Abowd, C. G. Atkeson, J. Hong, S. Long, R. Kooper, and M. Pinkerton. Cyberguide: A Mobile Context-Aware Tour Guide. *Wireless Networks*, 3(5):421–433, 1997.

[3] G. D. Abowd, C. G. Atkeson, J. Brotherton, T. Enqvist, P. Gulley, and J. LeMon. Investigating the Capture, Integration and Access Problem of Ubiquitous Computing in an Educational Setting. In *Proceedings of ACM SIGCHI Conference on Human Factors in Computing Systems, April 18-23, 1998, Los Angeles, CA, USA*, pages 440–447, 1998.

[4] R. Ahmed and S. B. Navathe. Version Management of Composite Objects in CAD Databases. In *Proceedings of ACM SIGMOD International Conference on Management of Data, May 29-31, 1991, Denver, CO, USA*, pages 218–227, 1991.

[5] I. Ahn. Towards an Implementation of Database Management Systems with Temporal Support. In *Proceedings of International Conference on Data Engineering, February 5-7, 1986, Los Angeles, CA, USA*, pages 374–381, 1986.

[6] I. Ahn and R. T. Snodgrass. Partitioned Storage for Temporal Databases. *Information Systems*, 13(4):369–391, 1988.

[7] G. Ariav. A Temporally Oriented Data Model. *ACM Transactions on Database Systems*, 11(4):499–527, 1986.

[8] R. Audi, editor. *The Cambridge Dictionary of Philosophy*. Cambridge University Press, 1999.

[9] C. W. Bachman. Data Structure Diagrams. *ACM SIGMIS Database*, 1(2):4–10, 1969.

[10] M. Baldauf, S. Dustdar, and F. Rosenberg. A Survey on Context-Aware Systems. *International Journal of Ad Hoc and Ubiquitous Computing*, 2(4):263–277, 2007.

[11] F. Bancilhon, P. Kanellakis, and C. Delobel, editors. *Building an Object-Oriented Database System: The Story of O_2*. Morgan Kaufmann Publishers, 1992.

[12] Y. Bar-Hillel. Indexical Expressions. *Mind*, 63(251):359–379, 1954.

[13] P. Barna, G.-J. Houben, and F. Frăsincar. Specification of Adaptive Behavior Using a General-Purpose Design Methodology for Dynamic Web Applications. In *Proceedings of Adaptive Hypermedia and Adaptive Web-Based Systems, August 24-26, 2004, Eindhoven, The Netherlands*, pages 283–286, 2004.

[14] D. S. Batory and W. Kim. Modeling Concepts for VLSI CAD Objects. *ACM Transactions on Database Systems*, 10(3):322–346, 1985.

[15] H. Baumeister, N. Koch, and L. Mandel. Towards a UML Extension for Hypermedia Design. In *Proceedings of International Conference on the Unified Modeling Language, October 28-30, 1999, Fort Collins, CO, USA*, pages 614–629, 1999.

[16] H. Baumeister, A. Knapp, N. Koch, and G. Zhang. Modelling Adaptivity with Aspects. In *Proceedings of International Conference on Web Engineering, July 27-29, 2005, Sydney, Australia*, pages 406–416, 2005.

[17] J. Baus, A. Krüger, and W. Wahlster. A Resource-Adaptive Mobile Navigation System. In *Proceedings of International Conference on Intelligent User Interfaces, January 13-16, 2002, San Francisco, CA, USA*, pages 15–22, 2002.

[18] D. Beckett, editor. RDF/XML Syntax Specification (Revised). http://www.w3.org/TR/rdf-syntax-grammar/, February 2004.

[19] D. Beech and B. Mahbod. Generalized Version Control in an Object-Oriented Database. In *Proceedings of International Conference on Data Engineering, February 1-5, 1988, Los Angeles, CA, USA*, pages 14–22, 1988.

[20] N. Belkatir and J. Estublier. Experience with a Data Base of Programs. In *Proceedings of ACM SIGSOFT/SIGPLAN Software Engineering Symposium on Practical Software Development Environments, December 9-11, 1986, Palo Alto, CA, USA*, pages 84–91, 1987.

[21] R. Belotti. SOPHIE – Context Modelling and Control. Diploma thesis, Swiss Federal Institute of Technology Zurich (ETH Zurich), Zurich, Switzerland, 2004.

[22] R. Belotti, C. Decurtins, M. Grossniklaus, M. C. Norrie, and A. Palinginis. Modelling Context for Information Environments. In *Proceedings of International Workshop on Ubiquitous Mobile Information and Collaboration Systems, June 7-8, 2004, Riga, Latvia*, pages 43–56, 2004.

[23] R. Belotti, C. Decurtins, M. Grossniklaus, M. C. Norrie, and A. Palinginis. Interplay of Content and Context. In *Proceedings of International Conference on Web Engineering, July 28-30, 2004, Munich, Germany*, pages 187–200, 2004.

[24] R. Belotti, C. Decurtins, M. Grossniklaus, and M. C. Norrie. An Infrastructure for Reactive Information Environments. In *Proceedings of International Conference on Web Information Systems Engineering, November 20-22, 2005, New York, NY, USA*, pages 347–360, 2005.

[25] R. Belotti, C. Decurtins, M. Grossniklaus, M. C. Norrie, and A. Palinginis. Interplay of Content and Context. *Journal of Web Engineering*, 4(1):57–78, 2005.

[26] G. Benelli, A. Bianchi, P. Marti, D. Sennati, and E. Not. HIPS: Hyper-Interaction within Physical Space. In *Proceedings of IEEE International Conference on Multimedia Computing and Systems, June 7-11, 1999, Florence, Italy*, pages 1075–1078, 1999.

[27] M. Benerecetti, P. Bouquet, and C. Ghidini. On the Dimensions of Context Dependence: Partiality, Approximation, and Perspective.

In *Proceedings of International and Interdisciplinary Conference on Modeling and Using Context, July 27-30, 2001, Dundee, Scotland, UK*, pages 59–72, 2001.

[28] Y. Bernard, M. Lacroix, P. Lavency, and M. Vanhoedenaghe. Configuration Management in an Open Environment. In *Proceedings of European Software Engineering Conference, September 9-11, 1987, Strasbourg, France*, pages 35–43, 1987.

[29] T. Berners-Lee and M. Fischetti. *Weaving the Web: The Original Design and Ultimate Destiny of the World Wide Web by its Inventor.* Harper San Francisco, 1999.

[30] G. Biegel and V. Cahill. A Framework for Developing Mobile, Context-Aware Applications. In *Proceedings of IEEE International Conference on Pervasive Computing and Communications, March 19-23, 2004, Orlando, FL, USA*, pages 361–365, 2004.

[31] A. Binemann-Zdanowicz, R. Kaschek, K.-D. Schewe, and B. Thalheim. Context-aware Web Information Systems. In *Proceedings of Asian-Pacific Conference on Conceptual Modelling, January 18-22, 2004, Dunedin, New Zealand*, pages 37–48, 2004.

[32] A. F. Bobick, S. S. Intille, J. W. Davis, F. Baird, C. S. Pinhanez, L. W. Campbell, Y. A. Ivanov, A. Schütte, and A. Wilson. The KidsRoom: A Perceptually-Based Interactive and Immersive Story Environment. *Presence: Teleoperators and Virtual Environments*, 8(4):369–393, 1999.

[33] A. Bongio, S. Ceri, P. Fraternali, and A. Maurino. Modeling Data Entry and Operations in WebML. In *Selected Papers from the Third International Workshop WebDB 2000 on the World Wide Web and Databases*, pages 201–214, 2001.

[34] C. Boyle and A. O. Encarnacion. MetaDoc: An Adaptive Hypertext Reading System. *User Modeling and User-Adapted Interaction*, 4(1):1–19, 1994.

[35] D. Brickley and R. V. Guha, editors. RDF Vocabulary Description Language 1.0: RDF Schema. `http://www.w3.org/TR/rdf-schema/`, February 2004.

[36] J. A. Brotherton and G. D. Abowd. Lessons Learned from eClass: Assessing Automated Capture and Access in the Classroom. *ACM Transactions on Computer-Human Interaction*, 11(2): 121–155, 2004.

[37] B. Brown and E. Laurier. Designing Electronic Maps: An Ethnographic Approach. In L. Meng, A. Zipf, and T. Reichenbacher, editors, *Map Design for Mobile Applications*, pages 247–262. Springer Verlag, 2004.

[38] P. J. Brown. The Stick-e Document: A Framework for Creating Context-Aware Applications. *Electronic Publishing*, 8(2-3):259–272, 1995.

[39] P. J. Brown. Triggering Information by Context. *Personal and Ubiquitous Computing*, 2(1):18–27, 1998.

[40] P. J. Brown, J. D. Bovey, and X. Chen. Context-Aware Applications: From the Laboratory to the Marketplace. *IEEE Personal Communications*, 4(5):58–64, 1997.

[41] P. Brusilovsky. Methods and Techniques of Adaptive Hypermedia. *User Modeling and User-Adapted Interaction*, 6:87–129, 1996.

[42] P. Brusilovsky, E. W. Schwarz, and G. Weber. ELM-ART: An Intelligent Tutoring System on World Wide Web. In *Proceedings of International Conference on Intelligent Tutoring Systems, June 12-14, 1996, Montréal, Canada*, pages 261–269, 1996.

[43] J. A. Bubenko. The Temporal Dimension in Information Modeling. In *Architecture and Models in Data Base Management Systems (Proceedings of IFIP Working Conference on Modelling in Data Base Management Systems, January 3-7, 1977, Nice, France)*, pages 93–118, 1977.

[44] J. A. Bubenko. Information Modelling in the Context of System Development. In *Information Processing 80 (Proceedings of IFIP Congress 80, October 6-9, 1980, Tokyo, Japan, October 14-17, 1980, Melbourne, Australia)*, pages 395–411, 1980.

[45] P. Büchler. XSLGui – A Graphical Template Editor for Web Content Managament. Diploma thesis, Swiss Federal Institute of Technology Zurich (ETH Zurich), Zurich, Switzerland, 2003.

[46] J. Burrell and G. K. Gay. Collectively Defining Context in a Mobile, Networked Computing Environment. In *Proceedinsg of ACM SIGCHI Conference on Human Factors in Computing Systems, March 31-April 5, 2001, Seattle, WA, USA*, pages 231–232, 2001.

[47] J. Burrell and G. K. Gay. E-Graffiti: Evaluating Real-World Use of a Context-Aware System. *Interacting with Computers*, 14(4): 301–312, 2002.

[48] P. Butterworth, A. Otis, and J. Stein. The GemStone Object Database Management System. *Communications of the ACM*, 34(10): 64–77, 1991.

[49] M. J. Carey and D. J. DeWitt. A Data Model and Query Language for EXODUS. *ACM SIGMOD Record*, 17(3):413–423, 1988.

[50] S. Casteleyn, O. De Troyer, and S. Brockmans. Design Time Support for Adaptive Behavior in Web Sites. In *Proceedings of ACM Symposium on Applied Computing, March 9-12, 2003 Melbourne, FL, USA*, pages 1222–1228, 2003.

[51] P. Castro and R. R. Muntz. Managing Context Data for Smart Spaces. *IEEE Personal Communications*, 7(5):44–46, 2000.

[52] P. Castro, P. Chiu, T. Kremenek, and R. R. Muntz. A Probabilistic Room Location Service for Wireless Networked Environments. In *Proceedings of International Conference on Ubiquitous Computing, September 30-October 2, Atlanta, GA, USA*, pages 18–34, 2001.

[53] D. Caswell and P. Debaty. Creating Web Representations for Places. In *Proceedings of International Symposium on Handheld and Ubiquitous Computing, September 25-27, 2000, Bristol, England, UK*, pages 114–126, 2000.

[54] S. Ceri, P. Fraternali, and S. Paraboschi. Data-Driven, One-To-One Web Site Generation for Data-Intensive Applications. In *Proceedings of International Conference on Very Large Data Bases, September 7-10, 1999, Edinburgh, Scotland, UK*, pages 615–626, 1999.

[55] S. Ceri, P. Fraternali, and A. Bongio. Web Modeling Language (WebML): A Modeling Language For Designing Web Sites. *Computer Networks*, 33(1-6):137–157, 2000.

[56] S. Ceri, P. Fraternali, A. Bongio, M. Brambilla, S. Comai, and M. Matera. *Designing Data-Intensive Web Applications*. The Morgan Kaufmann Series in Data Management Systems. Morgan Kaufmann Publishers Inc., 2002.

[57] S. Ceri, F. Daniel, and M. Matera. Extending WebML for Modeling Multi-Channel Context-Aware Web Applications. In *Proceedings of International Workshop on Multichannel and Mobile Information Systems, December 13, 2003, Roma, Italy*, pages 225–233, 2003.

[58] S. Ceri, P. Dolog, M. Matera, and W. Nejdl. Adding Client-Side Adaptation to the Conceptual Design of e-Learning Web Applications. *Journal of Web Engineering*, 4(1):21–37, 2005.

[59] S. Ceri, F. Daniel, and F. M. Facca. Modeling Web Applications Reacting to User Behaviors. *Computer Networks*, 50(10):1533–1546, July 2006.

[60] S. Ceri, F. Daniel, F. M. Facca, and M. Matera. Model-driven Engineering of Active Context-Awareness. *World Wide Web*, 2007. On-line first: `http://dx.doi.org/10.1007/s11280-006-0014-5`.

[61] S. Ceri, F. Daniel, M. Matera, and F. M. Facca. Model-driven Development of Context-Aware Web Applications. *ACM Transactions on Internet Technology*, 7(2), 2007.

[62] H. Chen, T. Finin, and A. Joshi. An Ontology for Context-Aware Pervasive Computing Environments. *The Knowledge Engineering Review*, 18(3):197–207, 2003.

[63] H. L. Chen. *An Intelligent Broker Architecture for Pervasive Context-Aware Systems*. PhD thesis, University of Maryland, Baltimore County, Baltimore, MD, USA, 2004.

[64] P. P.-S. Chen. The Entity-Relationship Model – Toward a Unified View of Data. *ACM Transactions on Database Systems*, 1(1):9–36, 1976.

[65] K. Cheverst, N. Davies, K. Mitchell, and A. Friday. Experiences of Developing and Deploying a Context-Aware Tourist Guide: The GUIDE Project. In *Proceedings of International Conference on Mobile Computing and Networking, August 6-11, 2000, Boston, MA, USA*, pages 20–31, 2000.

[66] K. Cheverst, N. Davies, K. Mitchell, A. Friday, and C. Efstratiou. Developing a Context-Aware Electronic Tourist Guide: Some Issues and Experiences. In *Proceedings of ACM SIGCHI Conference on Human Factors in Computing Systems, April 1-6, 2000, The Hague, The Netherlands*, pages 17–24, 2000.

[67] P. Chiu, J. Boreczky, A. Girgensohn, and D. Kimber. LiteMinutes: An Internet-based System for Multimedia Meeting Minutes. In *Proceedings of International World Wide Web Conference, May 1-5, 2001, Hong Kong, Hong Kong*, pages 140–149, 2001.

[68] J. Clark, editor. XML Stylesheet Language Transformations (XSLT). http://www.w3.org/TR/xslt, November 1999.

[69] J. Clifford and A. U. Tansel. On an Algebra for Historical Relational Databases: Two Views. In *Proceedings of ACM SIGMOD International Conference on Management of Data, May 28-31, 1985, Austin, TX, USA*, pages 247–265, 1985.

[70] J. Clifford and D. S. Warren. Formal Semantics for Time in Databases. *ACM Transactions on Databases Systems*, 8(2):214–254, 1983.

[71] CODASYL Data Base Task Group. *April 1971 Report*. Association for Computing Machinery (ACM), 1971.

[72] E. F. Codd. A Relational Model of Data for Large Shared Data Banks. *Communications of the ACM*, 13(6):377–387, 1970.

[73] M. H. Coen. Design Principles for Intelligent Environments. In *Proceedings of National Conference on Artificial Intelligence, July 2630, 1998, Madison, WI, USA*, pages 547–554, 1998.

[74] R. Conradi and B. Westfechtel. Version Models for Software Configuration Management. *ACM Computing Surveys*, 30(2):232–282, 1998.

[75] J. Coutaz, J. L. Crowley, S. Dobson, and D. Garlan. Context is Key. *Communications of the ACM*, 48(3):49–53, 2005.

[76] R. D. Cronk. Tributaries and Deltas. *BYTE*, 17(1):177–186, 1992.

[77] P. Dadam, V. Y. Lum, and H.-D. Werner. Integration of Time Versions into a Relational Database System. In *Proceedings of International Conference on Very Large Data Bases, August 27-31, 1984, Singapore, Republic of Singapore*, pages 509–522, 1984.

[78] P. De Bra and L. Calvi. AHA! An Open Adaptive Hypermedia Architecture. *The New Review of Hypermedia and Multimedia*, 4 (26):115–139, 1998.

[79] P. De Bra, G.-J. Houben, and H. Wu. AHAM: A Dexter-based Reference Model for Adaptive Hypermedia. In *Proceedings of ACM Conference on Hypertext and Hypermedia, February 21-25, 1999, Darmstadt, Germany*, pages 147–156, 1999.

[80] P. De Bra, A. Aerts, B. Berden, B. de Lange, B. Rousseau, T. Santic, D. Smits, and N. Stash. AHA! The Adaptive Hypermedia Architecture. In *Proceedings of ACM Conference on Hypertext and Hypermedia, August 26-30, 2003, Nottingham, England, UK*, pages 81–84, 2003.

[81] A. de Spindler, M. C. Norrie, M. Grossniklaus, and B. Signer. Spatio-Temporal Proximity as a Basis for Collaborative Filtering in Mobile Environments. In *Proceedings of International Workshop on Ubiquitous Mobile Information and Collaboration Systems, June 5-6, 2006, Luxembourg, Grand Duchy of Luxembourg*, pages 912–926, 2006.

[82] O. De Troyer and S. Casteleyn. Designing Localized Web Sites. In *Proceedings of International Conference on Web Information Systems Engineering, November 22-24, 2004, Brisbane, Australia*, pages 547–558, 2004.

[83] O. De Troyer and C. J. Leune. WSDM: A User-Centered Design Method for Web Sites. *Computer Networks and ISDN Systems*, 30 (1-7):85–94, 1998.

[84] R. De Virgilio and R. Torlone. A General Methodology for Context-Aware Data Access. In *Proceedings of ACM International Workshop on Data Engineering for Wireless and Mobile Access, June 12, 2005, Baltimore, MD, USA*, pages 9–15, 2005.

[85] R. De Virgilio and R. Torlone. Management of Heterogeneous Pro-
     files in Context-Aware Adaptive Information System. In *Proceed-
     ings of On the Move to Meaningful Internet Systems Workshops,
     October 31-November 4, 2005, Agia Napa, Cyprus*, pages 132–141,
     2005.

[86] R. De Virgilio and R. Torlone. Modeling Heterogeneous Context
     Information in Adaptive Web Based Applications. In *Proceedings
     of the International Conference on Web Engineering, July 11-14,
     2006, Palo Alto CA, USA*, pages 56–63, 2006.

[87] R. De Virgilio, R. Torlone, and G.-J. Houben. A Rule-based Ap-
     proach to Content Delivery Adaptation in Web Information Sys-
     tems. In *Proceedings of the International Conference on Mobile
     Data Management, May 9-13, 2006, Nara, Japan*, pages 21–24,
     2006.

[88] N. M. Delisle and M. D. Schwartz. Neptune: A Hypertext System
     for CAD Applications. In *Proceedings of ACM SIGMOD Inter-
     national Conference on Management of Data, May 28-30, 1986,
     Washington, D.C., USA*, pages 132–143, 1986.

[89] N. M. Delisle and M. D. Schwartz. Contexts – A Partitioning Con-
     cept for Hypertext. *ACM Transactions on Information Systems*, 5
     (2):168–186, 1987.

[90] A. K. Dey, G. D. Abowd, and D. Salber. A Context-based Infras-
     tructure for Smart Environments. In *Proceedings of International
     Workshop on Managing Interactions in Smart Environments, De-
     cember 13-14, 1999, Dublin Ireland*, pages 114–128, 1999.

[91] K. R. Dittrich and R. A. Lorie. Version Support for Engineering
     Database Systems. *IEEE Transactions on Software Engineering*,
     14(4):429–437, 1988.

[92] K. R. Dittrich, W. Gotthard, and P. C. Lockemann. DAMOKLES –
     A Database System for Software Engineering Environments. In
     *Proceedings of an International Workshop on Advanced Program-
     ming Environments, June 16-18, 1986, Trondheim, Norway*, pages
     353–371, 1986.

[93] P. Dourish. *Where the Action Is: The Foundations of Embodied
     Interaction*. MIT Press, 2001.

[94] D. J. Ecklund, E. F. Ecklund, Jr., R. O. Eifrig, and F. M. Tonge. DVSS: A Distributed Version Storage Server for CAD Applications. In *Proceedings of International Conference on Very Large Data Bases, September 1-4, 1987, Brighton, UK*, pages 443–454, 1987.

[95] R. Elmasri, G. T. J. Wuu, and Y.-J. Kim. The Time Index: An Access Structure for Temporal Data. In *Proceedings of International Conference on Very Large Data Bases, August 13-16, 1990, Brisbane, Queensland, Australia*, pages 1–12, San Francisco, CA, USA, 1990. Morgan Kaufmann Publishers Inc.

[96] F. Espinoza, P. Persson, A. Sandin, H. Nyström, E. Cacciatore, and M. Bylund. GeoNotes: Social and Navigational Aspects of Location-Based Information Systems. In *Proceedings of International Conference on Ubiquitous Computing, September 30-October 2, 2001, Atlanta, GA, USA*, pages 2–17, 2001.

[97] J. Estublier. Work Space Management in Software Engineering Environments. In *Proceedings of Workshop on System Configuration Management, March 25-26, 1996, Berlin, Germany*, pages 127–138, 1996.

[98] J. Estublier and R. Casallas. Three Dimensional Versioning. In *Selected papers from the ICSE SCM-4 and SCM-5 Workshops on Software Configuration Management*, pages 118–135, 1995.

[99] F. M. Facca, S. Ceri, J. Armani, and V. Demaldé. Building Reactive Web Applications. In *Special Interest Tracks and Posters of International World Wide Web Conference, May 10-14, 2005, Chiba, Japan*, pages 1058–1059, 2005.

[100] P. Fahy and S. Clarke. CASS – Middleware for Mobile Context-Aware Applications. In *Proceedings of Workshop on Context Awareness, June 6, 2004, Boston, MA, USA*, 2004.

[101] M. Fernández, D. Florescu, J. Kang, A. Levy, and D. Suciu. STRUDEL: A Web Site Management System. In *Proceedings of ACM SIGMOD International Conference on Management of Data, May 13-15, 1997, Tucson, AZ, USA*, pages 549–552, 1997.

[102] M. Fernández, D. Suciu, and I. Tatarinov. Declarative Specification of Data-intensive Web Sites. In *Proceedings of Conference on*

Domain-Specific Languages, October 3-6, 1999, Austin, TX, USA, pages 135–148, 1999.

[103] M. Fernández, D. Florescu, A. Levy, and D. Suciu. Declarative Specification of Web Sites with STRUDEL. *The VLDB Journal*, 9 (1):38–55, 2000.

[104] Z. Fiala and G.-J. Houben. A Generic Transcoding Tool for Making Web Applications Adaptive. In *Proceedings of CAISE'05 Forum, June 13-17, 2005, Porto, Portugal*, pages 15–20, 2005.

[105] Z. Fiala, M. Hinz, K. Meissner, and F. Wehner. A Component-based Approach for Adaptive, Dynamic Web Documents. *Journal of Web Engineering*, 2(1-2):58–73, 2003.

[106] Z. Fiala, F. Frăsincar, M. Hinz, G.-J. Houben, P. Barna, and K. Meissner. Engineering the Presentation Layer of Adaptable Web Information Systems. In *Proceedings of International Conference on Web Engineering, July 26-30, 2004, Munich, Germany*, pages 459–472, 2004.

[107] Z. Fiala, M. Hinz, G.-J. Houben, and F. Frăsincar. Design and Implementation of Component-based Adaptive Web Presentations. In *Proceedings of Symposium on Applied Computing, March 14-17, 2004, Nicosia, Cyprus*, pages 1698–1704, 2004.

[108] G. W. Fitzmaurice. Situated Information Spaces and Spatially Aware Palmtop Computers. *Communications of the ACM*, 36(7): 39–49, 1993.

[109] A. Fitzpatrick, G. Biegel, S. Clarke, and V. Cahill. Towards a Sentient Object Model. In *Proceedings of Workshop on Engineering Context-Aware Object-Oriented Systems and Environments, November 5, 2002, Seattle, WA, USA*, 2002.

[110] A. Fox and E. A. Brewer. Reducing WWW Latency and Bandwidth Requirements by Real-time Distillation. *Computer Networks and ISDN Systems*, 28(7-11):1445–1456, 1996.

[111] A. Fox, S. D. Gribbe, E. A. Brewer, and E. Amir. Adapting to Network and Client Variability via On-Demand Dynamic Distillation. *Computer Architecture News*, 24(Special Issue):160–170, 1996.

[112] F. Frăsincar. *Hypermedia Presentation Generation for Semantic Web Information Systems.* PhD thesis, Technische Universiteit Eindhoven, Eindhoven, The Netherlands, June 2005.

[113] F. Frăsincar, P. Barna, G.-J. Houben, and Z. Fiala. Adaptation and Reuse in Designing Web Information Systems. In *Proceedings of International Conference on Information Technology: Coding and Computing, April 2-4, 2004, Las Vegas, NV, USA*, pages 387–391, 2004.

[114] F. Frăsincar, G.-J. Houben, and P. Barna. Hera Presentation Generator. In *Special Interest Tracks and Posters of International World Wide Web Conference, May 10-14, 2005, Chiba, Japan*, pages 952–953, 2005.

[115] S. K. Gadia. A Homogeneous Relational Model and Query Languages for Temporal Databases. *ACM Transactions on Database Systems*, 13(14):418–448, December 1988.

[116] E. Gamma, R. Helm, R. Johnson, and J. Vlissides. *Design Patterns: Elements of Reusable Object-Oriented Software.* Addison-Wesley Longman Publishing Co., 1995.

[117] F. Garzotto, P. Paolini, and D. Schwabe. HDM – A Model-Based Approach to Hypertext Application Design. *ACM Transactions on Informations Systems*, 11(1):1–26, 1993.

[118] I. P. Goldstein and D. G. Bobrow. Extending Object Oriented Programming in Smalltalk. In *Proceedings of ACM Conference on LISP and Functional Programming, August 25-27, 1980, Stanford University, CA, USA*, pages 75–81, 1980.

[119] M. Grossniklaus. CMServer – An Object-Oriented Framework for Website Development and Content Management. Diploma thesis, Swiss Federal Institute of Technology Zurich (ETH Zurich), Zurich, Switzerland, 2001.

[120] M. Grossniklaus and M. C. Norrie. Information Concepts for Content Management. In *Proceedings of International Workshop on Data Semantics and Web Information Systems, December 11, 2002, Singapore, Republic of Singapore*, pages 150–159, 2002.

[121] M. Grossniklaus, M. C. Norrie, and P. Büchler. Metatemplate Driven Multi-Channel Presentation. In *Proceedings of International Workshop on Multichannel and Mobile Information Systems, December 13, 2003, Roma, Italy*, pages 234–242, 2003.

[122] M. Grossniklaus, M. C. Norrie, B. Signer, and N. Weibel. Putting Location-Based Services on the Map. In *Proceedings of International Symposium on Web and Wireless Geographical Information Systems, December 4-5, 2006, Hong Kong, China*, pages 1–11, 2006.

[123] T. Gu, H. K. Pung, and D. Q. Zhang. A Middleware for Building Context-Aware Mobile Services. In *Proceedings of Vehicular Technology Conference (Spring), May 17-19, 2004, Milan, Italy*, pages 2656–2660, 2002.

[124] R. V. Guha and J. McCarthy. Varieties of Contexts. In *Proceedings of International and Interdisciplinary Conference on Modeling and Using Context, June 23-25, 2003, Stanford, CA, USA*, pages 164–177, 2003.

[125] B. Gulla, E.-A. Karlsson, and D. Yeh. Change-Oriented Version Descriptions in EPOS. *Software Engineering Journal*, 6(6):378–386, 1991.

[126] R. M. Gustavsen. Condor – An Application Framework for Mobility-Based Context-Aware Applications. In *Proceedings of Workshop on Concepts and Models for Ubiquitous Computing, September 29, 2002, Göteborg, Sweden*, 2002.

[127] A. Haake. CoVer: A Contextual Version Server for Hypertext Applications. In *Proceedings of ACM European Conference on Hypertext Technology, November 30-December 4, 1992, Milan, Italy*, pages 43–52, 1992.

[128] A. Haake. Under CoVer: The Implementation of a Contextual Version Server for Hypertext Applications. In *Proceedings of ACM European Conference on Hypermedia Technology, September 19-23, 1994, Edinburgh, Scotland, UK*, pages 81–93, 1994.

[129] A. Haake and J. M. Haake. Take CoVer: Exploiting Version Support in Cooperative Systems. In *Proceedings of ACM SIGCHI*

Conference on Human Factors in Computing Systems, April 24-29, 1993, Amsterdam, The Netherlands, pages 406–413, 1993.

[130] A. Haake and D. L. Hicks. VerSE: Towards Hypertext Versioning Styles. In *Proceedings of ACM Conference on Hypertext, March 16-20, 1996, Bethesda, MD, USA*, pages 224–234, 1996.

[131] A. N. Habermann and D. Notkin. Gandalf: Software Development Environments. *IEEE Transactions on Software Engineering*, 12 (12):1117–1127, 1986.

[132] F. Halasz and M. Schwartz. The Dexter Hypertext Reference Model. *Communications of the ACM*, 37(2):30–39, 1994.

[133] A. Harter, A. Hopper, P. Steggles, A. Ward, and P. Webster. The Anatomy of a Context-Aware Application. *Wireless Networks*, 8 (2-3):187–197, 2002.

[134] R. L. Haskin and R. A. Lorie. On Extending the Functions of a Relational Database System. In *Proceedings of ACM SIGMOD International Conference on Management of Data, June 2-4, 1982, Orlando, FL, USA*, pages 207–212, 1982.

[135] C. Heath and P. Luff. Disembodied Conduct: Communication Through Video in a Multi-Media Office Environment. In *Proceedings of ACM SIGCHI Conference on Human Factors in Computing Systems, April 27-May 2, 1991, New Orleans, LA, USA*, pages 99–103, 1991.

[136] S. Helal, B. Winkler, C. Lee, Y. Kaddoura, L. Ran, C. Giraldo, S. Kuchibhotla, and W. Mann. Enabling Location-Aware Pervasive Computing Applications for the Edlerly. In *Proceedings of IEEE International Conference on Pervasive Computing and Communications*, pages 531–536, 2003.

[137] S. Helal, W. Mann, H. El-Zabadani, J. King, Y. Kaddoura, and E. Jansen. The Gator Tech Smart House: A Programmable Pervasive Space. *Computer*, 38(3):50–60, 2005.

[138] G. D. Held, M. R. Stonebraker, and E. Wong. INGRES – A Relational Data Base System. In *Proceedings of National Computer Conference, May 19-22, 1975, Anaheim, CA, USA*, pages 409–416, 1975.

[139] R. Hennicker and N. Koch. A UML-Based Methodology for Hypermedia Design. In *Proceedings of International Conference on the Unified Modeling Language, October 2-6, 2000, York, England, UK*, pages 410–424, 2000.

[140] K. Henricksen. *A Framework for Context-Aware Pervasive Computing Applications*. PhD thesis, University of Queensland, Brisbane, Australia, 2003.

[141] D. L. Hicks, J. J. Leggett, P. J. Nürnberg, and J. L. Schnase. A Hypermedia Version Control Framework. *ACM Transactions on Information Systems*, 16(2):127–160, 1998.

[142] T. Hofer, W. Schwinger, M. Pichler, G. Leonhartsberger, J. Altmann, and W. Retschitzegger. Context-Awareness on Mobile Devices – The Hydrogen Approach. In *Proceedings of Annual Hawaii International Conference on System Sciences (Track 9)*, pages 10–19, 2003.

[143] F. Hohl, U. Kubach, A. Leonhardi, K. Rothermel, and M. Schwehm. Next Century Challenges: Nexus – An Open Global Infrastructure for Spatial-Aware Applications. In *Proceedings of ACM/IEEE International Conference on Mobile Computing and Networking, August 15-20, 1999, Seattle, WA, USA*, pages 249–255, 1999.

[144] J. I. Hong and J. A. Landay. A Context/Communication Information Agent. *Personal and Ubiquitous Computing*, 5(1):78–81, 2001.

[145] J. I. Hong and J. A. Landay. An Infrastructure Approach to Context-Aware Computing. *Human Computer Interaction*, 16(2-4):287–303, 2001.

[146] G.-J. Houben, P. Barna, F. Frăsincar, and R. Vdovják. Hera: Development of Semantic Web Information Systems. In *Proceedings of International Conference on Web Engineering, July 14-18, 2003, Oviedo, Spain*, pages 529–538, 2003.

[147] S. S. Intille. Designing a Home of the Future. *IEEE Pervasive Computing*, 1(2):76–82, 2002.

[148] G. Jaeschke and H.-J. Schek. Remarks on the Algebra of Non First Normal Form Relations. In *Proceedings of the ACM SIGACT-SIGMOD Symposium on Principles of Database Systems, March 29-31, 1982, Los Angeles, CA, USA*, pages 124–138, 1982.

[149] C. S. Jensen and R. T. Snodgrass. Temporal Data Management. *IEEE Transactions on Knowledge and Data Engineering*, 11(1): 36–44, 1999.

[150] Y. Jin, S. Decker, and G. Wiederhold. OntoWebber: Model-Driven Ontology-Based Web Site Management. In *Proceedings of International Semantic Web Working Symposium, July 29-August 1, 2001, Stanford University, CA, USA*, pages 529–547, 2001.

[151] S. Jones and P. J. Mason. Handling the Time Dimension in a Data Base. In *Proceedings of International Conference on Data Bases, July 2-4, 1980, Aberdeen, Scotland*, pages 65–83, 1980.

[152] R. José and N. Davies. Scalable and Flexible Location-Based Services for Ubiquitous Information Access. In *Proceedings of International Symposium on Handheld and Ubiquitous Computing, September 27-29, 1999, Karlsruhe, Germany*, pages 52–66, 1999.

[153] J. W. Kaltz and J. Ziegler. A Conceptual Model for Context-Aware Web Engineering. In *Proceedings of International Workshop on Modelling and Retrieval of Context, September 20-21, 2004, Ulm, Germany*, 2004.

[154] D. Kaplan. On the Logic of Demonstratives. *Journal of Philosophical Logic*, 8(1):81–98, 1979.

[155] G. Kappel, W. Retschitzegger, and W. Schwinger. Modeling Customizable Web Applications – A Requirement's Perspective. In *Proceedings of International Conference on Digital Libraries, November 13-16, 2000, Kyoto, Japan*, pages 168–179, 2000.

[156] R. H. Katz. Toward a Unified Framework for Version Modeling in Engineering Databases. *ACM Computing Surveys*, 22(4):375–409, 1990.

[157] R. H. Katz and E. E. Chang. Managing Change in a Computer-Aided Design Database. In *Proceedings of International Conference*

on Very Large Data Bases, September 1-4, 1987, Brighton, UK, pages 455–462, 1987.

[158] R. H. Katz and T. J. Lehman. Database Support for Versions and Alternatives of Large Design Files. *IEEE Transactions on Software Engineering*, SE-10(2):191–200, 1984.

[159] R. H. Katz, M. Anwarrudin, and E. E. Chang. A Version Server for Computer-Aided Design Data. In *Proceedings of ACM/IEEE Conference on Design Automation, June 1986, Las Vegas, NV, USA*, pages 27–33, 1986.

[160] C. D. Kidd, R. Orr, G. D. Abowd, C. G. Atkeson, I. A. Essa, B. MacIntyre, E. D. Mynatt, T. Starner, and W. Newstetter. The Aware Home: A Living Laboratory for Ubiquitous Computing Research. In *Proceedings of International Workshop on Cooperative Buildings, Integrating Information, Organization, and Architecture, October 1-2, 1999, Pittsburgh, PA, USA*, pages 191–198, 1999.

[161] T. Kindberg, J. Barton, J. Morgan, G. Becker, D. Caswell, P. Debaty, G. Gopal, M. Frid, V. Krishnan, H. Morris, J. Schettino, B. Serra, and M. Spasojevic. People, Places, Things: Web Presence for the Real World. *Mobile Networks and Applications*, 7(5): 365–376, 2002.

[162] M. Kirchhof and S. Linz. Component-based Development of Web-enabled eHome Services. *Personal Ubiquitous Computing*, 9(5): 323–332, 2005.

[163] C. Kiss, editor. Composite Capability/Preference Profiles (CC/PP): Structure and Vocabularies 2.0. `http://www.w3.org/TR/CCPP-struct-vocab2/`, April 2007.

[164] P. Klahold, G. Schlageter, R. Unland, and W. Wilkes. A Transaction Model Supporting Complex Applications in Integrated Information Systems. In *Proceedings of ACM SIGMOD International Conference on Management of Data, May 28-31, 1985, Austin, TX, USA*, pages 388–401, 1985.

[165] P. Klahold, G. Schlageter, and W. Wilkes. A General Model for Version Management in Databases. In *Proceedings of International*

Conference on Very Large Data Bases, August 25-28, 1986, Kyoto, Japan, pages 319–327, 1986.

[166] M. R. Klopprogge. Term: An Approach to Include the Time Dimension in the Entity-Relationship Model. In *Proceedings of International Conference on Entity-Relationship Approach, October 12-14, 1981, Washington, DC, USA*, pages 477–508, 1981.

[167] A. Kobler. *The eXtreme Design Approach*. PhD thesis, Swiss Federal Institute of Technology Zurich (ETH Zurich), Zurich, Switzerland, 2001.

[168] A. Kobler and M. C. Norrie. OMS Java: Lessons Learned from Building a Multi-Tier Object Management Framework. In *Proceedings of Workshop on Java and Databases: Persistence Options, November 2, 1999, Denver, CO, USA*, 1999.

[169] A. Kobler, M. C. Norrie, B. Signer, and M. Grossniklaus. OMS Java: Providing Information, Storage and Access Abstractions in an Object-Oriented Framework. In *Proceedings of International Conference on Object Oriented Information Systems, August 27-29, 2001, Calgary, Canada*, pages 25–34, 2001.

[170] A. Kobsa, D. Müller, and A. Nill. KN-AHS: An Adaptive Hypertext Client of the User Modeling System BGP-MS. In *Readings in Intelligent User Interfaces*, pages 372–380. Morgan Kaufmann, 1998.

[171] N. Koch. *Software Engineering for Adaptive Hypermedia System*. PhD thesis, Ludwig-Maximilians-University Munich, Munich, Germany, 2000.

[172] N. Koch and M. Wirsing. The Munich Reference Model for Adaptive Hypermedia Applications. In *Proceedings of International Conference on Adaptive Hypermedia and Adaptive Web-Based Systems, May 29-31, Malaga, Spain*, pages 213–222, 2002.

[173] P. Korpipää, J. Mäntyjärvi, J. Kela, H. Keränen, and E.-J. Malm. Managing Context Information in Mobile Devices. *IEEE Pervasive Computing*, 2(3):42–51, 2003.

[174] G. Kortuem, M. Bauer, and Z. Segall. NETMAN: The Design of a Collaborative Wearable Computer System. *Mobile Networks and Applications*, 4(1):49–58, 1999.

[175] B. Kreller, D. Carrega, J. Shankar, P. Salmon, S. Bottger, and T. Kassing. A Mobile-Aware City Guide Application. In *Proceedings of ACTS Mobile Communications Summit, June 8-11, 1998, Rhodes, Greece*, pages 60–65, 1998.

[176] M. Lacroix and P. Lavency. Preferences: Putting More Knowledge into Queries. In *Proceedings of International Conference on Very Large Data Bases, September 1-4, 1987, Brighton, England, UK*, pages 217–225, 1987.

[177] C. Lamb, G. Landis, J. Orenstein, and D. Weinreb. The Object-Store Database System. *Communications of the ACM*, 34(10):50–63, 1991.

[178] A. Lampen and A. Mahler. An Object Base for Attributed Software Objects. In *Proceedings of European Unix Systems User Group Conference, October 3-7, 1988, Cascais, Portugal*, pages 95–106, 1988.

[179] P. Lavency and M. Vanhoedenaghe. Knowledge Based Configuration Management. In *Proceedings of Annual Hawaii International Conference on System Sciences (Software Track), January, Kailua-Kona, HI, United States*, pages 83–92, 1988.

[180] D. B. Leblang and R. P. Chase, Jr. Computer-Aided Software Engineering in a Distributed Workstation Environment. *ACM SIG-SOFT Software Engineering Notes*, 9(3):104–112, 1984.

[181] A. Leonhardi, U. Kubach, K. Rothermel, and A. Fritz. Virtual Information Towers – A Metaphor for Intuitive, Location-Aware Information Access in a Mobile Environment. In *Proceedings of IEEE International Symposium on Wearable Computers, October 18-19, 1999, San Francisco, CA, USA*, pages 15–20, 1999.

[182] A. Lombardoni. *Towards a Universal Information Platform: An Object-Oriented, Multi-User, Information Store*. PhD thesis, Swiss Federal Institute of Technology Zurich (ETH Zurich), Zurich, Switzerland, 2006.

[183] N. A. Lorentzos and R. G. Johnson. TRA: A Model for Temporal Relational Algebra. In *Temporal Aspects of Information Systems (Proceedings of IFIP Working Conference on Temporal Aspects in Information Systems, May 13-15, Sophia-Antipolis, France)*, pages 95–108, 1988.

[184] V. Y. Lum, P. Dadam, R. Erbe, J. Günauer, P. Pistor, G. Walch, H.-D. Werner, and J. Woodfill. Designing DBMS Support for the Temporal Dimension. In *Proceedings of ACM SIGMOD International Conference on Management of Data, June 18-21, 1984, Boston, MA, USA*, pages 115–130, 1984.

[185] A. Mahler. Variants: Keeping Things Together and Telling Them Apart. In *Configuration Management*, pages 73–97, 1995.

[186] N. Marmasse and C. Schmandt. Location-Aware Information Delivery with ComMotion. In *Proceedings of International Symposium on Handheld and Ubiquitous Computing, September 25-27, 2000, Bristol, England, UK*, pages 157–171, 2000.

[187] M. Marx and C. Schmandt. CLUES: Dynamic Personalized Message Filtering. In *Proceedings of ACM Conference on Computer Supported Cooperative Work, November 16-20, 1996, Boston, MA, USA*, pages 113–121, 1996.

[188] S. Meyer and A. Rakotonirainy. A Survey of Research on Context-Aware Homes. In *Proceedings of Australasian Information Security Workshop Conference on ACSW Frontiers, February 1, 2003, Adelaide, Australia*, pages 159–168, 2003.

[189] D. B. Miller, R. G. Stockton, and C. W. Krueger. An Inverted Approach to Configuration Management. *ACM SIGSOFT Software Engineering Notes*, 14(7):1–4, 1989.

[190] G. A. Miller, R. Beckwith, C. Fellbaum, D. Gross, and K. J. Miller. Introduction to WordNet: An On-line Lexical Database. *International Journal of Lexicography*, 3(4):235–244, 1990.

[191] M. Milosavljevic and J. Oberlander. Dynamic Hypertext Catalogues: Helping Users to Help Themselves. In *Proceedings of ACM Conference on Hypertext and Hypermedia, June 20-24, 1998, Pittsburgh, PA, United States*, pages 123–131, 1998.

[192] R. Mohan, J. R. Smith, and C.-S. Li. Adapting Multimedia Internet Content for Universal Access. *IEEE Transactions on Multimedia*, 1(1):104–114, 1999.

[193] R. Motschnig-Pitrik and L. Nykl. The Role and Modeling of Context in a Cognitive Model of Rogers' Person-Centred Approach. In *Proceedings of International and Interdisciplinary Conference on Modeling and Using Context, July 27-30, 2001, Dundee, Scotland, UK*, pages 275–289, 2001.

[194] M. C. Mozer. The Neural Network House: An Environment that Adapts to its Inhabitants. In *Proceedings of AAAI Spring Symposium on Intelligent Environments, March 23-25, 1998, Stanford University, Palo Alto, CA, USA*, pages 110–114, 1998.

[195] B. P. Munch, J.-O. Larsen, B. Gulla, R. Conradi, and E.-A. Karlsson. Uniform Versioning: The Change-Oriented Model. In *Proceedings of International Workshop of Software Configuration Management, May 21-22, 1993, Baltimore, MD, USA*, pages 188–196, 1993.

[196] E. D. Mynatt, I. Essa, and W. Rogers. Increasing the Opportunities for Aging in Place. In *Proceedings of Conference on Universal Usability, November 16-17, 2000, Arlington, VA, USA*, pages 65–71, 2000.

[197] K. S. Nagel, C. D. Kidd, T. O'Connell, A. K. Dey, and G. D. Abowd. The Family Intercom: Developing a Context-Aware Audio Communication System. In *Proceedings of International Conference on Ubiquitous Computing, September 30-October 2, 2001, Atlanta, GA, USA*, pages 176–183, 2001.

[198] S. B. Navathe and R. Ahmed. A Temproal Relational Model and a Query Language. *Information Sciences*, 49(1–3):147–175, 1989.

[199] P. J. Nicklin. Managing Multi-Variant Software Configuration. In *Proceedings of International Workshop on Software Configuration Management, June 12-14, 1991, Trondheim, Norway*, pages 53–57, 1991.

[200] M. C. Norrie. An Extended Entity-Relationship Approach to Data Management in Object-Oriented Systems. In *Proceedings of Inter-*

national Conference on the Entity-Relationship Approach, Arlington, TX, USA, pages 390–401, 1994.

[201] M. C. Norrie. Distinguishing Typing and Classification in Object Data Models. In H. Kangassalo, H. Jaakkola, S. Ohsuga, and B. Wangler, editors, *Information Modelling and Knowledge Bases VI*, pages 399–412. IOS Press, 1995.

[202] M. C. Norrie and A. Palinginis. From State to Structure: An XML Web Publishing Framework. In *Proceedings of CAiSE'03 Forum, June 16-20, 2003, Klagenfurt/Velden, Austria*, pages 137–140, 2003.

[203] M. C. Norrie and A. Palinginis. Empowering Databases for Context-Dependent Information Delivery. In *Proceedings of International Workshop on Ubiquitous Mobile Information and Collaboration Systems, June 16-17, 2003, Klagenfurt/Velden, Austria*, pages 90–101, 2003.

[204] M. C. Norrie and A. Palinginis. Versions for Context Dependent Information Services. In *Proceedings of Conference on Cooperative Information Systems, November 3-7, 2003, Catania-Sicily, Italy*, pages 503–515, 2003.

[205] M. C. Norrie, B. Signer, and N. Weibel. General Framework for the Rapid Development of Interactive Paper Applications. In *Proceedings of Workshop on Collaborating over Paper and Digital Documents, November 4, 2006, Banff, Canada*, pages 9–12, 2005.

[206] M. C. Norrie, B. Signer, and N. Weibel. Print-n-Link: Weaving the Paper Web. In *Proceedings of the ACM Symposium on Document Engineering, October 10-13, 2006, Amsterdam, The Netherlands*, pages 34–43, 2006.

[207] M. C. Norrie, B. Signer, M. Grossniklaus, R. Belotti, C. Decurtins, and N. Weibel. Context-Aware Platform for Mobile Data Management. *Wireless Networks*, 2007. On-line first: `http://dx.doi.org/10.1007/s11276-006-9858-y`.

[208] Objectivity, Inc. Objectivity/DB. `http://www.objectivity.com`, 2000.

[209] Open Text Corporation. Livelink Enterprise Content Management. http://www.opentext.com, 2006.

[210] R. Oppermann and M. Specht. A Context-Sensitive Nomadic Exhibition Guide. In *Proceedings of International Symposium on Handheld and Ubiquitous Computing, September 25-27, 2000, Bristol, England, UK*, pages 127–142, 2000.

[211] K. Østerbye. Structural and Cognitive Problems in Providing Version Control for Hypertext. In *Proceedings of ACM European Conference on Hypertext Technology, November 30-December 4, 1992, Milan, Italy*, pages 33–42, 1992.

[212] Y. Papakonstantinou, H. Garcia-Molina, and J. Widom. Object Exchange Across Heterogeneous Information Sources. In *Proceedings of International Conference on Data Engineering, March 6-10, 1995, Taipei, Taiwan*, pages 251–260, 1995.

[213] J. Pascoe. The stick-e Note Architecture: Extending the Interface Beyond the User. In *Proceedings of International Conference on Intelligent User Interfaces, January 6-9 1997, Orlando, FL, USA*, pages 261–264, 1997.

[214] J. Pascoe. Adding Generic Contextual Capabilities to Wearable Computers. In *Proceedings of IEEE International Symposium on Wearable Computers, October 19-20, 1998, Pittsburgh, PA, USA*, pages 92–99, 1998.

[215] J. Pascoe, D. R. Morse, and N. Ryan. Developing Personal Technology for the Field. *Personal and Ubiquitous Computing*, 2(1): 28–36, 1998.

[216] J. Pascoe, N. Ryan, and D. Morse. Issues in Developing Context-Aware Computing. In *Proceedings of International Symposium on Handheld and Ubiquitous Computing, September 27-29, 1999, Karlsruhe, Germany*, pages 208–221, 1999.

[217] P. F. Patel-Schneider, P. Hayesand, and I. Horrocks, editors. OWL Web Ontology Language: Semantics and Abstract Syntax. http://www.w3.org/TR/owl-absyn/, February 2004.

[218] P. Persson, F. Espinoza, P. Fagerberg, A. Sandin, and R. Cöster. GeoNotes: A Location-based Information System for Public

Spaces. In K. Höök, D. Benyon, and A. Munro, editors, *Designing Information Spaces: The Social Navigation Approach*, pages 151–173. Springer Verlag, 2003.

[219] M. Petrovic, M. Grossniklaus, and M. C. Norrie. Role-Based Modelling of Interactions in Database Applications. In *Proceedings on International Conference on Advanced Information Systems Engineering, June 5-9, 2006, Luxembourg, Grand Duchy of Luxembourg*, pages 63–77, 2006.

[220] N. Pissinou, K. Makki, and Y. Yesha. On Temporal Modeling in the Context of Object Databases. *ACM SIGMOD Record*, 22(3): 8–15, 1993.

[221] J. Plaice and W. W. Wadge. A New Approach to Version Control. *IEEE Transactions on Software Engineering*, 19(3):268–276, 1993.

[222] A. Ranganathan and R. H. Campbell. An Infrastructure for Context-Awareness Based on First Order Logic. *Personal Ubiquitous Computing*, 7(6):353–364, 2003.

[223] A. Ranganathan, R. H. Campbell, A. Ravi, and A. Mahajan. ConChat: A Context-Aware Chat Program. *IEEE Pervasive Computing*, 1(3):51–57, 2002.

[224] T. Reichenbacher. The World in Your Pocket – Towards a Mobile Cartography. In *Proceedings of International Cartography Conference, August 6-10, 2001, Bejing, China*, volume 4, pages 2514–2521, 2001.

[225] T. Reichenbacher. Adaptive Concepts for a Mobile Cartography. *Journal of Geographical Sciences*, 11(Supplement):43–53, 2001.

[226] C. Reichenberger. VOODOO – A Tool for Orthogonal Version Management. In *Selected Papers from the ICSE SCM-4 and SCM-5 Workshops on Software Configuration Management*, pages 61–79, 1995.

[227] F. Rice. Introducing the Office (2007) Open XML File Formats. http://msdn.microsoft.com/en-us/library/ms406049.aspx, May 2006.

[228] G. Rivera. *From File Pathnames to File Objects*. PhD thesis, Swiss Federal Institute of Technology Zurich (ETH Zurich), Zurich, Switzerland, 2001.

[229] J. F. Roddick and J. D. Patrick. Temporal Semantics in Information Systems – A Survey. *Information Systems*, 17(3):249–267, 1992.

[230] M. Román, C. Hess, R. Cerqueira, A. Ranganathan, R. H. Campbell, and K. Nahrstedt. A Middleware Infrastructure for Active Spaces. *IEEE Pervasive Computing*, 1(4):74–83, 2002.

[231] G. Rossi, D. Schwabe, and R. Guimarães. Designing Personalized Web Applications. In *Proceedings of International World Wide Web Conference, May 1-5, 2001, Hong Kong, China*, pages 275–284, 2001.

[232] D. Rotem and A. Segev. Physical Organization of Temporal Data. In *Proceedings of International Conference on Data Engineering, February 3-5, 1987, Los Angeles, CA, USA*, pages 547–553, 1987.

[233] J. R. Rumbaugh, M. R. Blaha, W. Lorensen, F. Eddy, and W. Premerlani. *Object-Oriented Modeling and Design*. Prentice Hall, 1990.

[234] J. R. Rumbaugh, I. Jacobson, and G. Booch. *The Unified Modeling Language Reference Manual*. Addison-Wesley Longman, 1999.

[235] N. Ryan, J. Pascoe, and D. R. Morse. Enhanced Reality Fieldwork: The Context-Aware Archaeological Assistant. In *Proceedings of Conference on Computer Applications and Quantitative Methods in Archaeology, April, 1997 Birmingham, England, UK*, 1997.

[236] N. Ryan, J. Pascoe, and D. R. Morse. FieldNote: A Handheld Information System for the Field. In *Proceedings of International Workshop on Telegeoprocessing, May 6-7, 1999, Lyon, France*, pages 156–163, 1999.

[237] D. Salber, A. K. Dey, and G. D. Abowd. The Context Toolkit: Aiding the Development of Context-Enabled Applications. In *Proceedings of ACM SIGCHI Conference on Human Factors in Computing Systems, May 15-20, 1999, Pittsburgh, PA, USA*, pages 434–441, 1999.

[238] N. Sarnak, R. L. Bernstein, and V. Kruskal. Creation and Maintenance of Multiple Versions. In *Proceedings of International Workshop on Software and Configuration Control, January 27-29, 1988,
Grassau, Germany*, pages 264–275, 1988.

[239] N. Sawhney and C. Schmandt. Nomadic Radio: Speech and Audio Interaction for Contextual Messaging in Nomadic Environments. *ACM Transactions on Computer-Human Interaction*, 7(3):
353–383, 2000.

[240] H.-J. Schek and P. Pistor. Data Structures for an Integrated Data
Base Management and Information Retrieval System. In *Proceed-
ings of the International Conference on Very Large Data Bases,
September 8-10, 1982, Mexico City, Mexico*, pages 197–207, 1982.

[241] K.-D. Schewe and B. Thalheim. Modeling Interaction and Media
Objects. In *Proceedings of International Conference on Applications of Natural Language to Information Systems, June 28-29,
2001, Madrid, Spain – Revised Papers*, pages 313–324, 2001.

[242] K.-D. Schewe and B. Thalheim. Reasoning About Web Information
Systems Using Story Algebras. In *Proceedings of East-European
Conference on Advances in Databases and Information Systems,
September 22-25, 2004, Budapest, Hungary*, pages 54–66, 2004.

[243] B. N. Schilit and M. M. Theimer. Disseminating Active Map Information to Mobile Hosts. *IEEE Network*, 8(5):22–32, 1994.

[244] B. N. Schilit, N. Adams, and R. Want. Context-Aware Computing
Applications. In *Proceedings of IEEE Workshop on Mobile Com-
puting Systems and Applications, December 8-9, 1994, Santa Cruz,
CA, USA*, pages 85–90, 1994.

[245] B. N. Schilit, D. M. Hilbert, and J. Trevor. Context-Aware Communication. *IEEE Wireless Communications*, 9(5):46–54, 2002.

[246] C. Schmandt, N. Marmasse, S. Marti, N. Sawhney, and S. Wheeler.
Everywhere Messaging. *IBM Systems Journal*, 39(3-4):660–677,
2000.

[247] A. Schmidt. Implicit Human Computer Interaction Through Context. *Personal and Ubiquitous Computing*, 4(2-3):191–199, 2000.

[248] A. Schmidt, M. Beigl, and H.-W. Gellersen. There Is More to Context Than Location. *Computer and Graphics*, 23(6):893–901, 1999.

[249] A. Schmidt, A. Takaluoma, and J. Mäntyjärvi. Context-Aware Telephony Over WAP. *Personal and Ubiquitous Computing*, 4(4): 225–229, 2000.

[250] D. Schwabe and G. Rossi. An Object Oriented Approach to Web-based Applications Design. *Theory and Practice of Object Systems*, 4(4):207–225, 1998.

[251] D. Schwabe, G. Rossi, and S. D. J. Barbosa. Systematic Hypermedia Application Design with OOHDM. In *Proceedings of ACM Conference on Hypertext, March 16-20, 1996, Washington, DC, USA*, pages 116–128, 1996.

[252] C. Schwank. A Content Management Component for EdFest. Semester thesis, Swiss Federal Institute of Technology Zurich (ETH Zurich), Zurich, Switzerland, 2005.

[253] B. Schwarzentrub. Multi-Variant Programming. Semester thesis, Swiss Federal Institute of Technology Zurich (ETH Zurich), Zurich, Switzerland, 2006.

[254] E. Sciore. Using Annotations to Support Multiple Kinds of Versioning in an Object-Oriented Database System. *ACM Transactions on Database Systems*, 16(3):417–438, 1991.

[255] E. Sciore. Versioning and Configuration Management in an Object-Oriented Data Model. *The VLDB Journal*, 3(1):77–106, 1994.

[256] A. Segev and A. Shoshani. Logical Modeling of Temporal Data. In *Proceedings of ACM SIGMOD International Conference on Management of Data, May 27-29, 1987, San Francisco, CA, USA*, pages 454–466, 1987.

[257] Y. Shi, W. Xie, G. Xu, R. Shi, E. Chen, Y. Mao, and F. Liu. The Smart Classroom: Merging Technologies for Seamless Tele-Education. *IEEE Pervasive Computing*, 2(2):47–55, 2003.

[258] F. Siegemund. A Context-Aware Communication Platform for Smart Objects. In *Proceedings of International Conference on Pervasive Computing, April 18-23, 2004, Linz/Vienna, Austria*, pages 69–86, 2004.

[259] B. Signer. *Fundamental Concepts for Interactive Paper and Cross-Media Information Spaces*. PhD thesis, Swiss Federal Institute of Technology Zurich (ETH Zurich), Zurich, Switzerland, 2006.

[260] B. Signer, M. Grossniklaus, and M. C. Norrie. Java Framework for Database-Centric Web Engineering. In *Proceedings of Workshop on Web Engineering, May 1, 2001, Hong Kong, China*, pages 42–49, 2001.

[261] B. Signer, M. C. Norrie, M. Grossniklaus, R. Belotti, C. Decurtins, and N. Weibel. Paper-Based Mobile Access to Databases. In *Demonstration Proceedings of ACM SIGMOD International Conference on Management of Data, June 27-29, Chicago, IL, USA*, pages 763–765, 2006.

[262] A. Singh, A. Trivedi, K. Ramamritham, and P. Shenoy. PTC: Proxies that Transcode and Cache in Heterogeneous Web Client Environments. *World Wide Web*, 7(1):7–28, 2004.

[263] J. R. Smith, R. Mohan, and C.-S. Li. Transcoding Internet Content for Heterogeneous Client Devices. In *Proceedings of International Symposium on Circuits and Systems, May 31-June 3, 1998, Monterey, CA, USA*, pages 599–602, 1998.

[264] R. Snodgrass. The Temporal Query Language TQuel. In *Proceedings of ACM SIGACT-SIGMOD Symposium on Principles of Database Systems, April 2-4, 1984, Waterloo, Ontario, Canada*, pages 204–213, 1984.

[265] R. Snodgrass and I. Ahn. A Taxonomy of Time Databases. In *Proceedings of ACM SIGMOD International Conference on Management of Data, May 28-31, 1985, Austin, TX, USA*, pages 236–246, 1985.

[266] L. F. G. Soares, G. L. D. S. Filho, R. F. Rodrigues, and D. C. Muchaluat. Versioning Support in the HyperProp System. *Multimedia Tools and Applications*, 8(3):325–339, 1999.

[267] Y. Stavrakas and M. Gergatsoulis. Multidimensional Semistructured Data: Representing Context-Dependent Information on the Web. In *Proceedings of International Conference on Advanced Information Systems Engineering, May 27-31, 2002, Toronto, Canada*, pages 183–199, 2002.

[268] Y. Stavrakas, M. Gergatsoulis, and P. Rondogiannis. Multidimensional XML. In *Proceedings of International Workshop on Distributed Communities on the Web, June 19-21, 2000, Quebec City, Canada*, pages 100–109, 2000.

[269] Y. Stavrakas, K. Pristouris, A. Efandis, and T. Sellis. Implementing a Query Language for Context-Dependent Semistructured Data. In *Proceedings of East-European Conference on Advances in Databases and Information Systems, September 22-25, 2004, Budapest, Hungary*, pages 173–188, 2004.

[270] A. Steiner. *A Generalisation Approach to Temporal Data Models and their Implementations.* PhD thesis, Swiss Federal Institute of Technology Zurich (ETH Zurich), Zurich, Switzerland, 1998.

[271] G. Stevenson, P. Nixon, and S. Dobson. Towards a Reliable, Wide-Area Infrastructure for Context-Based Self-Management of Communications. In *Proceedings of IFIP Workshop on Autonomic Communications, October 3-5, 2005, Athens, Greece*, pages 115–128, 2005.

[272] T. Strang and C. Linnhoff-Popien. A Context-Modeling Survey. In *Proceedings of Workshop on Advanced Context Modelling, Reasoning and Management, September 7, 2004, Nottingham, England, UK*, 2004.

[273] Y. Sumi, T. Etani, S. Fels, N. Simonet, K. Kobayashi, and K. Mase. C-MAP: Building a Context-Aware Mobile Assistant for Exhibition Tours. In *Community Computing and Support Systems, Social Interaction in Networked Communities (based on the Kyoto Meeting on Social Interaction and Communityware, June 8-10, 1998, Kyoto, Japan)*, pages 137–154, 1998.

[274] M.-R. Tazari, M. Grimm, and M. Finke. Modelling User Context. In *Proceedings of International Conference on Human-Computer Interaction, June 22-27, 2003, Crete, Greece*, pages 293–297, 2003.

[275] B. Thalheim and A. Düsterhöft. SiteLang: Conceptual Modeling of Internet Sites. In *Proceedings of International Conference on Conceptual Modeling, November 27-30, 2001, Yokohama, Japan*, pages 179–192, 2001.

[276] R. H. Thomason. Type Theoretic Foundations for Context, Part 1: Contexts as Complex Type-Theoretic Objects. In *Proceedings of International and Interdisciplinary Conference on Modeling and Using Context, September 9-11, 1999, Trento, Italy*, pages 351–360, 1999.

[277] V. J. Tsotras and B. Gopinath. Optimal Versioning of Objects. In *Proceedings of International Conference on Data Engineering, February 3-7, 1992, Tempe, AZ, USA*, pages 358–365, 1992.

[278] TYPO3 Association. TYPO3. http://www.typo3.org, 2005.

[279] R. Vdovják. *A Model-driven Approach for Building Distributed Ontology-based Web Applications*. PhD thesis, Technische Universiteit Eindhoven, Eindhoven, The Netherlands, June 2005.

[280] R. Vdovják, F. Frăsincar, G.-J. Houben, and P. Barna. Engineering Semantic Web Information Systems in Hera. *Journal of Web Engineering*, 1(1-2):3–26, 2003.

[281] Versant, Corp. Versant Object Database. http://www.versant.com, 2004.

[282] Vignette Corporation. Vignette Enterprise Content Management. http://www.vignette.com, 1996.

[283] W. W. Wadge, G. Brown, M. C. Schraefel, and T. Yildirim. Intensional HTML. In *Proceedings of International Workshop on Principles of Digital Document Processing, March 29-30, 1998, Saint Malo, France*, pages 128–139, 1998.

[284] R. Want, A. Hopper, V. Falcão, and J. Gibbons. The Active Badge Location System. *ACM Transaction on Information Systems*, 10 (1):91–102, 1992.

[285] J. Warmer and A. Kleppe. *The Object Constraint Language: Precise Modeling with UML*. Addison-Wesley Longman, 1999.

[286] M. J. Weal, D. T. Michaelides, M. K. Thompson, and D. C. DeR-
      oure. The Ambient Wood Journals: Replaying the Experience.
      In *Proceedings of ACM Conference on Hypertext and Hypermedia,
      August 26-30, 2003, Nottingham, England, UK*, pages 20–27, 2003.

[287] J. N. Weatherall and A. Hopper. Predator: A Distributed Location
      Service and Example Applications. In *Proceedings of International
      Workshop on Cooperative Buildings, Integrating Information, Or-
      ganization, and Architecture, October 1-2, 1999, Pittsburgh, PA,
      USA*, pages 127–139, 1999.

[288] Web Models s.r.l. WebRatio Site Development Studio. `http://
      www.webratio.com`, 2001.

[289] M. Weiser. The Computer for the Twenty-First Century. *Scientific
      American*, 265(3):94–104, 1991.

[290] A. Wexelblat. Communities Through Time: Using History for So-
      cial Navigation. In *Community Computing and Support Systems,
      Social Interaction in Networked Communities (based on the Ky-
      oto Meeting on Social Interaction and Communityware, June 8-10,
      1998, Kyoto, Japan)*, pages 281–298, 1998.

[291] E. J. Whitehead, Jr. Goals for a Configuration Management Net-
      work Protocol. In *Proceedings of International Symposium on Sys-
      tem Configuration Management, September 5-7, 1999, Toulouse,
      France*, pages 186–203, 1999.

[292] E. J. Whitehead, Jr. *An Analysis of the Hypertext Versioning Do-
      main*. PhD thesis, University of California, Irvine, CA, USA, 2000.

[293] D. Widdows. A Mathematical Model for Context and Word-
      Meaning. In *Proceedings of International and Interdisciplinary
      Conference on Modeling and Using Context, June 23-25, 2003,
      Stanford, CA, USA*, pages 369–382, 2003.

[294] J. F. H. Winkler. Version Control in Families of Large Programs. In
      *Proceedings of International Conference on Software Engineering,
      March 30-April 2, 1987, Monterey, CA, USA*, pages 150–161, 1987.

[295] T. Winogard. Architectures for Context. *Human Computer Inter-
      action*, 16(2-4):401–419, 2001.

[296] A. P. Würgler. *OMS Development Framework: Rapid Prototyping for Object-Oriented Databases.* PhD thesis, Swiss Federal Institute of Technology Zurich (ETH Zurich), Zurich, Switzerland, 2000.

[297] A. Zeller and G. Snelting. Unified Versioning Through Feature Logic. *ACM Transactions on Software Engineering and Methodology*, 6(4):398–441, 1997.

[298] Zope Corporation. Zope Content Management Framework. `http://www.zope.org`, 2006.

[299] S. Zweifel. Graphical Authoring Tools for Web Content Management. Diploma thesis, Swiss Federal Institute of Technology Zurich (ETH Zurich), Zurich, Switzerland, 2002.

Curriculum Vitae

Particulars

Name	Michael Grossniklaus
Date of Birth	June 22, 1976
Birthplace	Basel, BS, Switzerland
Citizenship	Zurich, ZH, Switzerland
	Beatenberg, BE, Switzerland

Education

1983–1987	Christoph Merian Primary School, Basel
1987–1995	Holbein Grammar School, Basel
1995	Matura Type D, Holbein Grammar School, Basel
1996–2001	Study of Computer Science at the Swiss Federal Institute of Technology Zurich (ETH Zurich)
2001–2007	Research and teaching assistant supervised by Prof. Dr. Moira C. Norrie in the Global Information Systems research group at the Swiss Federal Institute of Technology Zurich (ETH Zurich)

Work Experience

1995–1996	Software development at Sandoz Pharma AG and Novartis AG, Basel, Switzerland
2000	Internship as software developer at Obtree Technologies Inc., Basel, Switzerland

www.ingramcontent.com/pod-product-compliance
Lightning Source LLC
LaVergne TN
LVHW062308060326
832902LV00013B/2099